Science and the Open Society

Science and the Open Society

The Future of Karl Popper's Philosophy

Mark Amadeus Notturno

Foreword by

George Soros

CEU PRESS

Central European University Press

Published in 2000 by
Central European University Press

Október 6. utca 12
H-1051 Budapest
Hungary

400 West 59th Street
New York, NY 10019
USA

Distributed in the United Kingdom and Western Europe by
Plymbridge Distributors Ltd., Estover Road, Plymouth, PL6 7PZ,
United Kingdom

ISBN 963-9116-69-6 *Cloth*
ISBN 963-9116-70-X *Paperback*

Library of Congress Cataloging in Publication Data
A CIP catalog record for this book is available upon request

Printed in Hungary by AKAPRINT

For Karl—
the two of them

I may be wrong and you may be right, and by an effort, we may get nearer to the truth.

Karl R. Popper

Revolutions close with a total victory for one of the two opposing camps. Will that group ever say that the result of its victory has been something less than progress? That would be like admitting that they had been wrong and their opponents right. To them, at least, the outcome of revolution must be progress, and they are in an excellent position to make certain that future members of their community will see past history in the same way.

Thomas S. Kuhn

An open society (that is, a society based on the idea of not merely tolerating dissenting opinions but respecting them) and a democracy (that is, a form of government devoted to the protection of an open society) cannot flourish if science becomes the exclusive possession of a closed set of specialists.

Karl R. Popper

The controversial question whether philosophy exists, or has any right to exist, is almost as old as philosophy itself. Time and again an entirely new philosophical movement arises which finally unmasks the old philosophical problems as pseudo-problems, and which confronts the wicked nonsense of philosophy with the good sense of meaningful, positive, empirical science. And time and again do the despised defenders of 'traditional philosophy' try to explain to the leaders of the latest positivistic assault that the main problem of philosophy is the critical analysis of the appeal to the authority of 'experience'—precisely that 'experience' which every latest discoverer of positivism is, as ever, artlessly taking for granted.

Karl R. Popper

Foreword

Many years ago, after I escaped from becoming a victim of the Holocaust in Hungary, I made my way to London, where I became acquainted with Karl Popper's ideas about science and open society, and then with Karl Popper himself. I read his books when I was a student at the London School of Economics—I was studying economics, not philosophy—and his books meant a lot to me. Many years later, after I had moved to the United States, I sent him a book of philosophy that I had written under the somewhat grandiose title *Burden of Consciousness*, to which I received a very enthusiastic reply. He said, 'I haven't quite finished it, but I'm really excited about it.' And so I went to see him. But when I introduced myself, he looked at me, or rather listened to me, and said, 'But you are not an American!' 'No,' I said. 'I am Hungarian.' He then said 'That's terribly disappointing.' At first I didn't know what to think. But then he explained, 'When I read your book I thought that, finally, somebody in America had really understood what I meant when I talked about Closed Society and Open Society. But you are Hungarian, you *lived* through it.'

While I was working on the *Burden of Consciousness* I was also making my career in the financial world. But after I had made more money than I thought I would need, I thought about how to put it to good use, and I remembered Karl Popper's ideas about science and the open society. It was at the time when the Soviet Union was showing cracks in its armor, and I thought that this was a unique opportunity to try to open its closed societies, with the hope that future generations would not have to live through what I had lived through. I began a foundation in Budapest. And then another in Poland. Before long I had started foundations in twenty or so different countries. I also decided to found an international university with campuses in Budapest, Warsaw, and Prague. And in June of 1994, just a few months before he died, the Central European University made Karl Popper the first recipient of its annual Open Society Prize, so that his name would now be connected with that prize for ever after.

A year or so before his death, Popper told me about an American who he thought had also understood what he meant, and asked me to support his work. This was a philosopher named Mark Notturno, who was then editing the unpublished papers in his archives. Notturno had already edited *The Myth of the Framework* and *Knowledge and the Body-Mind Problem* with the support of another foundation when Popper told me about his work. These books were not yet published, but Popper was convinced that he was the right man to edit his archives, and he asked for my support in order to insure that the job would actually be done. I met with Notturno, and liked his 'Popper Project', and agreed to support it. An agreement was soon worked out whereby Notturno would do his work at the Central European University in Budapest and the books that he produced from Popper's archives would be published jointly by Routledge and the CEU Press. Notturno, at the time, was working on a book called *An Introduction to Scientific Methods*, which was to be based upon ten years' worth of the lectures that Popper gave to his first year students at the London School of Economics. But shortly after Notturno moved to Budapest, Popper died. And shortly after that, his literary executors unexpectedly decided to terminate the project that he had asked me to support.

Science and the Open Society might never have been written had the Popper Project ended there. But Notturno and his wife Kira Viktorova, a Russian philosopher, were dedicated to my project of introducing open society into the countries of the former Soviet

Union, and they immediately began to redirect the project in an effort to help me with mine. Instead of devoting their time to archival research, they began to organize workshops on Popper's philosophy in Budapest for philosophers and scientists in the countries of the former Soviet Union. This soon led to summer schools, to workshops in other areas of philosophy, and then to workshops in different countries, and eventually to a doctoral support program in Philosophy at the CEU in Budapest. The Notturnos, as this book goes to press, have organized workshops, lectures, and summer schools on Popper's philosophy in more than fifteen of the countries in which I have established foundations, and in a number of other countries in which I have not. It is these workshops that have led to the publication of this book, which has been constructed from some of the lectures and talks that Notturno has given in the course of his work which I have supported.

In saying that I have supported his work, I want to be very clear that I do not mean that I agree with, or am responsible for, everything that Notturno says about open society—anymore than Notturno agrees with, or is responsible for, what I have to say about it myself. But I do mean that I agree with very much of what he says, and especially with the idea that we are free in an open society to express our disagreements and to discuss them critically.

George Soros

Preface

The essays collected in this volume have been written in defense of science and open society. If that is not always apparent, it is probably because I am critical of some of the popular misconceptions that are frequently associated with these ideas. I do not, for example, think that our scientific theories can be justified, or proven, or even confirmed by the success of their predictions. I do not think that open society is a product of combining democratic political processes with a market economy. And I am, perhaps, most critical of the view that science is a social institution in which such traditional philosophical values as truth, rationality, criticism, and freedom of thought play no role. I believe, on the contrary, that science and open society are related to each other primarily through the emphasis that each of them places upon these philosophical values—and that the attempt to replace them with political power, solidarity, commitment to belief, and consensus is one of the greatest contemporary threats to science and open society that I know.

The essays collected in this volume have also been written in defense of the philosophy of Karl Popper—a philosophy that is widely regarded in America as mistaken, and in any event *passé*, but that is today providing inspiration for the people in Central and Eastern Europe and Middle Asia who are struggling to build open societies in their countries. Popper was one of the twentieth century's greatest defenders of reason and the freedom of thought. I do not think that people in the West have understood his philosophy. And I fear that our open societies may now be in danger as a result. The future, however, is open. And I think that the future of Karl Popper's philosophy, as well as the future of science and the open society, will turn upon our recognition of our own fallibility, and upon our willingness to defend reason and the freedom of thought whenever they are attacked.

Mark Notturno
Vienna, 1999

Acknowledgements

The essays that form this book were written and rewritten over several years under conditions that might simultaneously be described as 'the best of times' and 'the worst of times'. I want to thank all of those who have helped me. Werner and Annette Baumgartner. George Soros. Jim Baer. Bill Newton-Smith. Steve Fuller. Michael Liston. Adam Chmielevski. Miles Davis and Ben Webster. Frances Pinter, Walda Metcalf and the staff at CEU Press. The Board of Directors of the Ianus Foundation. The directors and staff of the local Soros foundations and the universities and research institutions at which the essays have been presented. The editors and translators of the journals and books in which they have been previously published.

The essays themselves have been revised several times and, hopefully, improved by the criticism of hundreds of philosophers and scientists from over thirty countries. There are far too many of them to mention here by name. But their participation in our workshops and summer schools has forced me to rethink my positions on the topics discussed in this book time and again.

I owe the greatest debts, of course, to Karl Popper, who has inspired each of the essays in this volume, and to Kira Viktorova—my wife, colleague, best critic, and best friend—who has read and reread these essays almost as many times as I have myself, and who has taught me more about the Soviet Union than either of us would care to know.

Contents

Introduction

Since 1992 I have had the privilege of doing full-time research in The Karl Popper Archives, and since 1994 of being the director of the Popper Project at the Central European University in Budapest. My work, during this time, has been supported, with Popper's recommendation, first by the Ianus Foundation and then by the Soros Foundation. This support enabled me to edit Karl Popper's last two books, *The Myth of the Framework* and *Knowledge and the Body-Mind Problem*, while he was still alive. But what is, to my mind, much more important is that it has also enabled me to play a small role in George Soros' attempt to open the closed societies of the former Soviet Union and socialist bloc. The Popper Project has—with the support of the Central European University, the Higher Educational Support Program of the Open Society Institute, and the various 'local' foundations of the Soros network—offered workshops, seminars, lectures, and summer schools in thirty different cities of eighteen different countries during this time. Dr. Kira Viktorova, who is my assistant in the project, and I have tried to conduct our workshops, seminars, and summer schools as round-table Socratic-style critical discussions—something that was apparently unheard of in this part of the world. We have, through the generosity of the Soros Foundations, been able to distribute Popper's books in these countries, and to encourage their translation into languages in which they were once forbidden. We have tried through these activities to acquaint philosophers from both the East and the West with Popper's ideas and with his methods of critical inquiry.

We have tried to teach them about science and open society. And they, in many cases, have tried to teach us about science and closed society. We have all learned a lot.

The papers that are collected in this volume have been written in connection with this project. They have been presented at universities, research institutes, and foundations as far East as Kazakhstan and as far West as California. Previous versions of them have been published, and many of them have been translated into different languages. I have collected them here partly because philosophers in the East have asked me do so, and partly so that people in the West may have access to them too. I do not intend them to constitute a systematic exposition of Popper's philosophy. But I hope that they might, when taken together, indicate some of its most important aspects. I also hope that they will indicate some of the dangers that now confront reason and the freedom of thought—both in the East and in the West—as well as some of the reasons why Popper's ideas regarding science and open society are still important today and perhaps even more important than ever.

In my view, Popper's philosophy has been a missed opportunity. It was, until just very recently, forbidden in the Soviet Union. And it continues to be widely misunderstood, and misrepresented, in England and the United States. It is, first and foremost, an attempt to construct a non-authoritarian theory of science and society. But even those who have understood this have often evaluated it, and rejected it, by appealing to the very authoritarian ideas that it seeks to replace.

Popper's philosophy offers a middle way between two opposing authoritarian approaches to science and society—between irrationalist dogmatism, on the one hand, and irrationalist relativism, on the other. This is why it is important. It offers an account of how scientific knowledge can be objective and rational without being certain, without appealing to induction, and without grounding itself upon expert opinion, consensus, and the solidarity of belief. It offers an account in which truth, and not power, is still the regulative ideal of scientific inquiry and rational discussion. And it offers an account of how individuals in an open society can exercise their freedom of thought to rationally criticize the consensus of belief in their communities, and to keep their elected leaders in check, without leading to violence of one form or another.

Perhaps most important of all, it offers a vision of how men and women can still appeal to reason in what might be called 'The Post-Foundationalist Age.'

The papers that are collected in this volume explore these themes in greater detail. But I would like, in this introduction, to emphasize what I regard as the most distinctive feature of Popper's philosophy.

The most distinctive feature of Popper's philosophy, and the key to understanding his views on objectivity and rationality, is that *it does not regard scientific knowledge as justified true belief.* Popper believed that all of our knowledge is irreparably fallible, that it grows through criticism and trial and error, and that the claim that a theory is justified not only appeals to authority, but leads unwittingly to scepticism, misologism, and irrationalism when we learn that it is not.

Popper equated the rational attitude with the critical attitude, and he called his philosophy Critical Rationalism in order to emphasize this fact. But Critical Rationalism is best understood today in contrast with what might equally be called Uncritical Empiricism or Critical Irrationalism.

This, however, must be put into context.

Most philosophers regard scientific knowledge as justified true belief. They regard knowledge as objective and rational to the extent to which it is justified, and they regard an argument as a justification of knowledge to the extent to which it is rational and objective.

Indeed, the whole point of a justification is to give evidence that is as compelling for others as it is for ourselves.

The idea that we could give objective and rational justifications is what gave rise to the great foundationalist projects of the past. These all claimed to give objective and rational justifications that would be compelling for all rational beings. There have been many such projects in the history of western philosophy, because foundationalists, ironically enough, could not agree about what is or ought to be regarded as objective, rational, and compelling. But each of these projects conceived of science as a building that must be grounded, with the cement of logic, upon a firm foundation.

Foundationalists hoped to build story after story of knowledge upon their foundations so as to eventually produce a skyscraper of science in which the theories in the penthouse were just as objective, and rational, and certain as those in the basement. And they did not, insofar as this is concerned, differ too much in proclaiming that their favorite 'objective and rational foundations' were 'indubitable', and 'self-evident', and 'clear and distinct', and 'infallibly true', etc., etc.

ECONOMICS
SOCIOLOGY
PSYCHOLOGY
BIOLOGY
CHEMISTRY
PHYSICS
MATHEMATICS
THE INDUBITABLE, SELF-EVIDENT, CLEAR AND DISTINCT, INFALLIBLE ETC., ETC., OBJECTIVE AND RATIONAL FOUNDATIONS

But it is clear that there is something fundamentally wrong with the foundationalist picture, since the so-called 'objective and rational' foundations are characterized in terms of subjective, indeed *psychological*, predicates.

Uncritical Empiricism takes for granted that our knowledge is justified by empirical facts. This has a long history to it that begins with David Hume, who believed that experience is the only source of our ideas.

Hume criticized inductive inference as irrational. He argued that the knowledge that we gain through experience is based upon custom and habit, and he concluded that reason is and ought to be the slave of the passions. But Hume, nonetheless, uncritically accepted the idea that our knowledge is and must be justified—and this led him, despite his criticism of induction, to accept inductive inference as providing us with *psychological* justification for believing it. This is what made him an Uncritical Empiricist. But it is also what made him a Critical Irrationalist.

Today's empiricists also uncritically accept the idea that our scientific knowledge is justified. Many of them still appeal to invalid argument forms in an attempt to induce people to believe theories that do not actually follow from the 'evidence'. And those who do not say that scientific knowledge is based upon custom and habit tend to say that it is based upon consensus and solidarity instead.

None of this would be so bad, if they did not pretend that such arguments justified their beliefs as true—and if they did not try to impose their beliefs upon others.

In his *Logic of Scientific Discovery*, Popper showed what was wrong with foundationalism by arguing that the demand that we justify our knowledge by objective and rational argument leads led him, despite his criticism of induction, to accept inductive inference as providing either to infinite regress—in which the demand that we justify a statement is replaced by the demand that we justify the statements that are offered to justify it—or to attempts to cut short the infinite regress by 'grounding' our knowledge upon the authority of reason or the authority of experience. In the one case, the demand for justification leads to dogmatism. In the other, it leads to psychologism.

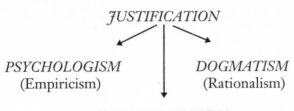

JUSTIFICATION

PSYCHOLOGISM
(Empiricism)

DOGMATISM
(Rationalism)

INFINITE REGRESS

In either case, it leads to a *reductio ad absurdum* of the idea that we can justify our knowledge with objective and rational logical arguments.

Most philosophers, when faced with this argument, have opted either for psychologism or for some form of dogmatism—ranging from the dogmatism of a priori valid truths to the dogmatism of the conventions of the scientific community.

In so doing, they have either weakened their concept of justification, because neither dogmatism nor psychologism can show that a statement is true; or they have weakened their concept of truth by defining it in terms of what is dogmatically or psychologistically justified.

Inductivists, insofar as this is concerned, have *doubly* weakened their concept of justification—first by appealing to *psychologism* to justify the *singular* statements that they use as premises in inductive arguments, and then by appealing to *dogmatism* by using invalid argument forms, in which the conclusion can be false even if all of the premises are true, to justify the *universal* theories that they would 'derive' as their conclusions.

Popper, when faced with these alternatives, is almost alone in having given up the idea that justification is a necessary condition for scientific knowledge. Our scientific knowledge, according to Popper, cannot and need not be justified.

But this changes everything.

Philosophers who say that scientific knowledge *cannot* be justified are usually regarded as sceptics. But if one believes, as Popper did, that we *do* have scientific knowledge, that it cannot be justified, but that it is, nonetheless, both *objective* and *rational*, then it follows that:

1. Scientific knowledge can no longer be regarded as justified true belief, *since no statement can be justified*;
2. The rationality of scientific knowledge can no longer be regarded as a product of its justification, *since no statement can be justified*;
3. The objectivity of scientific knowledge can no longer be regarded as a product of its justification, *since no statement can be justified*;
4. Scepticism—or the denial that we have knowledge—can no longer be regarded as the thesis that no statement can be justified, *since no statement can be justified*;
5. Justifying theories can no longer be regarded as a task for philosophy and science, *since no statement can be justified*;
6. Logical arguments can no longer be regarded as attempts to justify statements, *since no statement can be justified*; and
7. The criticism that a statement or theory is not justified can no longer be regarded as a criticism, *since no statement can be justified*.

So what is objective and rational scientific knowledge, if not justified true belief?

Popper believed that scientific knowledge consists of problems, and of hypothetical solutions to our problems. More precisely, he believed that it consists of *guesses* that we propose in our attempts to solve our problems.

What makes these guesses, or hypothetical solutions, *scientific* is that we try to examine them carefully and, through criticism, eliminate errors in them.

But a theory's ability to successfully answer criticism never means that it is justified or confirmed—though it may, of course, mean that we are, for the moment, justified in preferring it over its competitors.

Our attempts to eliminate the errors in our theories typically lead to new problems—if only 'How do I solve my original problem, given that my first guess doesn't work?'—and to new theories, or guesses, as to how we can solve them.

Popper summed up this process in his so-called 'tetradic schema':

$$P_1 \rightarrow TT \rightarrow EE \rightarrow P_2$$

where 'P_1' is the original problem; 'TT' is a tentative theory, or solution to the problem; 'EE' is error elimination, or criticism; and P_2 is a new problem that emerges as a result of criticism.

This is an over-simplified schema, since we often work with many different problems and many different tentative theories at the same time. But the schema is supposed to indicate the important role that problems have in scientific inquiry, and the fact that scientific inquiry is an open-ended and never-ending process.

Popper's non-foundationalist theory of science has immediate consequences for objectivity and rationality.

Foundationalists equate the rationality of scientific knowledge with its justification:

$$rationality = justification = logic$$

where 'logicality' may refer to either deductive or inductive arguments.

Popper, on the contrary, equated rationality with criticism:

$$rationality = criticism = logic$$

where 'logic' refers to only deductive arguments.

Popper criticized induction as logical inference, as methodology, and as psychology. He saw induction as a myth that was put forth primarily as a way of justifying the claim that statements are justified when they really are not. He saw it as a way of subordinating our reason to custom and habit (or consensus and solidarity). And he did not believe that humans reason inductively from experience as Hume had claimed. Contrary to Uncritical Empiricism, Popper believed that science appeals to experience to *criticize* its theories, and not to *justify* them. And his appeal to deductive logic as the organon of criticism in this process is a large part of what is supposed to make our scientific knowledge objective and rational.

This is because *deductively valid arguments are the only arguments that preserve truth from premises to conclusion.* This means that it is impossible—inconsistent or contradictory—for a valid deductive argument to have true premises and a false conclusion.

We criticize a statement by trying to show that some of its logical consequences are false. Criticism thus attempts to show that a theory is false by showing that it is *inconsistent*—either with itself, or with other statements that we hold to be true.

But here, it is important to understand that *with the exception of contradictions, logic alone cannot show that a statement is false.*

If two statements are contradictory, then one must be true and the other false. But this is not enough to tell us *which* is true and *which* is false. And *since no statement can be justified* (or shown to be true), it follows that the acceptance or rejection of criticism always involves a *judgment.*

It follows from this that *reason cannot compel belief.*

Rationality, according to Popper, is not so much a property of knowledge as a task for humans. What is rational is not so much the content of a theory or a belief as the way in which we hold it.

We are rational to the extent to which we are open to criticism, including self-criticism; and to the extent to which we are willing to change our beliefs when confronted with what we judge to be good criticism.

We are, in short, rational to the extent to which we are willing to appeal to reasons and argument, as opposed to violence and force, to resolve our disputes.

Similar remarks can be made about objectivity.

Dogmatism and psychologism were characteristic of the rationalist and empiricist epistemologies of the last century. And if there really were foundations that *everyone* agreed to be clear and distinct, self-evident, and indubitable, then no one would have worried too much about them. The problem, however, was that empiricists and rationalists differed not only with regard to their foundations, but also with regard to their criteria for recognizing foundations. And *that* simple disagreement between dogmatism and psychologism was itself enough to refute classical foundationalism.

But this, again, cannot be what Popper means by 'objectivity', *since no statement can be justified.*

So what *does* Popper mean by 'objectivity'?

Merely that our theories can be articulated in language and, as a result, understood and criticized by others.

These ideas—that objective rational knowledge is inherently fallible; and that we can never justify, but can only criticize it—are essential both to Popper's philosophy of science and to his concept of open society. Indeed, Popper characterized an open society as one that sets free the critical faculties of man, and he criticized Scientific Socialism on the grounds that no science could be as certain and as justified as the so-called Scientific Socialists thought.

Today, many people believe that Scientific Socialism is dead. But one of the leit-motifs underlying the articles collected in this volume is that a new, and perhaps, even more dangerous philosophy of science and society has already arisen to take its place and is now threatening to close our societies in the West. This new philosophy of science and society discourages individuals from thinking for themselves and advocates yet another form of 'groupthink'. Philosophers from the former Soviet Union understand what I am talking about when I call it Post-Communist Communism. Philosophers from the West may understand it better as The Scientific Institution. I have, in the articles collected in this volume, sometimes described it as Floating Foundationalism. But it is best described, in terms of the categories that I have developed in this introduction, as Uncritical Irrationalism.

The philosophers whom I regard as Uncritical Irrationalists agree that our knowledge cannot be shown to be true. But they continue to regard its justification as important and they conclude, apparently forgetting the whole point of giving a justification, that it is *only* the foundations that have to be accepted without it. They strongly believe that their own theories and beliefs are true—though they do not really like to use that word—and they strongly oppose any attempt to question them or to argue that they are not.

Whereas Socrates believed that the unexamined life was not worth living, the Uncritical Irrationalists now teach, without really examining the claim, that it is the only life really worth living after all.

But what is infinitely worse is that Uncritical Irrationalists would replace our philosophical and scientific values of truth, rationality, and the freedom of thought with political power, solidarity, and commitment to belief. They would advise us to forget about objective and rational criticism, and to focus instead upon such subjective and irrational contingencies as religious, ethnic, national, and sexual identities. These, they say, are the things that bind human beings together. And focussing upon them will, or so they believe, help us to construct a more just and humane society.

I believe that Uncritical Irrationalists have the very best of intentions. But I also believe that they are very short-sighted. They have been disillusioned by the exaggerated claims that foundationalists have made in the past regarding objectivity, rationality, and scientific knowledge. And they would now reject these ideals entirely in the name of what they think is a more human and humane approach. I think that they have not considered some of the very obvious and likely consequences of the approach that they suggest. And I believe that they would, were we to follow them, lead us, with the very best of intentions, down the primrose path to science—or, I should say, to The Scientific Institution—and to the closed society.

If I sometimes sound too critical of The Scientific Institution in these essays—if I seem to see it too easily as a closed society—it is only because I do not regard it as science itself, and because I have experienced too much of it already.

1 The Open Society and Its Enemies: Authority, Community, and Bureaucracy[1]

> *Once we begin to rely upon our reason, and to use our powers of criticism, once we feel the call of personal responsibilities, and with it the responsibility of helping to advance knowledge, we cannot return to a state of implicit submission to tribal magic.*
>
> Karl R. Popper

I

I had been told that Ernest Gellner was the author of the joke that *The Open Society and Its Enemies* should have been called *The Open Society by One of Its Enemies*. So I was not too surprised to see that the conference that he organized in Prague to celebrate the book's 50th anniversary was supposed to have a cutting edge. One of the conference themes that he announced was 'the relevance of the ideas and values of [*The Open Society and Its Enemies*] to the aftermath of a totalitarian collapse, as opposed to their initial relevance as an attempt to undermine a victorious or expanding totalitarianism.' A second was 'the validity or otherwise of the parallel drawn by Popper between the principles of an Open Society and of scientific enquiry.' And Gellner, in emphasizing that the conference should discuss criticisms of the Popperian tradition, raised the question, 'Has [Popper] underestimated the importance and value of communalist thinking?' as a third.

I think that it is fairly clear where Gellner himself stood on these issues. But his unexpected death, just a few days before our talks began, seemed to cast a long shadow over them. Some people said that Popper's book *had* helped to introduce open society into Central and Eastern Europe. But others said that his work, and the work of philosophers in general, had had little or no effect at all upon the collapse of Marxism. And still others said that *The Open*

Society and Its Enemies was, in any event, now obsolete—since Popper was not an expert in social science, since he had seriously underestimated the importance of community, and since communalist thinking is necessary to re-establish faith in the legitimacy of government.

All of this may or may not be true.

Marxism, we are told, is dead—despite the elections. And democracy, we are told, is on the rise—along with fascism and nationalism. Indeed, we are told that free speech is now so popular that you can publish almost anything you like in the Russian press—so long as you are willing to pay for it.

My own sense is that none of this has much to do with the growth of open society—and that our growing reliance upon the experts of The Scientific Institution who tell us these things may well portend the exact opposite. My own sense is that Plato, Hegel, and Marx were only figureheads for the real enemies of open society, enemies that are still very much with us, and that are now threatening to close our society even in the West. I am talking about authority, community, and bureaucracy. And I think that the question now confronting open society is not whether Popper underestimated the value of community and communalist thinking, but how we can organize our society on a large scale without subordinating the freedom of an individual to the authority of his community, and without completely losing it in a labyrinth of bureaucratic structures.

II

Let me begin by saying that Popper believed that science is our best kind of knowledge in the same way and for the same reasons that he believed that democracy is our best form of government. They have, to date, both shown themselves to be better than their competitors, and they have done so, by far and large, by the ways in which they have dealt with their competitors—or, perhaps more accurately, by the ideals that they have articulated and tried to approximate about how to deal with competitors. Both science and democracy try to change their leaders without violence through rational discussion. And both try to learn from their competitors instead of silencing them. Neither has always succeeded in achieving these goals. But each has succeeded with greater frequency than other forms of knowledge and government—though this, we should always remember, is an empirical fact that may change with changing conditions in the world.

It is very easy to misunderstand this, and to think that the essence of science and democracy somehow guarantees that they will always be better than their competitors. Popper, however, taught us to be less concerned with essence than with performance. So if the institutionalists are right that science no longer appeals to rational argument, and if the post-modernists are right that democracy silences those whom it cannot persuade, then we should, perhaps, at least question whether scientific knowledge and democracy are still the best available forms of knowledge and government that we have.

It is in the same vein that Popper regarded open society as the best available form of social life that we have—not as a Utopia that is inevitably better than its competitors, but as a *task* at which we must constantly work to avoid falling prey to its competitors. And here, we should always bear in mind that success at this task is inevitably and only a matter of degree. For the task itself is nothing less than the battle to preserve our freedom.

III

The battle to preserve our freedom has always been fought to defend the right of an individual to think and to speak for himself. It has always been fought against our enslavement by ideologies. And it has always been fought with the weapons of truth and rational argument, and with the simple idea that a false statement is false regardless of who says or believes that it is true.

I want to emphasize this point—that open society is the task to preserve our freedom—because most of the talk about open society that I hear these days seems to be confused about what it is. I hear, for example, frequent identifications of open society with democracy, and with *laissez faire* capitalism, and even with that 'politically correct' ideal of free speech in which everyone can say whatever they like—provided that they do not offend anyone else while doing so.

These are all distortions of Popper's view. Popper contrasted open society with closed society. But he did not *identify* it with any specific political or economic system. His experiences in Vienna had convinced him that the dangers in socialism were far more threatening than the problems that it was supposed to solve. But he was also well aware of the dangers in unrestrained capitalism— which he had learned about, along with the rest of Europe, from the experience of the nineteenth century. So while Popper opposed the means that Marxists advocated and employed to implement their social reforms, he did not oppose those social reforms themselves. And while he thought that democracy was the most likely of all the known political systems to protect an open society, he was also very careful to distinguish between the two.

The fact of the matter is that open society, as Popper understood it, is less concerned with the state and its economy than with the individual and his freedom. *'The state,'* Popper wrote, *'should exist for the sake of the human individual—for the sake of its free citizens and their free social life—that is, for the sake of the free society—and not the other way round.'*[2] And a citizen must, for this reason, combine the duty of loyalty that he owes to his state with:

> ...a certain degree of vigilance and even a certain degree of distrust of the state and its officers: it is his duty to watch and see that the state does not overstep the limits of its legitimate functions. For the institutions of the state are powerful, and where there is power there is always the danger of its misuse—and a danger to freedom. All power has a tendency to entrench itself and a tendency to corrupt, and in the last resort it is only *the traditions of a free society*—which include a tradition of almost jealous watchfulness on the part of its citizens—which can balance the power of the state by providing those checks and controls on which all freedom depends.[3]

Even democracy is to be valued as a means for safeguarding our freedom—by enabling us to get rid of our leaders without violence and bloodshed when they turn out to be not as good as we had hoped them to be—and as a means that will not work well unless the society that uses it *already* values freedom and tolerance:

> It seems to me of the greatest importance for a free society that democracy should be seen for what it is: that it should be understood without being idealized. And it seems to me especially important to realize that, as a rule, democracy will work fairly well in a society which values freedom and tolerance, but not in a society which does not understand these values. Democracy, that is, the majority vote, may help to preserve freedom, but it can never *create* freedom if the individual citizen does not care for it.[4]

IV

The fact of the matter is that *The Open Society and Its Enemies* is not so much a criticism of a political or economic system as it is a criticism of the idea that there can be anything like a science with theories so well-established that we could safely rely upon its experts, as gods amongst men, for the truth. Popper thought that it was this idea—and, indeed, only their *certainty* in this idea—that gave well-intentioned men and women the courage to undertake, in the name of 'scientific socialism' and at the behest of 'scientific experts,' the drastic social changes that were undertaken by the communists.

But scientific knowledge is simply not like that. And this, in a nutshell, is Popper's critique of scientific socialism. Scientific knowledge is inherently conjectural, and always fallible. So while there may be experts who know their way around a problem and who have good ideas about why this or that 'solution' may or may not work, none of their advice can be safely regarded as authoritative or final. We should thus be bold in proposing and testing new theories, but not in applying them to the world. We should, instead, practice 'piecemeal engineering'—the results of which are more easily reversed than global reforms—just in case the theories that we apply turn out to be false.

V

But what then is open society, if it is neither market society nor democratic society?

Popper characterized it as a society that sets free the critical powers of man and he contrasted it with the 'closed' or 'tribal' society with its submission to magical forces.[5]

This is the reason why open society has so little in common with the politically correct version of free speech. I do not think that everyone should be able to say whatever he likes without reproach. But rudeness should never be treated as a crime. And we should, under normal circumstances, be able to say what we think is true without fear of being punished for it. This applies especially to criticism. Free speech, in an open society, should be an instrument for discovering error, and not a shield behind which to hide it. It is unfortunate that many people regard criticism of their ideas as a personal offense. But free speech must take precedence over our desire not to offend. Open society is not necessarily polite society. And if avoiding offense becomes our primary concern, then it will quickly become impossible to say anything freely at all.

Here it would be tempting to identify open society with the scientific society, or with the rational society. And Popper, no doubt, was inclined to do so. But there are dangers of doing so straightaway. For the most popular philosophy of science of our day—I am speaking of the institutional theory of Thomas Kuhn—maintains that scientific enquiry begins where criticism leaves off, and that it is not criticism but the abandonment of critical discourse for faith in a paradigm that marks the transition to science.[6] And this, regardless of Kuhn's intentions, is actually a recipe for closed society. It is a philosophy that tries to convince us that no fundamental decision or responsibility on our part is required, that we really should not waste our time on criticism or on trying to understand, and that everything will and must go all right if we only fall into step behind The Scientific Institution and its experts.[7]

But when we begin to think of science as incommensurable frameworks that are constructed upon paradigms that cannot be rationally criticized either from within or without, when we say that accepting those paradigms is like converting to this or that religion,[8] then we are only a stone's throw away from a closed or tribal society with its submission to magical forces.

VI

This idea—that we should not submit to magic and its superstitions—is essential for understanding what open society is all about. There is much in the world that we may regard as magical, and rightly so. We stand in awe of the fact that the world should exist at all. And we are enchanted by feelings of déjà vu, telepathic experiences, and improbable synchronicities that we just cannot explain. But regardless of whether or not we can explain these things, the idea that scientists have special powers of understanding and a special kind of authority that others cannot question is an entirely different thing—as is the notion that scientific theories are justified by the consensus of expert opinion. These are *mystical* ideas that we should recognize as mystical and simply not accept.

Popper intended *The Open Society and Its Enemies* to be an assault upon intellectual authority and its superstitions. He thought that:

> An open society (that is, a society based on the idea of not merely tolerating dissenting opinions but respecting them) and a democracy (that is, a form of government devoted to the protection of an open society) cannot flourish if science becomes the exclusive possession of a closed set of specialists.[9]

And he described his book to his friends and associates in just these terms:

> The book is a very bold and challenging book, not so much in its style, but in its content. It attacks some of the greatest authorities of all times; and not only a few of them, such as Plato, Aristotle, Hegel, etc., but in fact a great number which are not named in the table of contents. And it does so with a recklessness which is excusable only in view of the fact that *I consider the destruction of the awe of the Great Names, the Great Intellectual Authorities, one of the necessary prerequisites of a recuperation of mankind.*[10]

The *Open Society*—and by this I mean both the society and the book—is opposed not just to this or that authority, and not just to Plato, Hegel, and Marx. It is, on the contrary, opposed to the very idea that there are cognitive authorities that we can rely upon for the truth.[11] So if we are going to understand open society as scientific or rational society, then we must also understand science and rationality in Popper's terms. We must think of science not as an institutionalized hierarchy of experts, but as a never-ending process of problem-solving in which we propose tentative solutions to our problems and then try to eliminate the errors in our proposals. We must think of rationality not in terms of justification, but in terms of criticism. And we must think of criticism not as an offense, or as a show of contempt or disdain, but as one of the greatest signs of respect that one mind can show to another.

VII

This brings me to Ernest Gellner's question whether Popper underestimated the importance and value of communalist thinking. This question strikes at the very heart of Popper's idea of open society. It is as if someone had asked whether he underestimated the value of induction. And please do not misunderstand. Popper may have underestimated the value of both of these things. But if he did, then a proper estimation will require that we jettison all that makes open society open and critical rationalism rational. For communalism, like inductivism, asks that we abandon the rationalist attitude and consider the person of the thinker—and whether or not he is 'one of us'—instead of the truth of his thought.[12]

Popper used to say that relativism is one of the greatest contemporary threats to reason and the rational attitude. I agree with Popper about many things, but not entirely about this. It is one thing to say that truth is relative, and another to believe that it is really true—let alone to understand what it could possibly mean. Most relativists seem to believe that relativism is *absolutely* true—which leads me to believe that it is not really truth, but our *beliefs* and *knowledge*, that they think is relative. But what they often really mean is that we are fallible and that even the most certain of our beliefs may be mistaken—something that would actually be impossible were truth really relative, as they say. Today, a far greater threat to reason and the rational attitude comes from people who are quite willing to acknowledge both that truth is absolute and that they know what is absolutely true. It does not say that truth is meaningless or without value. It says that rationality is but one value amongst many and not the one that counts most. It says that family, or ethnic identity, or communal solidarity, or nationality, or gender—the list goes on, and it is very long—are far more important. And it says that we are not only justified in dismissing reason when it conflicts with one of these values, but that it may actually be our duty to do so.

This is the communalist attitude. And it is far more closely related to inductivism than one might initially think. Inductivism may talk about reason and rationality. But it is, in the end, only his submission to the communalist attitude that gives an inductivist the impression that the conclusion of an inductive argument is supported by its premises. This is because the conclusion of an inductive argument simply does not follow from its premises. This means that it may be false even if all of the premises are true. So one must, in order to accept it *as justified by the argument*, invariably take what Kierkegaard used to call 'a little leap'. This statement is said to be true, and that one too. And this and that are then said to provide justification for a third that, quite simply, does not follow. And this is how little tyrannies begin. First someone takes a little leap and calls it 'justified'. And then, if nobody objects, he takes a bigger leap and calls that 'justified' too. In this way, he finally gets so good at leaping that all hell breaks loose.

Popper used to call a guess 'a guess'. But inductivists prefer to call a guess 'the conclusion of an inductive argument'. This, no doubt, adds an air of authority to it. But the fact that the 'conclusion' of an inductive argument may be false even if all of its premises are true means that it is a guess, regardless of what we may or may not like to call it.

What gives us the impression that 'arguments' like this 'justify' their 'conclusions'? In my view, it can only be the collective weight of the community of scientists that one would have to oppose by denying it.

In my view, it is our adherence to the methods of deductive logic and the law of non-contradiction that sets free our critical powers. These methods advise us to reject an argument if its conclusion does not follow from its premises, and they force us to reexamine our beliefs when the conclusions that follow from them seem to be false. It is only our respect for these methods, and for the idea of truth upon which they are based, that enables us, as individuals, to challenge the beliefs of our communities in ways that do not immediately lead to irrationalism and, ultimately, to violence of one form or another.

No argument can force us to accept the truth of any belief. But a valid deductive argument *can* force us to *choose* between the truth of its conclusion on the one hand and the falsity of its premises on the other. An inductive argument cannot do this. Its conclusion may be false even if all of its premises are true. So we can always reject its conclusion while accepting its premises as true. So it can never force us to choose in the way that a deductive argument can.

All of this may make inductive arguments attractive to people who do not like to choose, or who do not want to be forced. But my own sense is that it is better to be forced by the law of non-contradiction than it is to be forced by a community of believers. And my own sense is that the idea that an inductive argument justifies its conclusion deprives the individual of the rational means to challenge the will of a person or community that has taken that 'little leap.'

This idea—that reason should be used to criticize and to challenge instead of to justify and defend—is what connects Popper's critique of induction and his defense of democracy. The primary problem in political theory, according to Popper, is not 'Who is the most fit to rule?' It is 'How can we get rid of our rulers without bloodshed and revolution when we no longer think that they are fit to rule?' And the primary problem in epistemology, according to Popper, is not 'Which theory should we accept as true?' It is 'How can we get rid of a theory when we no longer think that it is true?' Popper favored democracy when it came to politics, *not* because it gives us the best leaders but because it enables us to challenge our leaders and to change them without bloodshed and revolution when we think that it best to do so. And this is also the reason why he was so opposed to induction when it came to science. Induction concerns itself entirely with justification—with establishing theories and keeping them in place—even though it is clear that inductive justification never entails their truth. No one ever talks about inductive criticism. And it is, for this reason, no surprise that those who predicate rationality upon induction must resort to revolution when they want to get rid of a theory that they no longer believe to be true.

Popper appreciated the importance and value of communalist thinking. But he also appreciated its power and its dangers. It is the kind of thinking that led some scientists in the twenties and thirties to dismiss Einstein's theories as 'Jewish Physics.' It is the kind of thinking that led Hitler to National Socialism. It is, in fact, the kind of thinking that has usually 'supported' racial, ethnic, and religious prejudices—and it is so regardless of the beneficial ends that can be achieved through it, regardless of who manifests it, and regardless of the individuals or groups against which it is directed. Someone once said that 'Prejudice is what holds society together.' But if there is just one doctrine that is central to open society, it is that the personal traits of a thinker have no implications whatsoever for the truth of his thought.

VIII

Some people, nonetheless, think that Popper underestimated the value of community *as a solution to the legitimacy problem*. This is the problem of what justifies the authority of the state and of why we should accept what our leaders have to say. Some political theorists have argued that a sense of shared community can contribute to the legitimacy of a state, since people are more willing to accept its authority when they feel that they have a stake in it. I must confess that I do not quite see what the willingness of a people to accept the authority of a state should have to do with its legitimacy. But I find the argument ironic in at least two ways. First, because the legitimacy problem asks for the very sort of justification that Popper thought is impossible to give. And second, because communalist thinking is not so much the solution to the legitimacy problem as its cause.

Popper, as we have already seen, believed that we should not simply accept what our leaders say, but should instead combine loyalty to our state with 'a certain degree of vigilance and even a certain degree of distrust of the state and its officers'— beause power corrupts and absolute power corrupts absolutely.

But if this is true, then we should *expect* that people who become officers of the state will also become corrupted, and we should prepare new leaders to replace them when they do. This is why it is our duty as citizens 'to watch and see that the state does not overstep the limits of its legitimate functions.' Even a well-designed and well-functioning democracy is not so much justified as the best of a bad lot. Its primary virtue is *not* that it provides us with the best leaders. It usually does not. Its primary virtue is that it provides us with a regular and peaceful mechanism for changing our leaders when we become dissatisfied with them.

Why cannot the state be justified? It is the same reason why scientific theories cannot be justified. And I can, perhaps, best explain it with a little story.

Once upon a time, a serious young student asked a wise old sage what supported the earth in its place and prevented it from falling through the heavens. The wise old sage answered immediately, saying that the earth was held in its place because it rested upon the shoulders of Atlas. The serious young student was not satisfied with this answer and asked the wise old sage what supported Atlas in *his* place and prevented *him* from falling through the heavens. The wise old sage thought for a moment, and said that Atlas was held in his place because he stood on the back of a giant turtle. The serious young student was even less satisfied with this answer and asked the wise old sage what supported this giant turtle in *its* place and prevented *it* from falling through the heavens. The old sage fixed the student with his eyes, and then said, very slowly, that the turtle was held in its place because it stood on the back of a giant elephant. When, at this point, the serious young student began to ask the wise old sage what supported the elephant in *its* place and prevented *it* from falling through the heavens, the old man put up his hand and abruptly stopped him. 'Won't work,' he said, 'there are elephants all the way down!'

The reason why we cannot justify the state is the same reason why we cannot justify our scientific theories. It is because there are not—and, indeed, *cannot* be—elephants all the way down.

My own sense is that the legitimacy of a state becomes a problem when people *cease* to believe in its objectivity. And my own sense is that people cease to believe in the objectivity of a state not because they suddenly realize that the elephants do not go all the way down, but because they begin to believe that the state is partial to some sub-community of elephants that benefit from it. A legitimacy problem existed in the Soviet Union because people always suspected that some comrades were more equal than others. And a legitimacy problem has existed in the United States, and now exists in the European Union, for much the same reason. But if I am right about this, then communalist thinking—be it the sort of communalist thinking that discriminates or the sort that is sensitive to discrimination—is far more likely to be the cause of the legitimacy problem than its solution.

IX

Popper likened the principles of open society to the principles of scientific enquiry. But he held that scientific objectivity has nothing to do with justification, and that it is not due entirely to the mental or psychological attitude of the individual scientist either. He thought, on the contrary, that the public character of science and its institutions imposes a mental discipline upon the individual scientist that preserves the objectivity of science and its tradition of critical discussion. But he also thought that 'institutions are always ambivalent in the sense that ... they also may serve the opposite purpose to the one intended':[13]

Institutions are like fortresses. They must be well designed *and* properly manned. But we can never make sure that the right man will be attracted by scientific research. Nor can we make sure that there will be men of imagination who have the knack of inventing new hypotheses.[14]

If The Scientific Institution fails to impose mental discipline upon the individual scientist, if it instead perverts the tradition of critically discussing new ideas into a tradition of deferring to experts, if it leads scientists to employ unscrupulous methods in order to survive, and if it appeals to communalist thinking and the pressure of community to keep its party hierarchy in line, then The Scientific Institution is not well-designed. And if the members of The Scientific Institution are motivated primarily by self-interest, if they are more concerned with their own advancement than they are with discovering truth and explaining phenomena that we do not understand, then no matter how well-designed The Scientific Institution might be, it has not been properly manned.

I think that this is almost where we are today. I think that the regulative ideal of power has all but replaced the regulative ideal of truth. And I think that we can no longer expect The Scientific Institution to police its scientists—any more than we can expect the police to police itself—because we can no longer regard The Scientific Institution as disinterested.

On the contrary, The Scientific Institution as it exists today forms a hybrid with Big Government, Big Business, and Big Education—not The Scientific Institution, but The Big-Science-Big-Business-Big-Government-Big-Education Institution—in which the interests that have traditionally been regarded as scientific might actually count last in a decision regarding the acceptance of a new theory or technology (let alone in a job decision, or a decision to publish a journal article). We can no longer assume that The Scientific Institution will impose mental discipline upon the individual scientist to preserve a tradition of critical discussion. If Kuhn is right, then the individual scientist who tries to critically discuss new ideas may well find himself imposing an unwanted mental discipline upon a community that will respond, apparently with Kuhnian approval, by ostracizing him.

There are many attractions of communalist thinking. But its primary vice is that it uses the power of community to punish individuals who criticize its authority. This is the way it has always been and, while I am not an inductivist, I see no reason to think that it is any different now.

I see, on the contrary, every reason to think that this kind of punitive communalist thinking has worked its way into the very fabric of the West. And it is very easy to see why. Nobody still believes that it is possible to prove that their theories are true. But this only makes it more important for authorities to protect their authority. For, they would otherwise, after all, cease to *be* authorities. And what better way for The Scientific Institution to protect its authority than to define knowledge and truth as what its experts believe, and to exclude those who dare to think otherwise?

But the idea that there are experts who have a special kind of authority that cannot be questioned—and especially not by non-experts—is the royal road to closed society. And for all the current talk about open society, it is the road upon which we are now travelling.

Let me give you just one example.

I remember that when the Soviet Union collapsed, one of my old philosophy professors who had predicted the event several years earlier—a probability theorist, and not a political analyst—remarked: 'It's really very simple. We ran a race with the Russians, and they got there first.'

The event, however, apparently took many of our western experts by surprise—so much so that there have actually been papers and conferences devoted to the question of *why* it took them by surprise. But most of the explanations that I have heard have focussed upon the difficulty of making predictions in the social sciences—though I assume that what people really mean by this is the difficulty of making *true* predictions. I have even heard political scientists give their students the *practical* advice not to make predictions—lest they be *blamed* when their predictions turn out to be false!

But I have yet to hear even one such expert explain that he was surprised by the collapse of the Soviet Union because it showed that his theory of the Soviet Union was false—a novel idea that might be worth pursuing for anyone who is really interested in open society.

This goes a long way toward explaining why our growing reliance upon experts of The Scientific Institution may lead to a closed society. The idea that fuels The Scientific Institution is that science begins where criticism leaves off. And the idea that fuels the open society is that science corrects its mistakes through criticism. These two ideas are at odds. They contradict each other. And we must choose between them.

X

Those of you who have been influenced by the so-called 'post-modernist' movement may feel that this choice is now obsolete. You may think that the so-called 'problem of representation' has shown that truth does not exist and that what we now call 'truth' is simply what you can convince other people to believe. I think that the major attraction of this philosophy lies in its dissatisfaction with authoritarian regimes, and in its claim to be new and avant-garde. But I also find it ironic that some of the very people who once told us that history is important because its laws determine the future, now tell us—after their historical predictions have turned out to be false—that history is important because we can rewrite the past.

It is as if Marxists have discovered that Marxism isn't true, and have concluded from this that there is no truth.

None of this is new or avant-garde. What post-modernists now call the 'problem of representation' is really the age-old epistemo-logical problem of knowing which, if any, of our representations are true. And their 'new' idea that our inability to prove that a statement is true means that truth does not exist is really the last vestige of that pre-post-modernist philosophy known as 'logical positivism'.

The names, I admit, have all been changed. And most post-modernists will laugh with scorn at the idea that the positivists are their intellectual ancestors. But their basic idea is that truth can exist only if we have an objective criterion for determining what is true. And this, unless I am very mistaken, is simply the verifiability criterion of meaning—French style—telling us, all over again, that a term is meaningless if we do not have a criterion for applying it, and that 'truth' is meaningless if we cannot verify that statements are true.

I have no doubt whatsoever that the people who advocate this philosophy have the very best of intentions. But it leads all too easily, and far too quickly, to a worse kind of authoritarianism than the ones it seeks to deconstruct.

Plato and Stalin both knew that they could rewrite the past. And neither of them had any problem of representation while rewriting it. We can certainly argue about whether the lies they told were noble or not. But at least they knew that they were lying when they told them.

XI

This brings me to the problem of bureaucracy. It is well known that Popper broke with the communists because he could not reconcile himself with their cavalier sacrifice of human life. Nevertheless Popper remained a socialist for several more years, until his experiences in Vienna convinced him that there are dangers in socialism that are far more threatening than the problems it is supposed to solve. Indeed, Popper told me only shortly before his death that he would still consider himself a socialist 'were it not for the power problem.'

But what, exactly, is the 'power problem'? And what, exactly, are the dangers that he saw in socialism? Popper once explained it to me like this:[15]

> When I was a young man I was an ardent socialist. But I revised my views— not on the general humanitarian issues, but on the practical possibilities of socialism—when there was a socialist government in Vienna.

It was immediately after the First World War. There was terrible hunger and homelessness in Vienna. Popper, at the time, was working in a home for destitute children. And he had been assigned, as one of his duties, the job of cleaning and binding their little cuts and scratches:

> I had a certain amount of material to bind their wounds, and I had some iodine, which was then the main thing that we put on a wound to disinfect it. Well, you know that little children come all the time with all sorts of things. And before long I needed a new bottle of iodine. For *this* I had to make an application to the magistrate! I first had to travel to the center of Vienna, some fifteen miles away, where our bureaucrats met. Then I was sent from there across town to a doctor. The doctor viewed me with great suspicion and questioned me for a long time, but he finally gave me a prescription. And with that I had to travel to a hospital at the other end of Vienna, where I was given a bottle of iodine like this!

Here Popper held up his hand with his thumb and forefinger spread about an inch apart:

> It was, of course, the last time that I asked the socialists for iodine! The amount of work that went into getting that little bottle of iodine, and the amount of lost time from my real work with the children, was so absolutely out of proportion, that I actually preferred, from then on, to pay for it out of my own pocket rather than undergo that sort of thing again.

Popper told me that this one experience had taught him 'a lot of things,' and that it led him to change his mind about socialism:

> I saw that we, social workers, who were really working with the people, were like the soldiers at the front. And there on top of us were the administrators. It taught me that the administrators were in the main interested in their own advancement rather than in helping us to help the children. And it taught me that the central problem of socialism would be the problem of dealing with bureaucracy. You have a certain idea to help people, and you even get some money to do so. But how do you make sure that three-quarters of it does not disappear before it ever reaches them? So much of this administration went into red tape and into nothing at all! That, of course, was very many years ago. But I have hardly ever found a socialist of any degree of power in his party who would even admit that this was a central problem.

Lenin may or may not have admitted that bureaucracy is a central problem for Marxism. But some people have seen the Soviet bureaucrats as a new ruling class—or community, if you will—that has exploited people as much as the capitalists of the past. Others have thought that it engendered the eventual transformation of socialist radicalism into a conservatism in which the party leaders became far more concerned with preserving their own power than with serving the needs of the people whom they were supposed to represent.

But my own sense is that bureaucracy is not a problem that is peculiar to socialism. My own sense is that bureaucrats everywhere are often more interested in preserving their own power and promoting their own advancement than in helping others. And my own sense is that socialism never quite cornered the market on red tape.

Bureaucracy can now be found in almost every state system, and in almost every large organization as well. I do not think that we can any longer pretend to defend its existence on the grounds of efficiency. But we may defend it by saying that the representatives of large organizations cannot know all of the people whom they serve, and must therefore institute rules to protect themselves against fraud. And we may also defend it by saying that it is really necessary if we are going to have large organizations at all.

However I do not think we can say that it promotes open society. You do not have to look too far into a bureaucracy to find most of the things that are characteristic of closed society. There is, first of all, its strict hierarchical authority structure with rigid procedural rules and superior-inferior relationships. This leads to the transformation of human beings into little computers, programmed to follow a set of well-defined rules and capable of performing limited tasks according to them, but unable, or at least unwilling, to think for themselves even so far as to distinguish between those rules and the ends that they are meant to serve. It leads to the transformation of civil servants into civil masters, and to what Popper used to call the tyranny of the petty official.[16] And it leads, in the end, to a consolidation of power in the hands of an oligarchic elite—or community, if you will—that is able to manipulate the rules, as well as information and communication, so as to deflect criticism and perpetuate its own power.

It is hard to imagine how any of this helps to set free the critical powers of man. But it is very easy to see how much of it has worked its way into The Scientific Institution.

Today we no longer believe that scientific knowledge can be rationally justified and many have 'inferred' from this that it also cannot be true. But philosophers of science continue to attribute authority to The Scientific Institution—while simultaneously acknowledging that this authority, and indeed even the membership of The Scientific Institution, is based upon nothing more than the consensus of its members. All of this, I think, is entirely in keeping with communalist bureaucratic thinking and with the 'progress' that The Scientific Institution is so often said to have made. For it means that The Scientific Institution, or at least the philosophers of The Scientific Institution, have finally demonstrated—have agreed amongst themselves—that the elephants do, indeed, go all the way down.

This, I think, is what Popper had in mind when he said that he would still regard himself as a socialist were it not for the power problem. And it is, I think, the threat that he saw in socialism that he regarded as far more dangerous than the problems that it was meant to solve. We have already seen what it has done in the Soviet Union. But it is, for all that, not a problem that is peculiar to socialism. It is, on the contrary, the far more general problem of bureaucracy.

The problem of bureaucracy is the problem of how to organize science and society on a large scale without losing the individual's freedom in a labyrinth of rigid and impersonal rules. It is the problem of how to use bureaucracy in such a way that the rules exist for the sake of the human individual—for the sake of free citizens and their free social life—and not the other way round.

It is important to understand this problem in the context of the collapse of the Soviet Union—in the context, that is, of the collapse of a social, political, and economic Leviathan that presented itself, and defended itself as scientific, and as the product of science and rational thinking—and as part of the contemporary critique of science and rationality. It is, in other words, important to understand that the contemporary critique of science and rationality is really very often a critique of The Scientific Institution. If we fail to understand this, then we are likely to make the same mistake that the communists made. We are likely, that is, to abandon science and rationality itself, and to replace it with The Institution.

The failure of the policies of *scientific* socialism cannot be denied. They range from the economic to the ecological—and they have left the people of the former Soviet Union devastated and the countries in which they live fifty years behind the rest of the industrialized world. But the simple fact of the matter is that these failures were not due to science and rationality—but to the *abandonment* of the scientific and rational attitude. They were due to the subordination of the critical attitude to the demands of ideology—or, to put it more accurately, to the demands of authority, community, and bureaucracy, and to the necessity of preserving their power.

The problem of bureaucracy is a problem that we have not yet solved and do not yet know how to solve. I do not think that we will solve it by following the experts of The Scientific Institution. But it is a problem that we should all be trying to solve, along with the problems of authority and community, because it continues to pose one of the greatest threats to our freedom and open society.

XII

There is one more problem that those of us who are interested in open society should be trying to solve. It is the practical problem of whether freedom and open society are worth paying money for. I am by no means being facetious in raising this problem, or in calling it 'practical.' Freedom, we all say, is priceless. 'Give me liberty or give me death!' But matters apparently change as soon as we are asked to pay money for it. For many people seem willing to put their freedom in jeopardy, if not to sacrifice it entirely, if they see an opportunity to make a few dollars by doing so.

It is well-known that corruption in the countries of the former (current?) socialist bloc is now reaching unprecedented levels. But the most disturbing thing about this corruption is that it is not only mafia racketeers and professional criminals who engage in it. Black market, bribery, and tax evasion are now the norm for ordinary working citizens who want simply to lead a decent bourgeois existence. I have even heard experts say that such corruption is and ought to be tolerated by the state because it facilitates a rapid transition to capitalism—and, *hence*(?!), to freedom.

Part of the fallacy here is the easy equation of freedom with the ability to acquire and manipulate material objects. This, no doubt, is a certain kind of freedom. But it is one that all too easily conflicts with the freedom to say what you think is true. This is the freedom that Popper thought was important for an open society. And it is a freedom that people seem all too willing to sacrifice when they step outside the law.

But could it possibly be true that this corruption is not only tolerated, but actually encouraged by the state?

Popper was wary of historical predictions. But even he was willing to predict the formation of black markets in states that did not enforce laws against them while pursuing policies that result in a shortage of commodities. It is, likewise, easy to see that there will be a good deal of tax evasion in a society in which the state raises its taxes exorbitantly but fails to prosecute those who evade them.

But why would a state encourage criminal activities amongst its citizens? Why would it enact laws that are difficult to obey, and sometimes even contradictory, and then make little or no effort to enforce them?

One simple answer that you can never entirely rule out is stupidity. Another—and it may be difficult to decide which of the two is the more charitable—is that the state has found an easy and effective way to control its citizens.

Those who engage in criminal activity will most likely want to keep a low profile. They will, as a consequence, be less likely to criticize their government. And if they do speak out, their culpability makes it very easy for the government to silence them.

In this way, a state can even perpetuate the myth that it is only the lawless among its citizens who are dissatisfied with it.

Earlier I drew a distinction between open society and market society. But if open society is not market society, then it is not black market society either. And states that legislate and enforce laws in ways that encourage criminal activities among their citizens—like the citizens who enable them to do so—must at least be suspected to be enemies of freedom and open society.

Notes

1 This is a revised version of a paper that was first presented at a conference that was held in Prague on 9–10 November 1995 to celebrate the fiftieth anniversary of the publication of Karl Popper's *The Open Society and Its Enemies*. It has since been presented, among other places, at the Open Society House of Culture and Communications, in Vilnius, Lithuania on 24 April 1997; at the Department of Philosophy and Methodology at Moscow State University in Moscow, Russia on 22 May 1997; and at the Institute of Philosophy and Social Theory at the University of Belgrade in Belgrade, Serbia on 19 March 1998. Prior English versions have been published in *Common Knowledge*, December, 1997, and in *Popper's Open Society After Fifty Years*, edited by Ian Jarvie and Sandra Pralong, Routledge, London, 1999. A Russian translation was published in *Voprosy Filosofii*, November 1997. Unauthorized English, Russian, and Ukrainian versions were published in *Political Thought*, 3–4, 1996. A second unauthorized Ukrainian version was published in *Demons of Peace and Gods of War. Social Conflicts in Post-communist World*, edited by Sergey Makeev, Kiev, 1997. The motto is from Karl R. Popper, *The Open Society and Its Enemies*, 1945. Reprinted by Routledge, London, 1998, vol. 1, p. 200.
2 Karl R. Popper, 'The Open Society and the Democratic State,' The Karl Popper Archives, Box 6, File 6.
3 Popper, 'The Open Society and the Democratic State.'
4 Popper, 'The Open Society and the Democratic State.'
5 See Popper, *The Open Society and Its Enemies*, vol. 1, p. 1. Popper's criticism of Plato, Hegel, and Marx was that they believed in historicism—the idea that there are laws of history that determine the course of human events—and that historicism is a belief in magic.
6 See Thomas S. Kuhn, 'Logic of Discovery or Psychology of Research?' in *Criticism and the Growth of Knowledge*, edited by Imre Lakatos and Alan Musgrave, Cambridge University Press, 1970, p. 6.

7 Compare this with what Popper says about historicism in vol. 2, page 279 of *The Open Society and Its Enemies*.

8 See, for example, Thomas S. Kuhn, *The Structure of Scientific Revolutions*, 1962, second edition, University of Chicago Press, Chicago, 1970. Kuhn, I should note, soon retreated from his original doctrine of incommensurability, though many of his followers in the social sciences have carried it much further.

9 Karl R. Popper, 'Science: Problems, Aims, Responsibilities,' in Karl R. Popper, *The Myth of the Framework*, edited by M.A. Notturno, Routledge, London, 1994, p. 110.

10 Karl Popper's letter to Frederick Hellin, 29 June 1943. The Karl Popper Archives, Box 28, File 7. Popper then went on to say:

> This is one of the reasons why it will be difficult to find an authority to recommend it. The established intellectual authorities will not like it, since it fights against the very idea of an established intellectual authority, and since it undermines their glory. It hits practically everybody, with very few exceptions ...
>
> Thus my book will not easily find support from those who are 'arrived,' nor from those who hope to 'arrive' one day.

11 This—as opposed to anything that you might find in the probability calculus—is the big difference between Carnap's idea of confirmation and Popper's notion of corroboration. Simply put, we cannot rely upon even the best corroborated of our theories.

12 See Popper, *The Open Society and Its Enemies*, vol. 2, pp. 235–236.

13 Karl R. Popper, 'Public Opinion and Liberal Principles,' in Karl R. Popper, *Conjectures and Refutations*, 1963. Reprinted by Routledge, London, 1991, p. 351.

14 Karl Popper, *The Poverty of Historicism*, 1957. Reprinted by Routledge, London, 1991, p. 157.

15 Popper once told me this story, I think back in 1985, during one of our walks around the Kenley aerodrome. Years later, I found that he had told virtually the same story to his Introduction to Scientific Method class twenty years before. I am sure he told it many times. I have reconstructed it here, in the first person, partly from memory and partly from the transcript of Popper's 29 November 1966 class lecture that exists in The Karl Popper Archives.

16 See Popper, *The Open Society and Its Enemies*, vol. 1, p. 4.

2   Tolerance, Freedom, and Truth: Fallibilism and the Opening of Closed Societies[1]

> *An open society (that is, a society based on the idea of not merely tolerating dissenting opinions but respecting them) and a democracy (that is, a form of government devoted to the protection of an open society) cannot flourish if science becomes the exclusive possession of a closed set of specialists.*
> Karl R. Popper

I

Many people, under the influence of positivist empiricism, still believe that we are wholly the products of our environments. I believe, contrary to this, that it is our task as free and rational beings to transcend whatever we can blame on our environments. This applies especially to tolerance, which many people advocate as a way to transcend our religious, ethnic, and racial prejudices. These prejudices have long been impediments to freedom, and tolerance, if generally practiced, would go a long way toward fostering a society that many people would regard as free. But I also think that it might, strangely enough, be at odds with the sort of society that Karl Popper regarded as open. I say 'strangely enough' because most proponents of open society say that it *requires* a tradition of tolerance—and because neither Popper nor I would say that an open society is, or ought to be, *intolerant*.

My sense, however, is that tolerance may actually undermine our attempts to learn from each other through criticism—and that accepting it as our ideal may undercut our attempts to open closed societies.

If all one means by 'open society' is a society that tolerates differences, then it is clear that open society requires a tradition of tolerance. Popper, however, thought that open society sets free the critical powers of man, that it is based upon an awareness of our own fallibility, and that it is impossible without a recognition that the ideas of others may be closer to the truth than our own. Popper, it is true, thought that *democracy* will not work well in societies that do not value freedom and tolerance. But democracy is not itself open society. And while it may be the form of government best able to protect an open society, we should always remember that it is the best of a bad lot, that it can be abused by authoritarians and manipulated by bureaucrats, and that open society is not a product of manipulation and abuse, but of a serious attempt to get at the truth, tempered by a serious belief in our own fallibility.

It is clear, however, that one can argue for tolerance from a premise of *infallibilism*—'We should tolerate these false ideas, though we are certain that they are false, because it would only do greater harm to try to suppress them'—and that one can also argue that we ought *not* to criticize ideas that differ from our own *because* we are fallible and *because* fallibility means that we should tolerate them instead.

Indeed, many relativists now regard it as a foregone conclusion that there actually is no truth for us to get closer to, that 'reason' is just another name for power, and that our only salvation from violent power struggles is tolerance and the *non-critical* attitude.

The question whether or not we should be persuaded by such arguments is the great philosophical problem of our time. I, for one, am not persuaded by them. But it is clear from the very fact that these arguments can be made that tolerance is perfectly compatible with closed society. I would, at this point, be tempted to describe open society as a higher development of freedom— were it not for the fact that my wife, who was born in Russia and studied philosophy with the communists, visibly cringes at the very mention of 'higher developments.'

So let me just try, instead, to explain how an open society differs from one that is *merely* free and why tolerance is not quite the right ideal for fostering it.

II

Tolerance is the patient forbearance of something that is disliked and, perhaps, even thought to be evil. It has been valued as an ethical ideal at least since the eighteenth century, when it was proposed, by enlightenment philosophers such as Locke and Voltaire, as an antidote to religious persecution. This, perhaps, is the reason why some people regard tolerance and persecution as opposites, and think that since persecution is always wrong, tolerance is always right and always rational. But things are not so simple. Locke, despite his arguments for tolerance, may be even better known for insisting that we should *not* tolerate atheists and Roman Catholics. Freedom and free society, according to Locke, may not depend upon the *specific* religious beliefs that we hold. But it does depend upon our having *some* belief in God—since those who do not believe in God cannot take valid oaths—and it also depends upon our not paying allegiance to foreign princes, such as the Pope.

We have, at least in the West, come a long way since Locke. But even today, most advocates of tolerance would agree that we should not tolerate everything. We should not, for example, tolerate injustice, or murder, or attempts to restrict our freedom. And we *need* not, everything else being equal, tolerate the intolerant.

This last idea, that we need not tolerate the intolerant, is Popper's solution to the so-called 'paradox of tolerance.' Popper used to illustrate this paradox by telling a story about a tribe of Indians who were so impartial in their tolerance that they even extended it to a den of man-eating tigers that lived nearby. The tigers were very happy for this. But the Indians slowly disappeared—and their policy of indiscriminate tolerance along with them.

The point of the story is that we might, if we are too tolerant, end up promoting intolerance.[2]

But isn't the open society open to *all* ideas? And shouldn't tolerance at least be our *ideal*? Doesn't Popper's critical rationalism—the tradition of reasoning together instead of fighting each other—*imply* that we should tolerate those who disagree with us? So if we are both critical rationalists and tolerant, and if those who are intolerant disagree with us about tolerance, then aren't we actually *committed* to tolerating their intolerance?

How could tolerance possibly be at odds with open society?

Popper wrote that rationalism implies the recognition of the claim to tolerance for all who are not intolerant themselves.[3] But he was clear that this does not imply that rationalism always works, or that we must tolerate the intolerant. On the contrary, Popper wrote that 'there are limits to the attitude of reasonableness':

> You cannot have a rational discussion with a man who prefers shooting you to being convinced by you… It is the same with tolerance. You must not, without qualification, accept the principle of tolerating all those who are intolerant; if you do, you will destroy not only yourself, but also the attitude of tolerance.[4]

This is because:

> Unlimited tolerance must lead to the disappearance of tolerance. If we extend unlimited tolerance even to those who are intolerant, if we are not prepared to defend a tolerant society against the onslaught of the intolerant, then the tolerant will be destroyed, and tolerance with them.[5]

But it does not imply that we should *always* suppress the utterance of intolerant philosophies:

> As long as we can counter them by rational argument and keep them in check by public opinion, suppression would certainly be most unwise. But we should claim the *right* to suppress them if necessary even by force; for it may easily turn out that they are not prepared to meet us on the level of rational argument, but begin by denouncing all argument; they may forbid their followers to listen to rational argument, because it is deceptive, and teach them to answer arguments by the use of their fists or pistols. We should therefore claim, in the name of tolerance, the right not to tolerate the intolerant. We should claim that any movement preaching intolerance places itself outside the law, and we should consider incitement to intolerance and persecution as criminal, in the same way as we should consider incitement to murder, or to kidnapping, or to the revival of the slave trade, as criminal.[6]

Some people think that there is a contradiction in this—if not in the idea of the tolerant refusing to tolerate the intolerant, then at least in the idea that they may suppress some instances of intolerance while being willing to tolerate others. But the paradox of tolerance is not that the tolerant are being intolerant when they refuse to tolerate intolerance. It is that they may, by being too tolerant, unwittingly promote intolerance in others—and with it their own demise.

This, I think, enables us to see what is really at stake when it comes to tolerance. The intolerant would forcibly restrict our freedom because of who we are, or because of what we believe and say. And there is no point appealing to reason or talking about contradictions when it comes to this. We must claim the right to forcibly oppose their intolerance if we are to keep any rights at all.

But while it is important for us to *claim* the right to suppress the intolerant, it may not be necessary or, indeed, desirable for us to *exercise* it. For if we risk our freedom by tolerating the intolerant, we also risk it by suppressing them.

This is what Popper meant when he said that there are times when the suppression of intolerant philosophies would be 'most unwise.' But there is no algorithm or general rule that can tell us when the risks of suppressing the intolerant outweigh the risks of tolerating them. We must, on the contrary, decide in each individual case whether and to what extent we should tolerate the intolerant.

There is, insofar as this is concerned, no contradiction in our decision to exercise our rights in some cases and not in others—anymore than there is a contradiction in a decision to marry one person and not another. We might, for example, think that the chances of national socialism gaining popular support in Illinois in 1998 are so remote that we would run a greater risk to our freedom by forbidding the Nazis from marching in Skokie than we would by allowing it. And we might decide that it would, in this case, be unwise for us *not* to tolerate their intolerance—while simultaneously opposing a similar march on the same day in Budapest if, for example, we were to think that the chances of national socialism gaining popular support there were different.

We are, after all, trying to bring about the open society, not the stupid society.

But it is not even clear that such discriminant tolerance is, or should be regarded as, our *ideal*. Tolerance may be the best that we can hope for in the real world. But tolerance would not be necessary in an ideal world at all. There would be nothing in an ideal world that we would dislike, nothing that we would regard as evil, and thus nothing that we would have to tolerate. And even in the real world, the people whom the tolerant would tolerate do not, themselves, usually *want* to be tolerated. They want, on the contrary, to be accepted, and not merely endured as unavoidable evils for the sake of civilized policy. And they want this even if they are, in most cases, willing to tolerate being tolerated.

I say all of this not because I wish to denigrate tolerance, but because I fear that it is too easy to get carried away on a wave of good feeling while talking about it.

The fact of the matter is that tolerance is always a dicey proposition. There is no doubt that tolerance feels better than intolerance. But good feelings seldom endure—there would be no need for tolerance if they did—and we may run a serious risk of actually losing our freedom if we tolerate those who would take it away.

All of that is on the one hand. On the other hand is the fact that we are not ourselves open, and we should not congratulate ourselves for being open or for opening closed societies merely because we are willing to restrain ourselves from suppressing ideas that differ from our own.

In my view, the basic ideal of open society is not really tolerance at all. I do not mean that people should be intolerant, or that tolerance is not important for freedom and free society. But I do mean that the ideals that fuel an open society are such that we have to do more than merely tolerate dissenting ideas if we want to open a closed one.

III

Tolerance is putting up with things that we do not like and with things that we think might even be evil. It is good to tolerate others, if tolerating others does not threaten our own freedom.

And we would like, if nothing else, for others to tolerate us. Tolerance, thus understood, is the ideal of that so-called 'negative' freedom, or freedom from coercion, which asks for nothing more than that we leave each other alone. I do not want to denigrate negative freedom, or to suggest in any way that it is unimportant. It is, on the contrary, essential for anyone who does not already have it. And tolerance, for this reason, should always be our first priority so long as there are intolerant people in the world who are persecuting others for their religious beliefs or for their ethnic and racial heritages or for simply being 'different.' It is, in the face of intolerance, a necessary condition for the freedom of anyone who would be persecuted without it. But it is still, for all that, a *minimum* condition.

And Popper, in any event, thought that open society is 'based on the idea of not merely tolerating dissenting opinions but respecting them.'[7]

But isn't respect the same as tolerance?

You can, of course, use a term to mean whatever you like. And I would not disagree with anyone who said that tolerance, qua respect or qua the absence of intolerance, is a prerequisite for open society. This, I think, is the way in which Popper himself often used the term, and why he said that open society is based upon respecting dissenting opinions and not merely tolerating them. It is, however, important to recognize that many people regard tolerance and respect as entirely different things.

Tolerance is a *negative* attitude. We put up with. We endure. We suffer. We try not to suppress or to persecute. We restrain ourselves from eliminating what we would otherwise eliminate, were it not for our feeling that we ought to be tolerant. Respect, on the other hand, is a positive attitude. We consider. We appreciate. We take seriously, value, and perhaps admire. We may, indeed, even try to emulate and to model ourselves upon those whom we respect.

These are different attitudes and they lead to different actions. Tolerance leads to our allowing differences to exist. But respect leads to our trying to learn from them. And here, the attempt to learn from beliefs that differ from our own may well conflict with the kind of negative freedom for which tolerance is a necessary condition. I do not, in an open society, ask to be left alone in the security of my own beliefs. And I do not leave others alone in the security of theirs. I try, on the contrary, to improve my situation by learning from others and from what they believe. This is not tolerance. It is respect. And I would even say that the ideal of open society is more closely aligned to positive freedom than it is to negative freedom, were it not for the fact that positive freedom has been held to be suspect ever since Isaiah Berlin linked it to authoritarianism and totalitarian regimes.

IV

Positive freedom, according to Berlin,[8] is not simply freedom from coercion. It is freedom to be the master of your own fate. It is freedom to govern yourself and to improve your situation, fulfilling yourself as best you can in the way you see fit. I do not know whether this distinction between negative and positive freedom is as sharp and unambiguous as Berlin suggests, or whether his idea that positive freedom leads to authoritarianism can really withstand scrutiny.

But it is clear that Berlin recognizes the distinction between tolerance and respect. For he writes that:

> Toleration ... implies a certain disrespect. I tolerate your absurd beliefs and your foolish acts, though I know them to be absurd and foolish.[9]

And he goes on to say that Mill would have agreed. For Mill, according to Berlin:

> ...believed that to hold an opinion deeply is to throw our feelings into it. He once declared that when we deeply care, we must dislike those who hold the opposite views. He preferred this to cold temperaments and opinions. He asked us not necessarily to respect the views of others—very far from it—only to try to understand and tolerate them; only tolerate; disapprove, think ill of, if need be mock or despise, but tolerate; for without conviction, without some antipathetic feeling, there was, he thought, no deep conviction; and without deep conviction there were no ends of life, and

then the awful abyss on the edge of which he had himself once stood would
yawn before us. But without tolerance the conditions for rational criticism,
rational condemnation, are destroyed.[10]

John Stuart Mill was a fallibilist. And I do not know whether this is
really a faithful representation of his view—any more than I know
whether Berlin really equates rational criticism with rational
condemnation, as his rhetoric would suggest. I do, however, know
that Popper's views on the matter were decidedly different.[11]

The aim in an open society is not to put up with ideas with
which we disagree. It is to take them seriously and to criticize
them—not necessarily as a way of condemning them, but as a way
of trying to understand them, and of testing whether or not they
are true, and learning from them, even if learning from them
means learning how and where they go wrong.

This is what Popper meant when he said that open society is
'based on the idea of not merely tolerating dissenting opinions but
respecting them.' Open society is based on respect for other people, for their freedom and autonomy as rational agents—or, as
Kant would have put it, for people as ends in themselves. It is not
that we regard their ideas as evils that we have to tolerate for
civility's sake. And it is not even that we regard them as the ideas of
other people who have just as much right to ideas as ourselves.
That, at best, would be paternalism. And it would have nothing at
all to do with a recognition of our own fallibility. Respect, on the
contrary, means that we take the dissenting opinions of others
seriously, and that we regard them as possibly true. It means, in
fact, that we treat them as potentially our own—since we want to
discover the truth and since we recognize that we may be in
error—and it means, for this reason, that we try to do everything
in our power to criticize them and to show that they are false.

Here it is ironic that Berlin recognizes a distinction between
tolerance and respect, but nonetheless characterizes a person's
desire for respect as a 'longing for status.' 'I may,' as Berlin puts it,
'feel unfree in the sense of not being recognized as a self-governing
individual human being,' or 'as a member of an unrecognized or
insufficiently respected group.' And:

I may, in my bitter longing for status, prefer to be bullied and misgoverned by some member of my own race or social class, by whom I am, nevertheless, recognized as a man and a rival—that is as an equal—to being well and tolerantly treated by someone from some higher and remoter group, who does not recognize me for what I wish to feel myself to be.[12]

Berlin then goes on to say:

Yet it is not with individual liberty, in either the 'negative' or in the 'positive' senses of the word, that this desire for status and recognition can easily be identified. It is something no less profoundly needed and passionately fought for by human beings—it is something akin to, but not itself, freedom; although it entails negative freedom for the entire group, it is more closely related to solidarity, fraternity, mutual understanding, need for association on equal terms, all of which are sometimes—but misleadingly—called social freedom.[13]

And he even writes that:

Unless this phenomenon is grasped, the ideals and behaviour of entire peoples who, in Mill's sense of the word, suffer deprivation of elementary human rights, and who, with every appearance of sincerity, speak of enjoying more freedom than when they possessed a wider measure of these rights, becomes an unintelligible paradox.[14]

The rhetoric here is brilliant—as is Berlin's idea that someone who is seeking respect as a self-governing individual is really seeking status. It is, no doubt, a tribute to the infinite resources of dialectic. But I call it ironic, because it is difficult to reconcile this paternalism—which Berlin, 'with every appearance of sincerity,' offers to the oppressed—with his own criticism of those who would, in the name of freedom and rationality, claim to know what would make an individual free better than that individual himself.

Our coming to respect dissenting ideas may well be described as an unfolding of freedom, in which our tolerance for dissenting opinions somehow leads us to a curiosity about them, and, eventually, to a respect for them, as we discover that they are no less plausible than our own.

But respect is not a logical consequence of tolerance and it is not even on a continuum with it. It is not that we begin to respect dissenting opinions by tolerating them more and more. And it is not even that we are open to ideas if we tolerate them, and then become more open as we begin to respect them. Our tolerance, on the contrary, has to be *replaced* by respect.

We do not respect ideas that we tolerate. And there is no need to tolerate ideas that we respect.

V

Here, it is important to see that tolerance, as an ideal, has nothing whatsoever to do with a recognition of our own fallibility or with a desire to learn from others.

Imagine someone who believes that he himself is fallible and that everyone else is fallible too. He believes that truth exists, and is both objective and absolute. And he would even try to discover what it is, if he only believed that someone could infallibly do so. But since he is convinced that no one can, he reasons that he might as well try to impose his own will upon everyone else as far possible.[15]

I see no contradiction in such a scenario and I conclude, as a result, that tolerance does not follow simply from an awareness of our own fallibility.

But why, then, do so many people think that it does?

The answer is that they unconsciously factor into the equation a respect for the freedom and autonomy of their fellow man—and that the tolerance that they advocate *as a response to an awareness of human fallibility* follows, in fact, directly from this respect for human freedom alone.

If a person believes in human freedom, then he believes that we should be able to think and act as we wish, provided, of course, that our thoughts and actions do not impinge upon the freedom of others. But this is simply to say that the thoughts and actions of people should be tolerated so long as they are not themselves intolerant. None of this has anything to do with fallibility. And since I have just suggested how fallibilism is compatible with outright intolerance, we can conclude that tolerance neither entails nor is entailed by it.

Tolerance also has nothing whatsoever to do with learning. We say that the prejudices and fears that lead to intolerance spring from ignorance and from erroneous beliefs about people who differ from ourselves. But tolerance advocates that we *endure* our fears and put up with the things against which we are prejudiced. It nowhere advocates that we remove our ignorance and our erroneous ideas—though it does sometimes talk as if the mere fact that we are now tolerant means that we are no longer ignorant or in error.

No, we tolerate dissenting opinions not because we want to learn from them, but because we do not want to restrict the freedom of the people who hold them. And we do not want to restrict the freedom of the people who hold them because we do not want them to try to restrict our own.

VI

Earlier I said that tolerance is consistent with both relativism and infallibilism. But it is easy to see that neither of these attitudes is compatible with the sort of respect that is necessary for open society. This is clear when it comes to infallibilism, since infallibilists believe that they already know the truth and have nothing to learn from others. But it is important to understand that relativists cannot really respect the views of others, since they do not even believe in truth, and hence cannot believe that their own beliefs may be false, or that the beliefs of others may be closer to the truth than their own.

A relativist may or may not like diversity. But he cannot think that he can *learn* the truth from others, because there is really no truth in his universe to learn.

This is why relativists can talk about diverse forms of life, paradigms, and linguistic frameworks while simultaneously denying the possibility of understanding them—let alone of comparing them critically in an effort to discover which of them is true. And this is the difference between tolerance and open society. It is, in a nutshell, the difference between leaving people alone and trying to get at the truth.

Popper regarded relativism as one of the greatest of the contemporary threats to open society. But I think that the so-called 'identity philosophies' pose a greater threat.

Many people today *say* that truth is relative, but most of them do not really believe what they say. When you question them, you typically find that it is not really *truth* that they think is relative, but our *knowledge* or *beliefs* about what is true. Indeed, if you question them long enough you may even find that what they really want to say is that our knowledge and beliefs are inherently fallible and subject to error—something that would actually be impossible were truth really relative, and something with which Popper certainly agreed.

Identity philosophers, on the other hand, may say that 'truth' is meaningful and that it means correspondence to the facts. They may even acknowledge the existence of foolproof criteria by which to determine whether or not a statement is true. But they believe, and this is what makes them identity philosophers, that they owe their primary allegiance to some group to which they belong. The thrust of their attack against truth is not that we cannot know what is true. It is that truth is but one value amongst many, and not the one that counts most for building a just society. They believe that when it comes to a choice between truth and solidarity, it is solidarity that counts—so that we are not merely justified in misrepresenting the truth, but that it may actually be our duty to do so if the solidarity of our community hangs in the balance.

But no one, I hope, would accuse identity philosophers of tolerating or respecting the views of others.

VII

Our attempt to get at the truth may lead people to regard open society as intolerant since it involves such uncomfortable things as criticism, confrontation, and culture clash, and since these things obviously do not leave people alone. But the idea that it is intolerant to be critical is one of the greatest of the confusions that have been foisted upon us by relativism. Make no mistake about it.

If we could with certainty discern the truth in all of its objectivity, then the only excuse for tolerating false ideas would be our disrespect for the people who hold them to be true. But we cannot discern the truth with certainty. And we think that an objective truth may nonetheless exist. We think that we have an obligation to try to discover what it is, even if we cannot know for sure, and an obligation to consider views that seem false—for the simple reason that they might actually be true. And if we are really serious about this, if we are not merely shamming our fallibility but really think that views that differ from our own might actually be true, then we will not merely tolerate these views. We will respect them.

We will, in other words, respect them enough to try to determine whether or not they are really true. And we will do this the only way we can: by deriving consequences from them and by checking to see whether and to what extent those consequences conflict with what we think is true.

All of this is already implicit in the motto 'I may be wrong and you may be right, and by an effort, we may get closer to the truth,'[16] which is the motto that Popper used to formulate his attitude of critical rationalism. And it is also implicit in the three ethical principles that he thought 'form the basis of every rational discussion, that is, of every discussion undertaken in the search for truth':[17]

1. The principle of fallibility: perhaps I am wrong and perhaps you are right. But we could easily both be wrong.
2. The principle of rational discussion: we want to try, as impersonally as possible, to weigh up our reasons for and against a theory: a theory that is definite and criticizable.
3. The principle of approximation to the truth: we can nearly always come closer to the truth in a discussion which avoids personal attacks. It can help us to achieve a better understanding; even in those cases where we do not reach an agreement.[18]

If we take this attitude and these three principles seriously, then we will not *merely* tolerate views that differ from our own. We will not, in fact, really *tolerate* them at all. We will, on the contrary, consider them seriously, and as very possibly true, and we will, for that reason, criticize them seriously, and as impersonally as possible, in an effort to test them, and to try to determine whether or not they are actually true.

And we will, in any event, regard dissenting opinions, and the people who hold them, with the utmost respect, since we will recognize a possibility of learning from them, and, hence, of increasing our own knowledge.

VIII

But what about the idea that positive freedom leads to authoritarianism?

Berlin says that the idea of positive freedom has repeatedly been used by social reformers to justify their attacks upon negative freedom. But it is not clear whether he thinks that these uses were themselves justified, or that he would deny that positive freedom is a fundamental human right.

Berlin says, for example, that the argument from libertarian motives to authoritarian designs is 'historically and psychologically intelligible,' 'if not logically valid.'[19] And he writes, apparently with approval, that John Stuart Mill 'was on his guard against those who, for the sake of being left in peace to cultivate their gardens, were ready to sell their fundamental human right to self-government in the public spheres of life.'[20] But if the link between positive freedom and authoritarianism is not logical, if it is merely historically and psychologically intelligible, then doesn't that mean that the one does not follow from the other at all? Doesn't it mean that it is not positive freedom that leads to authoritarianism—for if it were, then the link between them would be logical after all—but something else, perhaps when held in conjunction with positive freedom, but, then again, perhaps all by itself?

In my view, the authoritarianism that Berlin rightly criticizes is not so much a consequence of positive freedom as it is an addition to it. And the answer, when Berlin asks whether there is something amiss in the premises of an argument that leads from freedom to despotism, should be 'Not necessarily, since the conclusion does not really follow from them.' But what is interesting is that when Berlin restates his premises—so that we can see what exactly *is* amiss in them—we find not simply the idea that freedom is self-direction, but:

> ... first, that all men have one true purpose, and one only, that of rational self-direction; second, that the ends of all rational beings must of necessity fit into a single universal, harmonious pattern, which some men may be able to discern more clearly than others; third, that all conflict, and consequently all tragedy, is due solely to the clash of reason with the irrational or the insufficiently rational—the immature and undeveloped elements in life—whether individual or communal, and that such clashes are, in principle, avoidable, and for wholly rational beings impossible; finally, that when all men have been made rational, they will obey the rational laws of their own natures, which are one and the same in them all, and so be at once wholly law-abiding and wholly free.[21]

There is so much added to positive freedom here, and so much amiss, that I really do not know where to begin. But even so, the argument as stated does not quite entail authoritarianism—let alone *state* authoritarianism—not, at least, until we add that we know with certainty which men are able to discern the ends of all rational beings more clearly than others, and that we are willing and able to force compliance with these ends upon those who would otherwise resist them.

Everything is what it is. Positive freedom is what it is. And authoritarianism is what it is. And what Berlin rightly criticizes is not positive freedom, but that old Hegelian 'sleight of hand' that would first divide the self into its 'higher' and 'lower' halves and then equate the coercion of an individual 'for his own good' with the free choice of that individual's higher self. It is this idea that leads to authoritarianism—together with the notion that someone else who is in closer contact with knowledge, or science, or rationality, or God Himself, can judge better than you what your higher self really wants.

But the idea that I can judge better than you what would make you 'truly' free is not itself a consequence of positive freedom. And there is really no reason to mince words about it. This is authoritarianism pure and simple. And it is, in any event, utterly at odds with the fallibilism that fuels Popper's views on science and the open society.

Berlin may be right that positive freedom is a rationalist's doctrine and that rationality is 'knowing things and people for what they are.' But knowing things and people for what they are, for a *critical* rationalist, is knowing that we are all—the state and everyone in it—inherently fallible.

IX

If what I have been saying is true, then the attitude of tolerance—of enduring, or suffering, or putting up for civility's sake with something that we know to be wrong—is fundamentally at odds with the ideal of an open society: not because we should be intolerant, but because we cannot really be open to new ideas if we know from the start that they are wrong. We could, at the very best, say that the establishment of a tradition of tolerance is important as a first step for people who would like to move their societies away from intolerance. But it might be better, if we want to link this tradition to open society, to characterize it as a tradition of opposing intolerance.

We will not learn from different ideas if we *merely* tolerate them—instead of criticizing them and testing whether they are true—but we certainly will not learn from them if we cannot even hear what they are.

X

This, I think, goes a long way toward explaining one of the most disturbing phenomena in the practice of contemporary democracy. It is easy for 'democrats' to advocate tolerance and democratic process when the people they would tolerate pose no serious threat to their own power. But it is often a different story when these same 'democrats' are confronted with serious opponents who have widespread

support and may even win at the polls. And please do not misunderstand. We need not, and very often ought not, tolerate the
Hitlers and Stalins who pose a threat to our freedom. But we
certainly ought to respect the members of different political parties
that seek merely to reexamine our ends and the means that we have
adopted to achieve them. So it is disturbing to see 'democrats' and
'friends of the people' resort to dirty tricks to ensure their own re-
elections and the acceptance of their policies. It is disturbing to see
them misrepresent the facts. It is disturbing to see them try to silence,
compromise, and exclude their opponents from the political process.
It is disturbing to see them try to control and manipulate the discussion with techniques that are designed to deflect criticism rather
than to answer it. It is disturbing to see them doing all of this in the
name of 'democracy'. And it is impossible not to wonder whether
such 'friends of the people' can be anyone's real friends at all.

It is, perhaps, even more disturbing to find that many of us now
not only accept that this is what actually happens, but that we also
accept that it is what *ought* to happen—because it is, after all, 'part
of the game.'

I have already said that democracy is not itself open society. It is
probably the best political system that we have thus far invented
for protecting open society. But it is still the best of a bad lot, and
its primary virtue is that it provides a regular and non-violent way
to get rid of our leaders once we discover that they are not as good
as we had hoped them to be. I do not mean to diminish this virtue.
We see all around us the violent power struggles that take place in
states that do not have strong democratic traditions and many of us
live in constant fear that the violence of those power struggles may
someday touch our own lives and the lives of those we love.

*But this does not mean that we should tolerate 'democrats' who would
abuse our democratic traditions for the sake of their own power.*

The actions of these people speak louder than their words, and
their actions say that they are a threat to our freedom. Their
actions say that they believe that both the state and its citizens
should exist for the sake of their own political power. And their
actions tell us that they are enemies of freedom and open society,
and deserve neither our tolerance nor our respect.

XI

Here, someone might reasonably ask whether there is really any role for tolerance in an open society at all. My own view is that there is, but that it is very different from what most people think. Most people, when they think of tolerance, usually think about tolerating someone else. But I think that what we must really tolerate if we want to open our closed societies—and, especially, if we want to keep them open—is ourselves. We must somehow learn to tolerate our own fallibility and our own inability to be as good as we would like to be.

We are, as humans, all liable to make mistakes. Some of us are no doubt more liable than others. But none of us are infallible, and none of us likes the mistakes that he makes. Most of us, in fact, regard our mistakes as evils of one kind or another. Descartes thought that our errors were caused by sin. Kant believed that they were caused by madness. It is difficult to know whether this was a cause or an effect of their belief that knowledge is infallible. But it is easy to see why, with a legacy like that, we would prefer to deny our mistakes, or to cover them up, instead of acknowledging them and trying to learn from them.

In my view, the first thing that we must do if we really want to open closed societies is to accept and to learn how to tolerate the fact that we are fallible and liable to make mistakes without thereby tolerating the mistakes themselves. Popper thought that this was so important that he tried to formulate a new professional ethics in order to articulate it.[22] Our knowledge, he said, goes beyond what any *one* person can master. So there simply cannot be any authorities. It is impossible to avoid all mistakes. But it is our duty to try to do so. It is, in particular, the task of scientists to search for mistakes in even our best corroborated theories. But we must revise our attitude toward mistakes if we are to do this well. We must recognize that trying to cover up our mistakes is itself one of our greatest intellectual mistakes. We must, on the contrary, try to discover them and remember them if we are to avoid making them. We must develop and maintain a self-critical attitude in order to do this. But we must also learn to be grateful when others draw our attention to our mistakes. Indeed, we must understand that we need others to discover and correct our mistakes, just as they need us.

These are the principles of Popper's new professional ethics. But I would, in closing, like to add one of my own.

We must learn to tolerate the fact that we are human, that we cannot always realize our ideals, and that we must, sometimes, and despite our best efforts to respect others and their strange beliefs, settle for being merely tolerant.

Notes

1 This is a revised version of a paper that was first presented at the plenary session of the East-East Conference on Tolerance, which was held in Kharkov, 27-30 May 1996, and first published, in Ukrainian and English, in *Proceedings of the International Conference on Tolerance as a Cultural Universalia*, edited by A.V. Tyaglo and N.A. Busova, Kharkov, 1996. It has since been presented, among other places, at the Second Open Society Forum, entitled 'Tolerance in Society and Nature,' in Tallinn, Estonia on 18 April 1997; at the International Conference on 'Open Society—Possibilities and Perspectives' in Podgorica, Montenegro on 8 May 1997; and at the Soros Foundation in Almaty, Kazakhstan on 19 August 1998. An Estonian translation has been published in *II Avatud Ühiskonna Foorum: Sallivus*, edited by Kalle Kurg, Avatud Eesti Fond, Tallinn, 1998. The motto is from Karl R. Popper, 'Science: Problems, Aims, Responsibilities' in Karl R. Popper, *The Myth of the Framework*, edited by M.A. Notturno, Routledge, London, 1994, p. 110.
2 See Karl R. Popper, *The Open Society and Its Enemies*, 1945. Reprinted by Routledge, London, 1998, vol. 1, p. 265.
3 See Popper, *The Open Society and Its Enemies*, vol. 2, p. 238.
4 Karl R. Popper, 'Utopia and Violence' in Karl R. Popper, *Conjectures and Refutations*, 1963. Reprinted by Routledge, London, 1996, p. 357.
5 Popper, *The Open Society and Its Enemies*, vol. 1, p. 265.
6 Popper, *The Open Society and Its Enemies*, vol. 1, p. 265.
7 Popper, 'Science: Problems, Aims, Responsibilities,' p. 110.
8 See Isaiah Berlin, 'Two Concepts of Liberty' in Isaiah Berlin, *Four Essays on Liberty*, Oxford, New York, 1969.
9 Isaiah Berlin, 'John Stuart Mill and the Ends of Life' in *Four Essays on Liberty*, p. 184.
10 Berlin, 'John Stuart Mill and the Ends of Life,' p. 184.

11 After writing this paper, I came across a letter, dated 17 February 1959, that Popper wrote to Berlin about 'Two Concepts of Liberty.' After thanking Berlin for sending a copy of his paper, Popper writes, 'I have hardly ever read anything on the philosophy of politics with which I agreed so completely on all important issues.' But he goes on to say, 'Nevertheless I have some criticisms—in fact, a long list.' And he then singles out two points for special mention. The first is Berlin's picture of rationalism:

On p. 39 you state the basic assumptions of a kind of rationalism. Now I am sure you will believe me when I say that I was never in my life tempted to accept any of these four assumptions—on the contrary, I should say that ever since I could understand them— say, from my 17th year on—I would have turned from them in horror. Nevertheless I call myself a rationalist. Moreover, when you say 'Can it be that Hume is right, and Socrates mistaken?' I am far from convinced that Socrates would have accepted your four basic assumptions, although I agree that Hume would have rejected them.

But much as I admire Hume, he was the founder of irrationalism, together with Rousseau. I hasten to add that he was infinitely better than Rousseau, and surely not a romantic. But his irrationalism was that of a disappointed rationalist; and a disappointed rationalist is a man who expected too much from rationality.

On the bottom of p. 38 (note) you say: "I have never, I must own, understood what 'reason' means in this context." Nor have I. But does not this passage read like an anti-rationalist declaration? And is not anti-rationalism, or irrationalism, at least as great an enemy as an uncritical rationalism?

In my view, you yourself are a perfect example of a rationalist; for 'rationality' means, for me, the readiness to pay attention to criticism and argument—to other people's criticism of what one thinks and says, and to be highly critical of one's own views and predilections.

The second is Berlin's picture of positive freedom:

It is a marvellous ellaboration of the idea of being one's own master. But is there not a very different and very simple idea of positive freedom which *may* be complementary to negative freedom, and which does not need to clash with it? I mean, very simply, the idea to spend one's own life as well as one can; experimenting, trying to realise in one's own way, and with full respect to others (and their different valuations) what one values most? And may not the search for truth—*sapere aude*—be part of a positive idea of self-liberation? What have you against *sapere aude*? No doubt, the idea that anybody *is* wise, is dangerous and repugnant. But why should *sapere aude* be interpreted as authoritarian? It is, I feel, anti-authoritarian. When Socrates said, in the Apology, that the search for truth through critical discussion was a way of life (in fact, the best way of life he knew of)—was there anything objectionable in this?

I should be inclined to go even further: only those who have, more or less, adopted this Socratic way of life can fully understand such ideas as the idea of negative freedom.

(See Popper's correspondence with Isaiah Berlin in The Karl Popper Archives.)

12 Berlin, 'Two Concepts of Liberty,' p. 157.

13 Berlin, 'Two Concepts of Liberty,' p. 158.

14 Berlin, 'Two Concepts of Liberty,' p. 158.

15 Fallibilism may be described as a kind of *epistemological* relativism. (See my *Objectivity, Rationality, and the Third Realm*, Martinus Nijhoff, Dordrecht, 1985.) The danger, however, is the same. Such a relativist might argue that truth exists but cannot be the regulative ideal of action—as it could if someone could infallibly know it—and that in lieu of truth, the only regulative ideal strong enough to make a difference is power.

16 Popper, *The Myth of the Framework*, p. xii. See also, Popper, *The Open Society and Its Enemies*, vol. 2, p. 225.

17 Karl Popper, 'Toleration and Intellectual Responsibility' in Karl Popper, *In Search of a Better World*, translated by Laura J. Bennett, Routledge, London, 1992, p. 199.

18 Popper, 'Toleration and Intellectual Responsibility,' p. 199.

19 Berlin, 'Two Concepts of Liberty,' p. 152.

20 Berlin, 'John Stuart Mill and the Ends of Life,' p. 183.

21 Berlin, 'Two Concepts of Liberty,' p. 154.

22 See Popper, 'Toleration and Intellectual Responsibility,' pp. 201–202.

3   Education for an Open Society[1]

*All teaching on the University level (and if possible
below) should be training and encouragement in
critical thinking.*

Karl R. Popper

I

Karl Popper believed that teaching on the university level should be
training and encouragement in critical thinking. He also believed
that someone is well-educated only if he realizes how little he knows.
These two ideas are interrelated. For the purpose of critical thinking
is to discover our errors. And it is only by discovering our errors—
through self-criticism and through the criticisms of others—that we
recognize how little we know. No one else can teach us this. It is
something that we must learn for ourselves.

Popper also believed that institutions are necessary evils and that
we should not forget that they are evils simply because they are
necessary. I want to remind you of this, because I believe—and
Popper did too—that many of our educational institutions unwittingly create obstacles to learning, and that they are actually designed in such a way that education, in their hands, often degener-
ates into an authoritarian affair. This is not to say that *all* of our
educational systems are so designed, or that the students who are
educated in them never learn anything from them. But it is to say
that many of our schools and teachers unintentionally impede
learning, and that they do so in a way that unintentionally encourages the perpetuation of closed societies.

Why is this?

It is because most of our educational systems are designed in accordance with what Popper used to call 'the bucket theory of the

mind.' The mind, according to this theory, is like a bucket. And teaching occurs when someone fills our buckets with facts and theories.

Popper contrasted the bucket theory with his own idea that the mind is a searchlight. Our minds, according to this theory, have evolved as active problem-solving devices, and learning occurs when we search for solutions to our problems and for errors in the 'solutions' we find.

I want, with this in mind, to preface my paper by drawing a sharp distinction between teaching, on the one hand, and learning, on the other. This is a very simple distinction to see. All you need do is reflect upon the fact that someone can teach until he is blue in the face without anyone learning anything, and that someone can learn a great many things without ever being taught at all.

The fact of the matter is that many people do not want to be taught. They want to learn for themselves instead. And they actually resent and resist attempts to impose teaching on them. There are, of course, many cases in which students blossom under the right teacher. But there are too many cases in which a student's curiosity and interest in a problem are destroyed by the wrong one.

In my view, a teacher's primary responsibility is not to get in the way of learning.

This distinction, however simple, is essential if we want education for an open society. For unless I am seriously mistaken, the fact that so many of our societies are closed is, to a large extent, due to their preoccupation with teaching and their fear of techniques that facilitate learning.[2]

In what follows, I want to talk a bit about Popper's views on open society, and a bit about his views on education, and a bit about the way he actually taught—and I want to try, between this and that, to describe what education for an open society would look like.

II

Perhaps I should begin by putting this all into context. Popper characterized closed society as a magical or tribal society, and he contrasted it with open society, which sets free the critical powers of man.[3] The distinction, for Popper, had to do with an individual's freedom to make decisions, and with the responsibility and moral burden that it puts upon him for making them. Popper thought that individuals in open societies are confronted with personal decisions,[4] and that there is nothing quite like this in a closed society. There, everything is predetermined. Real moral choices do not exist, and the magical taboos of the tribe preclude the need for critical thinking and rational choice. Each individual knows his place in the tribe and exactly what he is expected to do. They are not encouraged to think for themselves or to make judgments of their own. They are taught, instead, to recognize and defer to the intellectual authorities of the tribe.

But is it really true that our educational institutions are designed in accordance with the bucket theory of the mind? And how, in any event, is the bucket theory of the mind related to authoritarianism and closed society?

My own sense is that the bucket theory and authoritarianism are so central to the way we think about education that they are actually 'hard-wired' into the architecture of the educational spaces that we create.

The vast majority of our classrooms consist of rows of small desks facing one large desk at the front of the room. At the small desks sit the students. At the large desk sits the teacher. The students all face the teacher. The teacher faces all the students. The message that is implicit in this design is loud and clear: 'The teacher is the expert and authority in this room. His are the only ideas to which you need to pay attention.'

There is a magic in this architecture. Each student knows his place and exactly what he is expected to do. He is expected to listen, to answer questions, and not to ask any of his own.

There is, however, another reason why our schools have degenerated into authoritarian affairs (if, indeed, they were ever non-authoritarian affairs in the first place). It is that many of them have taken upon themselves the mission of professional education, instead of what John Stuart Mill called 'education properly so called.' Instead of trying to produce 'capable and cultivated human beings,'[5] they try to produce employable workers. Instead of free men and women ready and able to think for themselves, our schools now try to train people to serve as obedient agents for others. And many of them make no bones about the fact.

This, perhaps, is the reason why our elementary school teachers so often place greater emphasis upon sitting correctly or keeping silent or not turning your head than upon anything that actually has to do with learning. And it is also the reason why our university students are often more concerned with their grades than with the content of their courses. It is why so few of them are interested in asking questions, or with problems and theories that will not be 'on the test', or with studying things that they do not already know.

Kant used to distinguish between what he called 'categorical' and 'hypothetical' imperatives. Categorical imperatives express values that we hold for their own sake. Hypothetical imperatives express values that we hold for the sake of something else.

The simple fact of the matter is that many of our students—like many of their parents and teachers—do not value learning for its own sake at all.

Most people regard education as a hypothetical imperative. They equate it with a university diploma. And they value it for the sake of getting a job—which they value for, and evaluate in terms of, the income and life style that it affords. Indeed, the growing recognition that a university diploma is neither a necessary nor sufficient condition for finding employment—that people can, and indeed do, acquire more money without it—has led some people to question whether education is in fact valuable at all.

But even people who value education for its own sake often believe that our teachers should be experts and authorities. Many people believe that the primary purpose of education—and the only justification for spending public funds on it—is to pass down our beliefs and traditions to our children. And many others believe that the primary purpose of education is to produce people who are experts in their fields. I do not want to contest this here. I will, in fact, go one step further and say that systematic education may even involve a certain amount of indoctrination.

But the most important tradition in an open society is the tradition of critical thinking. It is the tradition of not accepting something as true merely because it is the opinion of some authority. It is the tradition of questioning not only our experts and our teachers, but also ourselves. And if we want to preserve our open society, then this is a tradition that we must pass on to our children as well. It is a tradition that we must pass on to them along with our encouragement to question and reexamine and perhaps even reject all of the beliefs and traditions that we try to pass on to them.

Education may involve a certain amount of indoctrination. But our task in an open society is to insure that it does not become *mere* indoctrination.

III

But is it really true that the primary purpose of education is to produce experts in their fields? Popper would have disagreed. He would, in fact, have rejected the very notion that there are such things as fields for people to be experts in. Popper used to begin his first year course in scientific method by saying, 'This is a course in scientific method, and the first thing that I want to say is that this is a subject that does not exist.' He would jokingly appeal to his own authority, telling his students that this was something that he should know, since he was the only Professor of Scientific Method in the entire British Empire. And then, having made his point, he would sometimes invite them to speculate about *why* he was the only Professor of Scientific Method in the entire British Empire. But there was nothing special for Popper about scientific method. He used to tell his students that 'it is important to understand that academic subjects, in general, do not exist'—that they are fictions that are created by universities for the purpose of organizing their programs and justifying their existence:

> They are instituted by universities, because universities have to pay their professors. And in order to pay their professors they have to appoint them. So there has to be a certain fiction that one appoints a person who is an ex-

pert in a subject. And since he is supposed to be an expert in a subject, the subject itself must somehow exist. But all of this is a fiction. What really exist are *problems*—not subjects but *problems*. And when someone is interested in a problem and wants to solve it, then there is something that is really serious. *Subjects*, such as history or economics, are merely conveniences for university administrators. They are really more or less arbitrarily chosen collections of problems that have been ordered merely for the purpose of administering universities and examining students—a function that I think a university should not fulfill, though that is another matter.[6]

Popper believed that science consists of problems and that we learn by trying, and failing, to solve them. But if this is true, then an expert would have to be an expert not in a *subject* or in a *field*, but in a *problem* whose solutions might depend upon all sorts of things that range beyond the boundaries of what are typically recognized as academic fields.

But it is really more than this. Popper was sceptical of intellectual authority and of education that is based upon it. He believed that we should not rely upon experts, and proposed, as a new goal of liberal education, that we learn to distinguish between experts and charlatans instead. He criticized teachers who treat science as a 'body of knowledge,' saying that students learn intellectual honesty, a respect for truth, and a disregard for authority only if they experience for themselves how easy it is to make mistakes. He believed that this is something that we can learn only by making mistakes and by discovering the mistakes that we have made. And he believed that this is something that we can learn only through criticism.[7]

Popper thought that teaching at the university level should be training and encouragement in critical thinking. This is the sort of teaching that does not rely upon expert opinion. And it is a sort of teaching that seems decidedly out of fashion at a time when our logic books teach that arguments from authority are perfectly valid *so long as you argue from the right authority*, and at a time when the mere asking of a critical question can be taken as a sign of stupidity, if not disrespect. It is, however, the sort of teaching that Popper thought is necessary if we want education for an open society.

Why is this? It is, in a nutshell, because the primary enemy of the open society is the idea that there are sciences that are infallibly true and experts to whom we can safely appeal for the truth. If we want education for an open society, then we must 'set free the critical powers of man.' And in order to do this, we must understand that no science is infallibly true—and that criticism is not ridicule and scorn, but one of the greatest signs of respect that we can show to each other.

IV

Popper believed that we learn through trial and error, and that science, and learning in general, proceeds from problem to problem. He developed the following schema to express this idea:

$$P_1 \rightarrow TT \rightarrow EE \rightarrow P_2$$

Here P_1 is a problem that we want to solve, TT is a theory that we tentatively offer to solve it, EE is an attempt to eliminate errors through criticism, and P_2 is a new problem that results from our criticism.

The schema, of course, is an oversimplification. We typically work with several different problems at once and also with several different tentative solutions, all of which are interrelated in ways that simply cannot be captured by an arrow. Popper, in fact, would tell his students that there is no need even to begin with problems—that we can begin with theories or with criticism instead. But he would then explain that he preferred to emphasize problems because problems are generally ignored, and because he thought that they are essential for learning and for the growth of knowledge.

Popper used to talk about conjecture and refutation. But criticism, in my view, is really the setting of problems. We set problems by showing that our beliefs are contradictory and cannot all be true. And we try, in this way, to force ourselves to reexamine our beliefs and to choose between them.

Criticism can never force us to reject any particular belief as false or to accept any particular belief as true. But it can force us, if it is effective at all, to recognize that our beliefs are contradictory, and to reexamine them, and to try to decide how we should revise them in order to remove the contradiction.

This, in my view, is a large part of what the learning process is all about. But most people do not like to be criticized, and many do not like to criticize others. Some regard it as a sign of poor breeding, and others as a sign of disrespect. So we are often advised not to engage ourselves in criticism, either for fear of offending others or for fear of being offended ourselves. But this advice is detrimental. For criticism is not only one of our greatest signs of respect, it is also essential for learning. We run the risk, unless we engage ourselves in it and unless we take it seriously, of impeding not only our own learning, but also the learning of others.

V

There is a very interesting story about Niels Bohr that can be told in this connection. It is said that Bohr would never criticize a paper that he regarded as silly, but would instead nod his head in agreement, saying things like 'Sehr, sehr,' or 'Very interesting,' and 'We agree much more than you think.' Leon Rosenfeld was confused by this response the first time he attended a conference at Bohr's institute in Copenhagen. One of the speakers had presented some views that seemed quite erroneous to Rosenfeld:

> Bohr however, opposed them rather feebly (as I thought)... the phrase 'very interesting' recurred insistently, and [Bohr] concluded by expressing the conviction 'we agree much more than you think'.
>
> I was worried, the more so as the highbrow bench seemed to find it all right.

But Rosenfeld went to Bohr after the lecture, and Bohr quickly set him straight:

> I ventured later to explain my doubts to Bohr. I began cautiously to state that the speaker's argument did not seem to me quite justified. 'Oh,' said

Bohr 'it is pure nonsense.' So I knew that I had been led astray by a mere matter of terminology.[8]

Many of Bohr's biographers cite this reaction to silly papers as a manifestation of his great kindness—of his consideration for their authors and of his wish not to embarrass them. There can really be no doubt that this was Bohr's intent. But I find it difficult to imagine how it could possibly have worked. My own guess is that almost everyone in the room understood that Bohr's approval meant disdain. Indeed, I would think that the author of the 'silly' paper probably understood it best of all. For if we compare Bohr's 'Very interesting' with his well-publicized and intensely critical exchanges with Einstein and Schrödinger,[9] then it is easy to see that criticism from Bohr was a sign of respect. But I do not really care whether Bohr was being kind or whether the author of the silly paper felt embarrassed. The question that concerns me is whether anyone could possibly have *learned* anything from Bohr's response. It is whether his kindness and tact did anything to help anyone to understand *why* he thought the paper was silly.

My guess is that it did not. My guess is that Bohr's 'Very interesting' was understood not so much as showing that he was critical of the author's paper—as he was, for example, critical of Einstein's and Schrödinger's views—but as showing that he did not think that the paper was even worth the effort to criticize or discuss. And my guess is that others in the room, sensing Bohr's disdain and awed by his great authority—to which all of his biographers attest—followed his example and said 'Very interesting' too.[10]

The upshot is that the authors of silly papers probably left Copenhagen with the sense that their papers were silly, and perhaps even with gratitude that Bohr and the highbrow bench had not actually said so out loud, but with no understanding at all as to exactly why it was so.

Indeed, my guess is that the members of Bohr's institute who remained silent or who also said 'Very interesting' might not have understood why either.

It is interesting to compare Rosenfeld's story about Bohr with one that Bill Bartley told about Popper. Popper's seminars, according to Bartley, were:

> … intense confrontations between Popper and the person reading the paper, whether student or visiting scholar. At the first meeting of term, for example, the student managed to read about two paragraphs. Popper interrupted every sentence; nothing passed unchallenged: every word was important. He asked a question; the student dodged it. Popper asked the same question again. Again the student dodged it. Popper repeated the question once again. And the student answered at last. 'Were you then wrong in what you said first?' Popper inquired. The student evaded this unwelcome conclusion with a flow of words. Popper listened, then said, 'Yes. But were you then wrong in what you said first?' The student was learning, and admitted his error. 'Do you apologise?' Popper asked. The student did so, and Popper smiled broadly. 'Good,' he said. 'Then we can be friends.'

Bartley goes on to say that:

> Another student did not fare so well. He dodged Popper's questions, shifted his position without acknowledging it, avoided all criticism, appealed to the audience, tried to deliver a speech, became more and more incoherent … and belligerent. Popper finally asked him to leave. He refused. Popper then took him by the collar and ejected him from the seminar room.[11]

Bartley says that such behavior led A.J. Ayer to say that Popper was 'unfit to teach.' But he also says that he later heard Popper explain his teaching method. Popper thought that there is nothing easier than to nod sagely at a student and say that what he had written or said is 'interesting.' It is certainly easier than taking what he says seriously and trying to criticize it. But he also thought that it is not teaching, and that it does not involve learning.[12]

VI

The distinction between teaching and learning is the difference between Socrates and Plato. And it is a difference that goes far beyond their teaching styles. Plato regarded someone as wise if he knew a great deal. But Socrates regarded someone as wise if he knew that he knew nothing at all. Plato had a lot to teach. But Socrates was someone from whom you could really learn.

Popper had the greatest respect for Socrates. He regarded the *Apology* as the most beautiful philosophical work that he knew, and he attached the 'greatest significance' to the Socratic idea that the wisest of men is wise because he at least knows that he knows (almost) nothing at all.[13] Many people regard Socrates' interpretation of the oracle's judgment as paradoxical. But Popper regarded it as literally true. And he chastised Plato for teaching that it is not the man who is aware of his own ignorance, but the expert, who is wise.[14]

Popper was not alone in this. Søren Kierkegaard, who also admired Socrates, wrote that the Socratic teacher cannot bring the truth to his student, but must instead stand in relation to the student as a mere occasion: as an opportunity to learn, through the Socratic elenchus, that he does not know what he thinks he knows. Kierkegaard thought that this is the highest relationship that can exist between two people. Anything else is a lie and a seduction, since it pretends that the teacher is more like a god than a man. Kierkegaard thus thought that the Socratic teacher must constantly push his student away, so that neither he nor his student is seduced by the desire to attribute to the teacher a wisdom that goes beyond his knowledge that he knows almost nothing at all.[15]

'My own Error,' Kierkegaard wrote, 'is something I can discover only by myself, since it is only when I have discovered it that it is discovered, even if the whole world knew of it before.'[16]

This is the reason why Socrates was so unpopular.[17] And it is part of the reason why Popper had tortured relationships with his closest students. Both of them pushed their students away with brutal honesty, and by constantly pointing out their contradictions.

Many educators today regard the Socratic method as authoritarian and humiliating. And I agree that it may easily be so. But whether or not it actually is will depend as much upon the student as it will upon the teacher. If a teacher is out simply to propagate his own ideas, then he may easily close his ears and interpret any view other than his own as a mistake. And if a student is out only to get a grade or a recommendation, then he may easily decide to tell his teacher 'exactly what he wants to hear.' In either case, the Socratic method will quickly devolve into an authoritarian affair. But none of this involves teaching or learning. For this type of teacher and this type of student are obviously concerned with something else. Indeed, if people today regard education as a hypothetical imperative, then it is difficult to see how they could appreciate someone who teaches in the Socratic style.

A philosopher I know tells a story about a seminar that he took with Popper that unintentionally illustrates this point. Popper was visiting in America at the time, and the graduate students were appalled by his teaching method, which they described as 'authoritarian.' Many of them experienced the sort of criticism that Bartley describes and, not knowing that Popper regarded the grading system as an obstacle to serious education and that he rarely gave graduate students anything below an *A-*, began to fear for their grades. This philosopher says that he seriously considered quitting the course. But he thought that a good recommendation from Popper would carry a lot of weight toward getting him a job, and so he decided instead to tell Popper 'exactly what he wanted to hear.'

This man got his *A-*, and his letter of recommendation. But he apparently learnt very little from Popper. For he tells this story, without any embarrassment whatsoever, as an illustration of his own savvy in climbing the ladder of The Scientific Institution. There is, no doubt, a lesson in his story. But the lesson that it teaches—and indeed, the lesson that he presupposes his listeners already know—is not the one that Popper would like us to learn.

But is the Socratic method really authoritarian and humiliating as many educators claim?

VII

In my view, it is Bohr's method of dealing with silly papers, and not Popper's method of teaching, that is authoritarian. Bohr was often able, without offering an argument or criticism of any kind, to convince the members of his institute that a paper was silly. I cannot imagine how this could be possible were it not for the immense authority that the members of his institute attributed to him. In my view, it is Bohr's response to silly papers that is humiliating. For what can possibly be more humiliating for someone who is serious about his work than to have it dismissed as not even worthy of criticism?

In my view, the complaint that criticism is authoritarian and humiliating is most frequently heard from those who are trying to evade it—as are the complaints that a critic is simply making a 'debater's point,' or that he is arguing for argument's sake, or that he is out to gratify his ego.

These complaints are usually voiced when no other response can be offered. And they are, for that reason, very often projections of a person's own dogmatic tendencies onto his critic. I do not want to say that these complaints are never true. But the problem with them is that they do nothing whatsoever to answer the criticism that has been raised. They attempt, instead, to brush it aside by swaying the attention of the crowd from the issue that has been raised to the individual who has raised it.

But when we examine the character traits of a thinker, instead of the truth of his thought, we open up a Pandora's box of prejudices that makes it virtually impossible for us to be rational at all. Once our prejudices are released, it makes little difference what anyone says or does. Instead of appealing to reason, we give ourselves over to emotion. We know in advance that whatever certain people say or do is right, and whatever certain others say or do is wrong. Some people equate this sort of thing with criticism because it so often leads to condemnation. But it has nothing to do with criticism in my sense. It is, on the contrary, magic.

If there is just one thing that people who want to preserve open society should learn, it is that the traits of a thinker have no implications for the truth of his thought.

VIII

I do not think that Bohr's response to silly papers was unique. But I have focused upon it because Bohr, of all the scientists of the twentieth century, was one of the most responsible for our model of The Scientific Institution—and because I do not really think that it is an accident that the theory for which he is most often remembered, the Copenhagen interpretation of quantum mechanics, maintains that a rational understanding of atomic phenomena is impossible. I do not think that it would have been possible for the Copenhagen interpretation to gain the popularity that it has among physicists—whose task, after all, is to provide a rational explanation of the world—were it not for the great authority that physicists attributed to Bohr.

Bohr's authority, which for most physicists outweighed even the authority of Einstein, was undoubtedly due to the force of his personality, which seems to have made a great impression upon almost everyone he brought to study at his institute in Copenhagen. Even Schrödinger, who did not like his mysticism and did not regard his personality as ideal, wrote:

> There will hardly again be a man who will achieve such enormous external and internal success, who in his sphere of work is honored almost like a demigod by the whole world, and who yet remains—I would not say modest and free of conceit—but rather shy and diffident like a theology student. I do not necessarily mean that as praise, it is not my ideal of a man. Nevertheless, this attitude works strongly sympathetically compared with what one more often meets in stars of medium size in our profession.[18]

There was a kind of magic in Bohr's personality. Schrödinger did not fall completely, but even he went on to attribute the fact that Bohr 'talks often for minutes almost in a dreamlike, visionary and really quite unclear manner,' at least in part, to his great consideration—to his fear 'that the other might take a statement of his point of view as an insufficient appreciation of the other's.'[19]

Some physicists, however, regarded the deference that their colleagues paid to Bohr's authority as an impediment to their work. Max Born, for example, says that he found James Franck's reliance upon Bohr discouraging:

> Franck was an ardent admirer of Bohr and believed in him as the highest authority in physics. I sometimes found this rather exasperating. It happened more than once that we had discussed a problem thoroughly and

come to a conclusion. When I asked him after a while: 'Have you started to do that experiment?,' he would reply: 'Well, no; I have written first to Bohr and he has not answered yet.' This was at times rather discouraging for me, and even retarded our work to some degree.[20]

It is, in fact, difficult to see how Popper could be too far wrong when he wrote, in explaining why so many physicists were willing to accept Bohr's link between wave particle dualism and the theory of complementarity, that 'most of the physicists, theorists included, did not care too much, and simply relied on Bohr in a matter in which they did not feel competent.'[21] But many of those who relied upon Bohr's authority did care. And one need only think of how Paul Ehrenfest was brought to tears when he was forced to choose between the authority of Einstein and the authority of Bohr—he opted, in the end, for Bohr's—to realize that it is not always healthy.[22]

IX

Two lessons can be learned at once from the debate between Einstein and Bohr. The first, of course, is that appealing to experts solves nothing—if only because the experts themselves so often disagree. It is, indeed, only a novitiate's ignorance that fosters his belief that there is a consensus among the experts. The second is that even when there is a consensus among the experts—as there apparently was in the idea that Bohr had refuted Einstein in these debates—it is often based more upon impressions than upon reasons and understanding. I have already given the example of Ehrenfest. But almost every account that I have read of this debate speaks of the great impression that Bohr made upon the physicists at the 1927 Solvay Conference when, seemingly demolished by Einstein's thought experiment on Saturday and working with Heisenberg all through the night, he triumphantly showed the weakness in Einstein's argument at breakfast on Sunday. Bohr's reply to Einstein impressed most of those present as a reversal of tragic proportions. And it apparently did for Bohr what the discovery of

Neptune did for Newton. Many of them concluded that Bohr's ability to answer this one objection was—just because the objection had initially seemed so unanswerable—a conclusive proof of the Copenhagen interpretation. As Heisenberg later put it, 'The most important success of the Brussels meeting was that we could see that against *any* objections, against *any* attempts to disprove the theory, we could get along with it.'[23]

Einstein, of course, disagreed. He wrote:

> The soothing philosophy—or religion?—of Heisenberg-Bohr is so cleverly concocted that for the present it offers the believers a soft resting pillow from which they are not easily chased away. Let us therefore let them rest.[24]

But after Solvay there was suddenly the still popular picture of Einstein—old at 45—as the Moses who had brought the quantum physicists to Mt. Pisgah, but was unable to follow them to Copenhagen itself.

All of this is impressionism. It is no less impressionism because it occurs in physics. And we should not shrink from admitting that there has always been impressionism in science. Kepler was so impressed by the fact that there are only five perfect solids that he concluded that this must be the reason why there are only six planets. And he found 'good confirmation' of his theory in the fact that he could inscribe these solids into each other and, by so doing, explain the distances between the planetary orbits—almost—in terms of the space needed to fit the perfect solids in between. Had it not been for his laws of planetary motion—which were, of course, false—Kepler's theory would have probably been remembered, along with the theory of cosmic ice and the theory of interplanetary collisions, as part of the lunatic fringe of science.

But the problem with impressionism is not that it leads to such crazy theories. This, on the contrary, is what is good about it. The problem with impressionism is that it encourages us to suspend our critical faculties and to dismiss our critics out of hand because we know in advance that we can answer any and all of their objections.

X

Earlier I said that Popper characterized the closed society as a 'magical' society. To submit to this kind of impressionism—believing, perhaps, that there are experts with a special power of understanding that others cannot attain and a special authority that demands that we believe what they say—is really to submit to magic and its charms. It is the first step down the path to closed society. For it inevitably leads to the formation of schools that can, by appealing to someone's authority, ostracize those who dare to question them without any argument whatsoever.

Here, I want to be clear that this is bad regardless of whether the theory in question is true or false. Indeed, the recent suggestions that it was Galileo, and not Cardinal Bellarmino, who was in the wrong—because Galileo was disrespectful in his criticism, because he advocated his theory too strongly as the truth, and because 'we now know' that it was merely an instrument as Bellarmino insisted—entirely misses the point. No one should be imprisoned or silenced or persecuted for saying what he believes is true. And the open society will have plenty of enemies to fight, so long as there are people who are punished for their beliefs, and so long as our educational systems apologize for those who punish them.

XI

The aim of education, in my view, is to learn in very great detail how very little we know. This is what education for an open society is all about. If we want an open society, then we need to somehow instill the attitude that 'I may be wrong and you may be right, and that by an effort we may get nearer to the truth'—both in our students and in ourselves. We need also to instill a critical attitude, and the scepticism that goes with it, while preserving the idea that there is still a truth to which we can actually get nearer.

This is not a simple task. It is made difficult by the fact that we all believe that the statements that we believe are true—for otherwise we would not believe them at all. It is made more difficult by the fact

that few people enjoy criticism, and by the fact that our students believe that they will be punished by bad grades and poor recommendations if they express ideas that are critical of their teachers' ideas.
And it is made more difficult still by the fact that this belief of theirs
is, to a greater extent than we would like to admit, true.

But I think that the greatest obstacles to education for an open
society are our own ignorance of how little we know, and our own
unwillingness to acknowledge it even to ourselves.

So, instilling scepticism and the critical attitude in ourselves and
in our students will not be enough. We will also need to instill the
self-critical attitude in ourselves and in our students. And we will
need to reverse the contemporary wisdom that says that ignorance
is bad, but admitting it is stupid. This is perhaps the greatest obstacle to education that I know. It infects all levels of society, and
especially the professorial ranks of academia.

But even this self-critical attitude will not be enough. It may even,
on the contrary, have detrimental consequences of its own if it is not
accompanied by the logical tools that are necessary for critical
thinking. And by 'logical tools' I do not mean the first-order predicate calculus with identity. I mean something that is much less and,
simultaneously, much more. I mean a practical recognition of our
own fallibility, a desire to get closer to the truth, and an appreciation
of the fact that someone else may already be closer to the truth than
we are. I mean a respect for other people, and a respect for the law of
non-contradiction as a standard for critical thinking. I have already
explained what I mean by respect for other people. It is impossible
without an appreciation of our own fallibility and the fact that others
may be closer to the truth than we are. But I also think that impressionism and the submission to magic may result from a failure to
understand the nature of criticism and contradictions and what logical arguments can and cannot do.

XII

Criticism begins with two simple questions: 'What does it mean?'
and 'Is it really true?' We need an answer to the first of these

questions in order to seriously consider the second. But when we consider the second, we typically compare the statement in question, along with its consequences, with other statements that we think are true. In this way, we attempt to point out contradictions and, in so doing, to set problems for a theory by showing that it is inconsistent with other things that we believe are true.

This is where logic enters into the picture. Every criticism is an attempt to show that a given statement is inconsistent with something that we believe to be true. But only valid deductive arguments allow us to exercise rational control over a critical discussion. This is because valid deductive arguments are the only arguments in which the conclusions actually follow from the premises. In invalid and so-called 'inductive' arguments the *truth* of the conclusion is *consistent* with the truth of the premises. But *inconsistency*, ironically enough, is what really matters. In a valid deductive argument the *falsity* of the conclusion is *inconsistent* with the truth of the premises. And this inconsistency is what it means for the conclusion to follow from the premises. It means that we cannot simultaneously assert the truth of those premises and deny the truth of that conclusion without contradicting ourselves. It means that we must, if we want to avoid contradicting ourselves, choose between asserting the conclusion and denying the premises.

Here I want to be clear so as not to add to the harm that has been done by impressionism in logic.[25] Logical arguments cannot prove the truth of any statements other than tautologies. The best that an argument can do is to show that its conclusion is true *provided that its premises are true*—or, to put it differently, that *either* its conclusion is true *or* one or more of its premises are false.

A valid argument, for this reason, is not so much a proof as a choice. It presents us with a set of mutually exclusive alternatives. We can choose to accept its premises, in which case we must also accept its conclusion; or to reject its conclusion, in which case we must reject one or more of its premises; or to reject its premises, in which case we need do nothing at all vis-à-vis its conclusion.

But we cannot, without contradicting ourselves, choose to both accept its premises and reject its conclusion.

These alternatives are restricted by logical necessity. And the work of the argument is to clarify this restriction—as well as our alternatives—by showing that it is a contradiction to assert the premises of the argument while simultaneously denying its conclusion. But this does not justify or prove its conclusion. Logical arguments, contrary to popular belief, cannot force us to accept the truth of their conclusions. They can force us to choose, but they cannot make the choice for us.

A skillful teacher can use valid deductive arguments to force us to *reexamine* our beliefs by showing that and how our beliefs are contradictory. And he may help us, in this way, to recognize that we really do not know what we thought we knew. But he can do this only if we want to learn, only if we value truth and education, and only if we understand and respect the law of non-contradiction.

This is why the 'post-modern' disdain for truth and logic may easily lead to closed society. For it is only our respect for truth and criticism and the law of non-contradiction that enables us to learn anything at all. And this is the real lesson of post-modernism. The idea that there is nothing like truth or falsity to be right or wrong about is just another new way to evade criticism and the recognition of our errors and learning itself—this time by building it into our metatheory that there really is nothing for us to be mistaken about and, hence, nothing for us to learn.

XIII

Criticism, in an open society, is an attempt to find the contradictions in our beliefs and to choose between them instead of trying to cover them up. Education for an open society should encourage us to articulate our problems, to think up possible solutions to them, to try to criticize them ourselves, and, of course, to listen to the criticisms of others. All of this, I submit, is essential for learning.

There is, however, something else. In *The Lesson of This Century*, Popper tells the story of how he first began to question communism. He says that in 1919, after the peace treaty of Brest-Litovsk, he went to the Communist Party office and offered his services as an errand boy:

> It was an interesting meeting I had with them. They were very nice to me, spoilt me a little, and at first I trusted them. But very soon I found that a telegram from Moscow was enough for them to turn 180 degrees and say the opposite of what they had been saying the day before. Their attitude to people could also change completely from one day to the next. In other words, they had only one principle, and that was to support Moscow absolutely through thick and thin, without the slightest wavering. So when I found that out, my attitude to Communism was thrown into crisis.[26]

An awareness of our own fallibility, coupled with the desire to learn, means that there will be times when we will change our minds. It means that we may sometimes turn 180 degrees and say the opposite of what we had said before. And there is no reason whatsoever why such a change may not even occur overnight. But the attitude that Popper describes here seems to be something very different. It is difficult to believe that *these* changes had anything to do with fallibility or a desire to learn. Today we say that communism is dead and that open society is on the rise. There is much talk about the 'post-communist' world, the problems that people face, and the changes that they will have to make. But the attitude that Popper describes is very old and still very much alive. I do not think that it is, or ever was, peculiar to communists or communism. But I like to call it 'post-communist communism,' nonetheless. It is the attitude of telling the teacher whatever he wants to hear. And it is, regardless of whether the calls come from Moscow, London, or New York, one of the greatest threats that faces open society today.

XIV

I must confess, in closing, that I have somehow talked a great deal more about Niels Bohr than I had originally intended. I think that this is fitting for reasons that I have already mentioned. I have, of course, been critical of Bohr and of The Scientific Institution that he inspired. But I do not want to leave you with the impression that Bohr was an ineffective teacher, or that his teaching method was the same as his method of reacting to silly papers. On the contrary, C.F. von Weizsäcker, who worked at Bohr's institute, tells the following story about an interview he had with Bohr to discuss a paper that he had written. It is a story that shows that Bohr was capable, when he wanted to, of practicing the Socratic method with the best of them:

> I wrote up the paper in the course of some weeks and gave it to Bohr's secretary. Bohr himself could not be seen very much, since at that time he was very absorbed and busy in advisory work for the Danish government in tireless attempts to help German refugees.
>
> After a fortnight an interview with Bohr was arranged. He was late and looked infinitely tired. He pulled the paper from the pile and said 'Oh, very good, very good; that is a very nice piece of work, now everything is clear … I hope that you will publish it soon!' I thought to myself, 'The poor man! He probably has had almost no time to read the paper.' He continued: 'Just to clarify something, what is the meaning of the formula on page 17?' I explained it to him. Then he said 'Yes, I understand that, but then the footnote on page 14 must mean … so and so.' 'Yes—that is what I meant.' 'But then …' And so it went on. He had read everything. After an hour he was getting fresher all the time, and I came to a point where I had difficulty with an explanation. After two hours he was flourishingly fresh and complete master of the situation, full of naive enthusiasm, while I felt that I was getting tired and was being driven into a corner. In the third hour, however, he said, triumphantly but without any trace of malice, 'Now I understand it, now I understand the point … The point is that everything is exactly the opposite of what you said—that's the point!' With due reservations about the use of the word 'everything,' I agreed that it was so. When one has had such experiences with one's teachers several times, one has learned something that cannot be learned in any other way.[27]

Notes

1 This is a revised version of a paper that was first presented at the Popper Project's first workshop, which was held in Budapest from 6–14 June 1995. It has since been presented, among other places, at Semipalatinsk State University in Semipalatinsk, Kazakhstan on 14 December 1996; at the Institute for Pedagogical Research at the University of Belgrade in Belgrade, Serbia

on 19 March 1998, and at a Popper workshop that was held at Lake Sevan, Armenia from 8–11 June 1998. The motto is from Karl R. Popper, 'Normal Science and Its Dangers' in *Criticism and the Growth of Knowledge*, edited by Imre Lakatos and Alan Musgrave, Cambridge University Press, Cambridge, 1970, pp. 52–53.

2 Proposals for educational reforms typically focus upon teaching, and rarely, if ever, upon learning. We propose to improve education by getting new teachers, or by teaching new courses, or by teaching courses that we already teach in new ways, or by giving new tests to the teachers. The idea is that to improve education we must improve the teachers and teaching. The possibility that learning has little to do with teaching is apparently too threatening for teachers and school administrators to contemplate.

3 See Karl R. Popper, *The Open Society and Its Enemies*, 1945. Reprinted by Routledge, London, 1998, vol. 1, p. 1.

4 See Popper, *The Open Society and Its Enemies*, vol. 1, p. 173.

5 John Stuart Mill, 'On Education' in *John Stuart Mill: A Selection of His Works*, edited by John M. Robson, Odyssey, New York, 1966, p. 380. Mill wrote that:

> The proper function of a University in national education is tolerably well understood. At least there is a tolerably general agreement about what a University is not. It is not a place of professional education. Universities are not intended to teach the knowledge required to fit men for some special mode of gaining their livelihood. Their object is not to make skillful lawyers, or physicians, or engineers, but capable and cultivated human beings.

6 I have constructed this passage from introductory class lectures that Popper gave—on 8 October 1958 and on 11 October 1966—to the students in his first year course on Scientific Method. See Popper's unpublished course lectures on Scientific Method in The Karl Popper Archives.

7 See Popper, *The Open Society and Its Enemies*, vol. 2, pp. 283–284.

8 Quoted from Rosenfeld in Ruth Moore, *Niels Bohr: The Man, His Science, and the World They Changed*, The MIT Press, Cambridge, 1966, p. 383–387. Moore is quoting from Leon Rosenfeld's chapter in *Niels Bohr: His Life and Work*, John Wiley & Sons, New York, 1966. Moore, incidentally, goes on to say that Abraham Pais was also confused by Bohr's reaction when he became a research fellow at his institute:

> Bohr smoked one of his dozen or so pipes, and generally kept his eyes on the floor while Pais put some of his formulae on the blackboard. When Pais finished, Bohr said very little and the young physicist felt somewhat disheartened. Only later did he learn that Bohr's interest had been aroused. Bohr had not dismissed what Pais was saying with his usual equivalent of disapproval, 'very interesting, very interesting.'

9 It is said, for example, that Schrödinger caught a flu while visiting Bohr's institute, and that Bohr would burst into his room with criticisms even while he lay in bed trying to recover. (Pais, *Niels Bohr's Times*, p. 299.)

10 Remember, in this connection, Rosenfeld's reference to 'the highbrow bench.'
11 W.W. Bartley, III, *Unfathomed Knowledge, Unmeasured Wealth*, Open Court, La Salle, 1990, p. 155. Ian Jarvie, I should note, disputes 'Bartley's story of Popper expelling a student from his seminar by the scruff of his neck (Personal communication.):'

> Although such confrontations as Bartley described occurred, they were not personal and certainly not physical. I recollect him once inviting someone to leave, then showing him the door by literally opening it. Physicality was not his style... Popper did not threaten, he argued. His confrontations always had their roots in the recognition of academic standards and standards of conduct. Those confronted often took this personally, especially when intellectual dishonesty was the issue. Such a reaction is understandable but nevertheless mistaken. It was I guess a surprise for some to learn that practices they were familiar with from their colleagues and their own institutions were being put into question.

12 Bartley, *Unfathomed Knowledge, Unmeasured Wealth*, p. 155.
13 See Karl R. Popper, 'Einleitung 1978' in Karl R. Popper, *Die beiden Grundprobleme der Erkenntnistheorie*, zweite, verbesserte Auflage, herausgegeben von Troels Eggers Hansen, J.C.B. Mohr (Paul Siebeck), Tübingen, 1994, p. xv.
14 Popper ('Einleitung 1978,' p. xv, author's translation) wrote that:

> Socrates' pupil Plato abandoned the Socratic thesis of our ignorance, and with it the Socratic demand for intellectual modesty. Socrates and Plato both insisted that a statesman should be wise. But by this they meant something fundamentally different. For Socrates meant that the statesman ought to be aware of his ignorance. And Plato meant that he ought to be a thoroughly instructed and learned philosopher.

See also, Popper's discussion of Socrates and Plato, and the two meanings of philosophy, in *The Open Society and Its Enemies*, chapters 7 and 10.

15 Kierkegaard (Søren Kierkegaard, *Philosophical Fragments*, translated by David Swenson, revised by Howard V. Hong, Princeton University Press, Princeton, 1974, pp. 29–30.) in this connection, writes:

> ... the disciple gives occasion for the teacher to understand himself, and the teacher gives occasion for the disciple to understand himself. When the teacher dies he leaves behind him no claim upon the soul of the disciple, just as the disciple can assert no claim that the teacher owes him anything. And if I were a Plato in sentimental enthusiasm, and if my heart beat as violently as Alcibiades' or more violently than that of the Corybantic mystic while listening to the words of Socrates; if the passion of my admiration knew no rest until I had clasped the wondrous master in my arms— Socrates would but smile at me and say: 'My friend, how deceitful a lover you are! You wish to idolize me on account of my wisdom, and then to take your place as the friend who best understands me, from whose admiring embrace I shall never be able to tear myself free—is it not true that you are a seducer?' And if I still refused to understand him, he would no doubt bring me to despair by the coldness of his irony, as

he unfolded to me that he owed me as much as I owed him. Rare integrity, deceiving no one, not even one who would deem it his highest happiness to be deceived! How rare in our age, when all have transcended Socrates—in self-appreciation, in estimate of benefits conferred upon their pupils, in sentimentality of intercourse, in voluptuous enjoyment of admiration's warm embrace! Rare fruitfulness, seducing no one, not even him who exercises all the arts of seduction in order to be seduced!

16 Kierkegaard, *Philosophical Fragments*, p. 17.

17 See Plato, *Apology*, in *Five Dialogues*, translated by G.M.A. Grube, Hackett, Indianapolis, 1981, p. 27.

18 Pais, *Niels Bohr's Times*, p. 299. Popper says he was 'overwhelmed' by Bohr's personality, and wrote that when he first met Bohr—in 1936, shortly after publishing his *Logik der Forschung*–Bohr:

> ... impressed me as the most wonderful person I had ever met or would be likely to meet. He was everything a great and good man could be. And he was irresistible. I felt that I must be wrong about quantum mechanics, even though I certainly could not say that I now understood it, rationally, in Bohr's sense: I did not. But I was overwhelmed. (Karl R. Popper, *Quantum Theory and the Schism in Physics*, edited by W.W. Bartley, III, 1982. Reprinted by Routledge, London, 1992, p. 9.)

19 Pais, *Niels Bohr's Times*, p. 299.

20 Quoted from Born in Jagdish Mehra and Helmut Rechenberg, *The Historical Development of Quantum Theory*, Springer-Verlag, New York, p. 361.

21 Popper, I should note, prefaces this remark by saying:

> Murry Gell-Mann, one of the very few physicists who dares to criticize Bohr, puts it perhaps a little too bluntly when he says that 'Niels Bohr brainwashed a whole generation of theorists into thinking that the job' (that is, an adequate philosophical presentation of quantum mechanics) 'was done 50 years ago'. (Popper, *Quantum Theory and the Schism in Physics*, p. 10.)

22 Pais, *Niels Bohr's Times*, p. 409. Erhenfest later became so depressed by his inability to understand the developments in quantum physics that he committed suicide.

23 Pais, *Niels Bohr's Times*, p. 320. My italics.

24 Pais, *Niels Bohr's Times*, p. 320.

25 I am referring not only to the belief that a logical analysis of language could, in one way or another, resolve all of our philosophical problems by showing them to be nonsensical, but also to the seemingly more mundane idea that logic can justify our beliefs or, in one way or another, show that they are true.

26 Karl Popper, *The Lesson of This Century*, interviewed by Giancarlo Bosetti, Routledge, London, 1997, p. 15.

27 C.F. von Weizsäcker, 'A Reminiscence from 1932' in *Niels Bohr: A Centenary Volume*, edited by A.P. French and P.J. Kennedy, Harvard University Press, Cambridge, 1985, pp. 187–188.

4 Science and 'The Institution'[1]

I

Socrates, in Book V of the *Republic*, having just given Glaucon his account of the ideal of justice, expresses doubts concerning the possibility of its realization:

> A pattern, then ... was what we wanted when we were inquiring into the nature of ideal justice and asking what would be the character of the perfectly just man, supposing him to exist, and likewise, in regard to injustice and the completely unjust man. We wished to fix our eyes upon them as types and models, so that whatever we discerned in them of happiness or the reverse would necessarily apply to ourselves in the sense that whosoever is like them will have the allotment most like to theirs. Our purpose was *not* to demonstrate the possibility of the realization of these ideals.[2]

Glaucon is primed for these doubts, having already agreed that the just man need not 'conform in every way to the ideal,' but that it will 'suffice us if he approximate to it as nearly as possible and partake of it more than others.'[3] And he assents, in what immediately follows, to what Socrates calls 'the truth of the matter': that our words are no less well spoken if we find ourselves unable to prove that it is possible for a state to be governed in accordance with them.[4]

This paper is not so much about justice as it is about justification. But I cite this passage from the *Republic* because the attitude that Socrates expresses in it is one with which I agree, because it is an attitude that today seems largely forgotten, and because it is one that stands in diametrical opposition to the attitude that motivates contemporary attempts to 'institutionalize' science and philosophy. As one proponent of institutionalism has put it:

> The main problem with past work in evolutionary epistemology is not that it is evolutionary but that it is epistemology. As far as I can see, neither the content nor the methods of science can be 'justified' in the sense that generations of epistemologists have attempted to justify them. The reason that epistemologists have not been able to justify knowledge-claims in their sense of 'justify' is that no such justification exists. They want the impossible.[5]

Socrates was content to articulate ideals that are impossible to achieve. But this is just what institutionalists find problematic. They do not believe that epistemology *is* dead. But they would like us to believe that it *ought* to be.[6]

I will say little here about evolutionary epistemology or about the knowledge-claims made by science. I want instead to raise the question whether institutionalism is the best response to our inability to justify them.

I want, in particular, to question whether our traditional epistemological ideals of truth and justification are, or ought to be regarded as, problematic. I want to talk a bit about inductivism and about its relationship to the institutional theory of science. And I want to challenge the idea that the 'failure' of traditional epistemology to justify our knowledge is a *failure*—and also the ideas that epistemology and philosophy are the sorts of things that can die.

I hope, while doing all this, to present some of the basic ideas of Karl Popper's philosophy in what are, for all intents and purposes, non-Popperian terms. And I also hope to explain, without mentioning them too much by name, what I take to be the choice between Popper and Kuhn.

II

Perhaps I should begin by putting all of this into context. What is usually called 'The Scientific Revolution' began in Europe when free-thinkers began to say that the philosophical doctrines upheld by the Roman Catholic Church were not rationally justified and that belief in them rested solely upon the authority of the Church Fathers—which they then began to challenge. These ideas led to the characterization of rational knowledge as justified true belief and of religious faith as irrational dogma. They led to the burning of Giordano Bruno and to the imprisonment of Galileo. And it may, perhaps, be for these reasons that relations between science and religion have been somewhat strained ever since. But nearly four hundred years after 'The Scientific Revolution' began, Bertrand Russell warned that natural science showed every sign of becoming a new religion, governed by faith, and perhaps even hostile to rational discourse. And Russell, I think, was right. For the contemporary wisdom, at least amongst philosophers of science, is that the doctrines of science are *not* justified and that our belief in them rests solely upon the authority of 'The Scientific Institution,' which our 'institutionalized' philosophers of science say ought *not* to be challenged.

Today the most popular philosophy of science says that science is a social institution that begins where criticism leaves off, that there is no rational transition from one theory to the next, and that the best we can hope for are irrational paradigm shifts, fueled by political 'bandwagon effects,' that are more like religious conversions than anything else. Today scientists are said to value community, professionalism, and solidarity more than criticism, freethinking, and truth. And today we are told that the best that philosophy can offer is faith in 'The Institution.'

How have we arrived at this point?

Partly through the failures of the great foundationalist programs of the past, which have, from Descartes' through Carnap's, all capsized upon the problem of specifying an objective criterion of truth—and partly through the reluctance of philosophers and scientists, in the face of these failures, to relinquish their claims to cognitive authority.

It is thus not too surprising that many of today's theorists of truth and justification seriously propose the consensus of expert opinion as criteria for both.

But is this really the way we should go?

The great foundationalist programs of the past were attempts to justify our beliefs, where 'justify' meant showing them to be true, and 'true' meant corresponding to the facts. The collapse of foundationalism in the twentieth century is due to our discovery that it is impossible to justify our beliefs in this way. This is the great philosophical fact of the twentieth century. And the great epistemological problem posed by this fact is 'How should philosophers and scientists respond to it?'

Here, the idea that science is a social institution that justifies its theories by the consensus of belief amongst its members is one very popular response. And here I want to be clear that I agree with the institutionalists that the theories proposed by science cannot be justified in the way in which foundationalists thought, and that this has as much to do with how generations of epistemologists have understood 'justification' and 'truth' as it has to do with those theories themselves.

But unless my reading of the history of philosophy is seriously mistaken, it has been their traditional ideals of truth and justification that have enabled generation after generation of epistemologists to point this out.

This, in a nutshell, is why I am opposed to the attempt to institutionalize science and philosophy.

Institutionalists propose that we weaken our traditional ideals of truth and justification so that science can justify its theories. But I believe that these ideals have served, and continue to serve, an important epistemological function. And I believe that we should maintain them so that we can dispel the illusion, which recurs in every generation, that our scientific theories have been shown to be true.

III

Institutionalism enjoys the great popularity that it does, because it seems to be a more humane alternative to the infallibilism and authoritarianism that is associated with foundationalism. But this, I think, is an illusion. Far from being defenders of the right of the individual scientist to think and speak for himself, today's proponents of institutionalism take their lead from Francis Bacon, who, in addition to being the father of inductivism, proposed that science establish a 'Solomon's House' in which scientists would be brought together as a unified agency, or institution, that would speak with one authoritative voice.[7]

But does institutionalism really lead to authoritarian science? Didn't Karl Popper attribute scientific objectivity to its social institutions—to the friendly-hostile cooperation between its many scientists, and to the laboratories, journals, and conferences that they have created to pursue truth through rational discussion and criticism? But what else should we think when Thomas Kuhn says that science begins where criticism leaves off, that truth plays no role in it at all, and that scientists who persist in criticizing their colleagues should be drummed out of the profession?

Institutionalism, as it has now devolved, is a well-intentioned but inadequate and perhaps even dangerous response to the collapse of foundationalism. It is well-intentioned because it is meant to oppose irrationalism. But it is inadequate because it fails, despite its anti-foundationalist rhetoric, to rid itself of the foundationalist's *demand* that we justify our beliefs. And it is dangerous because this demand, in the absence of our traditional ideals of truth and justification, can easily lead to an even more authoritarian approach to science than the infallibilist one that it is supposed to replace. But in order to explain this, I will need to develop a bit more context.

IV

Most people remember Descartes as a sceptic—a little bit of irony since Descartes was, according to any literal interpretation of his work, one of the greatest opponents of scepticism in the history of Western Philosophy.

The idea that Descartes was a sceptic is undoubtedly due to the dramatic and recherche scenarios that he imagined in his *Meditations on First Philosophy* in order to doubt the veracity of his sense perceptions: his inability to determine whether he was sleeping or awake, and the possibility that God is an omnipotent evil deceiver. But people who remember Descartes as a skeptic apparently remember only his *first* meditation. They should also remember that Descartes' appeal to doubt was purely methodological; that it was not the *conclusion* of a philosophical investigation, but a *method* adopted to conduct one; and that Descartes intended his appeal to doubt to result not in scepticism, but in his uncovering the 'first foundations' of knowledge—that Archimedean bedrock point of certainty that would enable him to do 'great things,' namely, to establish something 'firm and lasting in the sciences.'[8]

Thus, while Descartes ends his first meditation wondering whether there is anything at all that he *cannot* doubt, he ends his sixth in wonder at how very little there is that he can. And along the way he 'proves,' beyond the shadow of a doubt, that he exists, that God exists too, that God is not an evil deceiver, and that he can never make a mistake so long as he uses his God-given intellect properly.

Descartes was able to 'prove' all of this by appealing repeatedly to his 'general rule' that everything that he clearly and distinctly perceives is true—which is, of course, another little bit of irony since it violates both the letter and the spirit of his sceptical method.

It is, for these reasons, not too surprising that people who do *not* remember Descartes as a sceptic, tend to remember him as not being sceptical *enough*.

I do not, for various reasons that I cannot go into here, think that Descartes intended his *Meditations on First Philosophy* to be interpreted literally. But the great foundationalist programs of the past have all been based upon two methodological principles that he introduced in them.

The first of these principles is 'Methodological Scepticism.' This is Descartes' first meditation resolution to doubt whatever he can doubt without contradiction. The second, which I call 'French Epistemology,'[9] is Descartes' fourth meditation claim, made to explain the possibility of error, that it is irrational and improper to accept anything that has not been shown to be true. These two principles have often been conflated, and I would like to clearly distinguish them here.

Methodological Scepticism says that *we should question or doubt* any statement that has not been justified. But French Epistemology says that *we should not accept* any statement that has not been justified.

Methodological Scepticism says that we should question any statement that has not been shown to be true, and that we should always remember that a belief that has not been shown to be true may turn out to be false no matter how familiar or obvious it may seem.

French Epistemology says that we should regard a statement as false, or at least that we should not accept it as true, unless or until it has been shown to be true.

Methodological Scepticism tells us how to arrive at certainty. French Epistemology tells us how to avoid mistakes.[10]

It is important, for what follows, to understand that these two principles state entirely different things—that it is possible to question or doubt a statement while simultaneously accepting it as true; and that it is possible to accept statements that have not been justified without ever questioning or doubting whether they are true.

It is important to understand this, because institutionalists typically make the same mistake in their response to the collapse of foundationalism. Instead of retaining Descartes' Methodological Scepticism and rejecting his French Epistemology, they reject his Methodological Scepticism and retain his French Epistemology.

V

The institutionalist approach to science is just one instance of a far more general response to the collapse of foundationalism that I call 'Floating Foundationalism.' Floating Foundationalism comes in many different varieties. But its basic move is to accept some statement or theory—paradigm, linguistic framework, form of life, belief or what have you—without justification, and to then use it as a foundation upon which to justify everything else. In doing so, Floating Foundationalism retains the demand, the purpose, and sometimes even the logical structure of justification. But it leaves the foundations themselves floating in mid-air. It acknowledges that justification is ultimately grounded upon something that is itself ungrounded and, according to French Epistemology, irrational. But it advises us not to question these things, but to 'commit' ourselves to them instead—and to proceed as if nothing has changed.

Indeed, the only real difference between Floating Foundationalism and traditional bedrock foundationalism is that Floating Foundationalism does not even pretend that its foundations are indubitably true or that the theories that are 'grounded' upon them always follow with logical necessity.

Some people regard this as an improvement. But in my view it raises serious and disturbing questions about the point of demanding justification.

I understand why we would want our theories to be justified, if 'justification' meant showing them to be true, and 'true' meant corresponding to the facts. And I understand, if this is what 'justification' and 'truth' mean, that we might still want our theories to be justified, even if we recognize that justifying them is an impossible dream.

But if a theory can be justified and not true, then why are we so concerned with justification? If a theory can be true but not correspond to the facts, then why should we be concerned with truth? What exactly turns on the justification of a belief if it's not its correspondence with the facts? And what, if anything, does all of this have to do with the institutionalist's distaste for criticism?

These questions, in my view, can all be answered in a word. The word is 'authority,' and in this context it refers to the cognitive authority that justification is supposed to provide for our beliefs.

This is why institutionalists recommend that we *commit* ourselves to a theory. And this is why they do not like criticism. If our knowledge is not grounded upon bedrock, then we better not rock the boat. But in my view, it is just this appeal to foundations that are not indubitably true and to arguments that are not logically valid that is likely to lead to infallibilism and authoritarianism.

Why so?

Because it is relatively easy, so long as we accept Methodological Scepticism, to argue against the claim that a certain theory is infallibly true. All you need do is to show that the claim that it is false involves no contradiction.

But how do you argue with a commitment?

VI

In my view, the contemporary attempt to ground rational belief upon irrational commitment suffers from a kind of bad faith. Justification once explained what made scientific belief rational. But the myth of the foundation is like every other myth: its power as a myth depends upon its being taken for the truth. Most of us no longer believe in a bedrock foundation of truth. But few of us believe that rationality is a matter of consensus. So Floating Foundationalism will not float for long. It is better to abandon our foundations entirely—and with them, the demand that we justify our theories.

But is it possible to do so without conceding to irrationalism?

I think that it is, but only if we retain our traditional ideals of truth and justification—only if we think that a true statement is one that corresponds to the facts and that a justified statement is one that has been shown to be true—and only if we give up French Epistemology.

What must go is not our questions and doubts regarding beliefs that have not been proven, but the idea that rational knowledge, and rationality in general, depends upon accepting only beliefs that have been justified as true.

VII

Karl Popper was one of the first philosophers to recognize this. Popper did not talk about French Epistemology, Floating Foundationalism, or Methodological Scepticism. But he was one of the first to give up the idea that rationality depends upon justification, and the first to associate it with criticism instead. Popper maintained that truth is correspondence to the facts and that justification is the demonstration of truth. But he also maintained that we have rational knowledge despite the fact that we can never justify our theories, or show that they are even probably true. And he was especially critical of inductivism and of the sort of institutionalism that pretends that justification and truth are matters of consensus.

These two things—institutionalism and inductivism—are more closely related than one might think. For it is only the pressure of 'The Institution' and its French Epistemology that supports the illusion that scientific theories are justified by inductive arguments. But in order to explain this, I will need to develop even a bit more context.

VIII

Popper argued that any attempt to justify our beliefs must lead either to psychologism, or to dogmatism, or to infinite regress. But neither psychologism nor dogmatism can demonstrate truth. And he concluded not only that it is impossible to justify our beliefs, but that attempts to do so may lead to authoritarianism of one form or another. This is what he meant when he called the positivists' appeal to the authority of experience 'artless.' For authority is authority—regardless of whether it is the authority of the Pope, or the authority of experience, or the authority of 'The Institution.' And it is useless as proof to anyone unwilling to defer to it.

But this inability to justify our beliefs is often obscured by an ambiguity that lies at the very heart of foundationalism. This ambiguity, when sorted out, reveals two very different justified true belief theories of knowledge. It is, in my view, the failure to recognize and distinguish these two theories that accounts, in part, for the survival of French Epistemology and for the popularity of the idea that beliefs can be justified by arguments that do not entail their conclusions.

IX

Most philosophers regard rational knowledge as justified true belief. But the two questions that they should immediately ask—but rarely, if ever, do—are 'What are we trying to justify when we try to justify true belief?' and 'What are we claiming is justified when we claim to have justified true belief?'

The obvious answer to these questions is 'a belief.' But the term 'belief' is importantly ambiguous. For it may refer either to the content of belief (to the *what* that is believed), or to the process of belief (to the *believing* itself).

It may, in other words, refer to an *object* that someone believes, or to a subject's *act* of believing it.

I will call epistemologies that appeal to the first of these senses of 'belief' *objectivist*, and epistemologies that appeal to the second of these senses *subjectivist*.

I do not wish to suggest that there is anything problematic or improper about either of these senses of 'belief'—or that one of them should, in and of itself, be preferred over the other. But I think that it is important to understand that this ambiguity gives rise to two very different 'justified true belief' theories of knowledge that differ both with regard to what we are justifying when we justify a belief, and with regard to what counts as a justification of it. For according to the objectivist theory, we are justifying a *statement* or *proposition*. But according to the subjectivist theory, we are justifying someone's *act of believing* a statement or proposition.

Justification, in an objectivist theory, is concerned with showing that a statement is true. But justification, in a subjectivist theory, is concerned with showing that someone acted properly in believing that a statement is true.

Descartes recognized that a statement and the act of believing a statement are two different things. But his French Epistemology makes the justification of the former a condition for the justification of the latter. It says that a person acts properly in believing a proposition only if the proposition that he believes has been shown to be true. It says, as Descartes says in his fourth meditation, that 'if I hold off from making a judgment when I do not perceive with sufficient clarity and distinctness what is in fact true, I clearly would be acting properly,' but that if I should make a judgment, 'and in so doing happen upon the truth by accident, I would still not be without fault.'[11]

I think that French Epistemology, together with this conflation of the justification of someone's act of believing a statement with the justification of the statement that he believes, is at the root of a good deal of epistemological confusion, and perhaps even at the root of inductivism itself. We are led by argument to the conclusion that we cannot justify the truth of statements. But we believe that we are, ourselves, rational in believing them. Since we believe that we are rational, we conclude that we are justified. And since we believe that we are justified, we conclude that the statements that we believe are justified too.

But even those who recognize this distinction may, nonetheless, think that subjective justification is the proper task of epistemology. Alan Musgrave, for example, has characterized the question 'What ought I to believe?' as 'the epistemic problem of problems'—and he has denied that any objectivist theory of knowledge can solve it.[12]

I agree with Musgrave that an objectivist theory cannot tell us what we ought to believe. But in my view, the question 'What ought I to believe?' ceases to be an epistemic problem *as soon as we realize that we are inherently fallible, and that all of our beliefs are subject to change.*

X

The question 'What ought I to believe?' owed its status as the epistemic problem of problems to the religious context in which Descartes raised it; to his belief that we could, if we acted properly, accept only beliefs that are true; and primarily to the metaphysical consequences of hellfire and damnation that followed as punishment for getting the answer wrong. But the significance of the question entirely changes as soon as we separate science from religion, and as soon as we acknowledge the inherent fallibility in all of our scientific beliefs.

It is perhaps understandable that Descartes introduced this question into a scientific context. For Descartes was either trying to move from a religious context to a scientific one or, if we interpret him literally, trying to ground a scientific context upon a religious one. It is, however, important to understand that if this 'epistemic problem of problems' ever made sense in a scientific context, it did so only because philosophers believed that we can show with certainty that at least some of the *statements* that we believe are true, and only because French Epistemology told us that it would be irrational for us to accept them without doing so.

I do not want to minimize the fact that the quest for certainty has dominated western philosophy since Descartes. And I do not want to deny that it may still have an influence upon the way we think. But most western philosophers and scientists today say that our beliefs are inherently fallible. And, 'What ought I to believe?,' for this reason, is no longer the epistemic problem of problems.

It's not that you can't continue to ask the question. It's just that your answer to it will no longer mean what it once did. For it will not insure your salvation with the Almighty. And it will not insure that your beliefs are true, or that you yourself are rational for believing them.

And this, I submit, is why 'What ought I to believe?' was the epistemic problem of problems in the first place.

As soon as we give up the idea that we can show that our theories are true, the epistemic problem of problems becomes not the problem of what to believe, but the problem of how to question. It becomes the problem of how to seriously question statements that we believe to be true.

This does not mean that we are now given license to take our mistakes lightly. But it does mean that we are given license to *expect* them. For it is only when we expect them that we will be ready to learn from them and to correct them.

The new epistemic problem of problems is how to seriously question or doubt a belief while simultaneously believing that it is true. It is the problem of how to retain Methodological Scepticism while rejecting French Epistemology.

This problem would be difficult enough to solve even under the best of circumstances. But it is made more difficult by the prevailing belief in inductivism, and by the fulfillment of Russell's prediction that natural science—I can only guess what he would have said about *social* science—could easily become a new religion. And it is made more difficult still by the institutional, but nonetheless eternal, hellfire and damnation that we risk whenever we challenge the prevailing consensus of 'The Institution.'

XI

Earlier I said that institutionalism and inductivism are more closely related than one might think. I am almost ready to explain why this is so. But I first need to explain the purpose of logical arguments, and the reason why inductive arguments are problematic.

Most people think that the purpose of an argument is to justify its conclusion—and to thereby establish its certainty—and that the problem with inductive arguments is that they fail to establish their conclusions with objective certainty since their conclusions may be false even if all of their premises are true. But this entirely confuses the issue, and it has even enabled inductivists to take the high ground in the debate, arguing that objective certainty is an impossible dream, and that inductive arguments are not, as a consequence, at fault for failing to achieve it.

But if the uncertainty of their conclusions were the problem with inductive arguments, then we would also have a similar problem with deductive arguments. For the premises of a deductive argument may be false. And the conclusion of a deductive argument may be false as well.

Contrary to what most people think, logical arguments cannot establish the truth, let alone the certainty, of their conclusions. And so contrary to what most people think, the problem with inductive arguments has nothing to do with the uncertainty of their conclusions.

The best that a logical argument can do is to *test* the truth of a statement. But it can do this only by showing that its falsity is inconsistent with the truth of other statements that can only be tested and never proved. Our so-called 'proof' methods are really techniques for testing consistency. And the demonstration that a 'conclusion' follows from a 'premise' shows only that the falsity of the 'conclusion' is inconsistent with the truth of the 'premise.'

That is all that is involved.

But so long as we regard contradictions as unacceptable, it is really quite a lot.

The inconsistency that marks a valid deductive argument—*the inconsistency, that is, between the truth of its premises and the falsity of its conclusion*—cannot force us to accept the truth of any belief. But it *can* force us, if we want to avoid contradicting ourselves, to re-examine our beliefs, and to *choose* between the truth of some beliefs and the falsity of others—because the falsity of the conclusion of a valid argument is inconsistent with the truth of its premises.

This fact—*that the best that a logical argument can do is to force us to choose between the truth of some beliefs and the falsity of others*—is the deep truth hidden in the so-called 'Law of the Conditional.'

Any argument can be expressed as a conditional statement in which the conclusion of the argument is taken as consequent and the premises of the argument are conjoined as antecedent.[13] And an argument is valid, insofar as this is concerned, if-and-only-if its so-called 'corresponding conditional' is a tautology. But the Law of the Conditional says that conditional statements are equivalent to disjunctions in which the negation of the conditional's antecedent forms one disjunct and the consequent of the conditional forms the other.[14]

And this is just another way of saying that what we call a *proof* actually presents us with the *choice* between accepting its conclusion and rejecting its premises.[15]

This should not be controversial. But logicians call arguments 'proofs.' And there is, to my mind, a big difference between a proof and a choice.

We construct logical arguments in order to persuade others of our beliefs. But the best we can do is to clarify a choice that they have to make. Inductive arguments, however, cannot even do this. Their conclusions never follow from their premises. There is no inconsistency between the truth of their premises and the falsity of their conclusions. So we can always accept their premises and reject their conclusions without contradicting ourselves. And this means that they can never force us even to reexamine our beliefs, let alone to choose between them, in the way that deductive arguments can.

The problem with inductive arguments is not that they cannot justify their conclusions. It is that *inductivists* tend to act *as if* they can. They tend, in other words, to be certain of the truth of their conclusions, and to dismiss as irrational anyone who has the temerity to challenge them.

But why, then, have so many people thought that inductive arguments justify their conclusions?

If what I have been saying is true, it is because they feel rational, and hence justified, in believing what they do, and because they infer from this that what they believe must be justified too.

I would not even regard this sort of subjective justification as problematic, were it not for the fact that inductivists typically move from the claim that *they* are justified, and hence, rational to believe what they do, to the claim that *we* must believe what they believe if we want to be rational too.

This is why institutionalism and inductivism are more closely related than one might think. It is why institutionalists are so opposed to criticism. And it is why the idea that inductive arguments justify their conclusions is so persuasive. Since the conclusion of an inductive argument never follows logically from its premises, an inductivist must inevitably take a little leap in order to accept it as true. The belief that he accepts is unjustified. But he feels safety in numbers, and more justified in accepting it if others whom he respects are willing to accept it too. The people whom he respects will at first be those with whom he agrees. But he will soon find that he respects those with whom he disagrees and is willing to defer to their judgment if he thinks that they can help him to advance. He will thus praise solidarity as constructive and denounce criticism as unprofessional. And he will do so especially if he has no other arguments with which to answer it. In this way, he may eventually reach the point where he is willing to accept a belief for no other reason than that his friends accept it too. And if he becomes powerful enough in 'The Institution,' he may even reach the point where he is willing to reject his friends for no other reason than that they question a belief that he thinks is true.

In my view, the persuasiveness of inductive arguments can only be due to the pressure that one has to resist if he wants to question or to criticize them. These are the pressures of 'The Institution.' And there is no reason to hide the fact. They are the pressures of authoritarianism, pure and simple.

XII

Popper and Kuhn both thought of science as a social institution. But Popper thought that its purpose was to facilitate our critical examination of competing ideas. And Kuhn thought that it was to forge solidarity of belief. Scientific institutions, according to Popper, exist to help scientists in their critical search for truth. But Kuhn thought that truth plays no role in science—and 'The Institution,' in its absence, now exists for the sake of itself.

Popper wrote that 'only political power, when it is used to suppress free criticism, or when it fails to protect it, can impair the functioning of these institutions, on which all progress, scientific, technological, and political, ultimately depends.'[16] But Kuhn did not believe in progress. And the institutions of science have now devolved into 'The Scientific Institution,' a tribal institution that not only wields political power, but whose effect is to suppress the freedom of thought.

XIII

But what about Socrates? And what, more importantly, about the failure of foundationalism? Should we really regard it as the death of epistemology? Or as the death of philosophy? Should it lead us to weaken our standards for truth and justification? And are epistemology and philosophy, in any event, really the sorts of things that can die?

Socrates, I am told, once said that the best that we can ever hope for is to be in the twilight zone between knowledge and ignorance, where the views that we hold happen to be true, but we are unable to know that they are. I do not know whether or not this is true. But I do know that Socrates believed that the unexamined life is not worth living, and that he examined life in a way that gave a new and deeper meaning to the Hellenic ideal to 'Know thyself.' Socrates' pursuit of this ideal gave western philosophy its first 'metaphysical research program'—and the western world its first philosophical hero. For Socrates' belief was no cocktail party platitude. It was, on the contrary, his reason for living—and his reason to forfeit his life when circumstances confronted him with the choice between death and a life left unexamined.

Socrates founded no institutions, received no grants, did not get tenure, and left no discernible positive doctrines. He never even published a book review.

But his pursuit of the philosophical life, or the life of critical examination, led him to cross-examine many of the so-called experts of the Athenian Scientific Institution and to catch them in embarrassing contradictions. And it was, in the end, their anger at being embarrassed that cost Socrates his life. But do not misunderstand. Socrates, despite what Aristotle might have said, was no philosophical martyr. For when faced with the alternatives of death and a life lived unexamined, Socrates *chose* to drink the hemlock, draining the cup 'calmly and easily,'[17] and criticizing Appollodorus and Crito for their unmanly displays of emotion.

This, Socrates insisted, was no cause for tears. This was a free man, who knew himself, exercising his freedom in the way he thought best.

The trumped up charges that cost Socrates his life were that he did not believe in the gods of Athens and that he had corrupted the youth of the city. They were, in other words, *political* charges, made by a politician, and by others who claimed to be patriotic men and to have the good of the community at heart—but who revealed under Socrates' critical examination that they were power hungry, and vain about their own authority, and that they did not quite know what they were talking about.

Socrates always tried to avoid politics. He believed in justice and thought that 'a man who really fights for justice must lead a private life if he is to survive for even a short time.'[18] But this did not prevent him from cornering men in the market place to cross-examine them on their views. And it did not prevent him from explaining to the jury at his trial and defense, begging them not to be angry at him for speaking the truth, that he would have died 'long ago' had he taken a part in politics, since 'no man will survive who genuinely opposes you or any other crowd.'[19]

The picture of Socrates at his apology—the picture of a free man choosing to speak the truth even when he was down on his luck—is what initially inspired many of us to devote our lives to philosophy and to science. Karl Popper, I know, regarded it as the most beautiful work of philosophy that he had ever read.

So how have things gotten so bad that we can today regard these quasi-political attempts to impose solidarity of belief and thought control as philosophy?

But what else should we really expect from 'The Institution'? What else should we expect when it says that science begins where criticism leaves off, or that those who criticize too much should be drummed out of the profession, or that truth and justification is really nothing more than the solidarity of belief amongst its experts?

If truth is nothing more than solidarity, then *all* of our questions are political questions—and the only question that matters is 'Which side are you on?'

I think that philosophers and scientists are faced today with a choice, but that very few of them are clear about what it is. Almost every philosopher and scientist that I know has, somewhere along the line, been faced with the choice to say what he thought was true or to say what he thought would further his career and status in what we today call 'The Institution.' I am sure that many of you have at some point been faced with it too. There is nothing new in this. Indeed, if Socrates is any guide, then it is the way things have always been. And it may, I readily admit, even be the way things will always be. But what *is* relatively new is the idea, proposed and even praised by the proponents of 'The Institution,' that this is the way things *ought* to be. And it is, I think, a tribute to the progress that 'The Scientific Institution' is so often said to have made. For today, twenty-four hundred years after Socrates drank the hemlock, the new-found wisdom of 'The Scientific Institution' is that the unexamined life is worth living after all. In my view, it is not 'The Institution' and its new found wisdom that we should choose. It is, on the contrary, science and the freedom of thought.

This is what philosophers and scientists have stood for since Socrates. It is what Popper stood for in our own century. And it is, I think, what philosophers and scientists should stand for always and everywhere.

In my view, the collapse of foundationalism has no implications whatsoever for truth. It does not show that truth does not exist. And it does not show that it is solidarity and consensus. What the collapse of foundationalism does show is that we do not know, and indeed cannot know, what we thought we knew. It shows that we are, even now, living in that twilight zone between knowledge and ignorance, where the views that we hold may be true, but where we are unable to know that they are.

It shows, if we could only appreciate the irony, that we really know nothing at all. And it shows why Kierkegaard was right to regard Socrates as the Master of Irony.

Socrates thought that the Delphic Oracle regarded him as the wisest of men because he alone knew that he knew nothing at all. But twenty-four hundred years after he drank the hemlock, we now have lovers of institutional wisdom who regard Socratic wisdom as a failure. My own view is that the failure of foundationalism is not the failure of epistemology. My own view is that it is its greatest success. It would mean that we could all stop worrying about the certainty of our beliefs, were it not for the fact that this Socratic Irony is something that is easily forgotten and must, apparently, be rediscovered in each and every generation.

In my view, philosophers and scientists ought to defend our traditional ideals of truth and justification—not because we believe that they can actually be realized and not because they are traditional. We should continue to defend them so that we will be able to recognize, in each and every generation, that they have not yet been achieved.

Notes

1 This is a revised version of a paper that was first published in *Divinatio: Studia Culturologica Series*, Volume 5, Autumn-Winter 1997. It has been presented, among other places, at Babes Bolyai University in Cluj, Romania on 26 October, 1996; at the Institute for Philosophy at the University of Wrocław in Wrocław, Poland on 28 April 1997; at the Institute of Public Administration at Moscow State University in Moscow, Russia on 23 May 1997; and at the Philosophy Faculty at the University of Bucharest in Bucharest, Romania on 5 March 1998. It also formed the basis for a summer school course on the philosophy of science that was held at the Soros Foundation in Almaty, Kazakhstan from 10–14 August 1998. The mottoes are from Thomas S. Kuhn, 'Logic of Discovery or Psychology of Research?' in *Criticism and the Growth of Knowledge*, edited by Imre Lakatos and Alan Musgrave, Cambridge University Press, Cambridge, 1970, p. 6; and Karl R. Popper, *Realism and the Aim of Science*, edited by W.W. Bartley III, 1983. Reprinted by Routledge, London, 1996, p. 7.

2 Plato, *Republic*, 472c. My italics.

3 Plato, *Republic*, 472b.

4 See Plato, *Republic*, 472e.

5 David Hull, *Science as Process*, Chicago, University of Chicago Press, 1988, pp. 12–13.

6 It is interesting to compare Hull's diagnosis of evolutionary epistemology with Hilary Putnam's statement (also cited by Hull) that what is 'wrong with evolutionary epistemology is not that the scientific facts are wrong, but that they don't answer any of the philosophical questions.' Hilary Putnam, 'Why Reason Can't be Naturalized' in *Synthesis*, 52, 1982, pp. 3–23.

7 It is interesting, in this connection to remember Bacon's description of one of the Solomon's House's directors of research (Francis Bacon, *The New Atlantis*, edited by James Spedding, Robert Leslie Ellis, and Douglas Denon Heath, Longman and Company, London, 1862–75, vol. III, pp. 114f.):

The day being come, he made his entry. He was a man of middle stature and age, comely of person, and had an aspect as if he pitied men. He was clothed in a robe of fine black cloth, with wide sleeves and a cape... He had gloves that were ... set with stone; and shoes of peach-coloured velvet... He was carried in a rich chariot without wheels, litter-wise; with two horses at either end, richly trapped in blue velvet embroidered; and two footmen on each side in the like attire. The chariot was all of cedar, gilt, and adorned with crystal; save that the fore-end had pannels of sapphires, set in borders of gold, and the hinder-end the like of emeralds of the Peru colour. There was also a sun of gold, radiant, upon the top, in the midst; and on the top before, a small cherub of gold, with wings displayed. The chariot was covered with cloth of gold tissued upon blue. He had before him fifty attendants, young men all, in white sattin loose coats to the mid-leg; and stockings of white silk; and shoes of blue velvet; and hats of blue velvet; with fine plumes of divers colours, set round like hat-bands. Next before the chariot went two men, bare-headed, in linen garments down to the foot, girt, and shoes of blue velvet; who carried the one a crosier, the other a pastoral staff like a sheep-hook; neither of them of metal, but the crosier of balm-wood, the pastoral staff of cedar. Horsemen he had none, neither before nor behind his chariot: as it seemeth, to avoid all tumult and trouble. Behind his chariot went all the officers and principals of the Companies of the City. He sat alone, upon cushions of a kind of excellent plush, blue: and under his foot curious carpets of silk of divers colours, like the Persian, but far finer. He held up his bare hand as he went, as blessing the people, but in silence.

8 René Descartes, *Meditations on First Philosophy*, translated by Donald A. Cress, Hackett, Cambridge, 1980, p. 57.

9 I call this principle 'French Epistemology' partly because Descartes introduced it (and Descartes was French), but primarily because the principle has an interesting analogue in a French judicial principle according to which issues of *reasonable doubt* in criminal cases may, contrary to Anglo-American custom, be resolved by evidence and argument bearing on prior convictions of the accused individual, his general behavior, and even his family history. But the directive that a person accused of a crime must be found *guilty beyond a reasonable doubt* has its origin in the principle of the presumption of innocence—the principle that an accused is presumed innocent until proven guilty (beyond a reasonable doubt)—and the two are often taken to be practically synonymous, if not legally equivalent.

The point is that an accused individual's prior criminal record, general behavior, or family history may, if sufficiently notorious, *practically* reverse the presumption of innocence in a French judicial proceeding. The person accused of a crime would, in such a case, still, in theory, be presumed innocent, and he would still, in theory, have to be proved guilty beyond a reasonable doubt. But the 'evidence' regarding his prior criminal record, general behavior, and family history might well be considered a sufficient rebuttal of the 'evidence' provided by the presumption of innocence, and might, thereby, render a *mere accusation* a 'proof beyond reasonable doubt.' In such a case, the burden of proof would be *practically* reversed. The prosecution would not need to prove that the defendant is guilty; the defendant would need to prove he is not.

10 This is, in fact, the reason why Descartes introduced it.

11 Descartes, *Meditations on First Philosophy*, p. 38.

12 Alan Musgrave, 'Popper on Induction' in *Philosophy of the Social Sciences*, December 1993, p. 526.

13 Thus, if an argument has the premises P_1, P_2, P_n and the conclusion C, then its corresponding conditional is $[(P_1 \ \& \ P_2 \ \& \ P_n) \rightarrow C]$. To give a hackneyed example: If all men are mortal and Socrates is a man, then Socrates is mortal.

14 So that $[(P_1 \,\&\, P_2 \,\&\, P_n) \to C]$ is equivalent to $[\sim(P_1 \,\&\, P_2 \,\&\, P_n) \lor C]$.

15 We can, if we take the argument one step further, conclude that all valid arguments are formally circular. For the so-called 'Law of Tautology' tells us that every tautology is materially equivalent to every other tautology. And this tells us that the corresponding conditional of every valid argument is materially equivalent to $(\sim P \lor P)$.

16 Karl R. Popper, *The Open Society and Its Enemies*, 1945. Reprinted by Routledge, London, 1998, vol. 2, p. 218.

17 Plato, *The Phaedo*, 117c.

18 Plato, *Apology*, 32a.

19 Plato, *Apology*, 31e.

5 Induction and Demarcation[1]

> *Science never pursues the illusory aim of making its answers final, or even probable. Its advance is, rather, towards an infinite yet attainable aim: that of ever discovering new, deeper, and more general problems, and of subjecting our ever tentative answers to ever renewed and ever more rigorous tests.*
>
> Karl R. Popper

I

Karl Popper regarded induction and demarcation as the two fundamental problems of epistemology. He claimed that he had solved both of them, and that his solutions were related to each other. But few philosophers, as Popper himself acknowledged, think that he has solved the problem of induction. And even those who think that he has solved the problem of demarcation often misconstrue what his solution actually is. This, I think, is because Popper presented these problems, and their solutions, in ways that can be easily misunderstood. He presented the problem of induction, for example, as a problem regarding the *justification* of scientific theories, while at the same time denying that deductive arguments can justify their conclusions. And he talked about *falsifiability* as the distinctive feature of scientific theories—while at the same time denying that conclusive falsifications are ever possible. In this way, he helped to obscure not only the problems of induction and demarcation, but also his own important and revolutionary solutions to them.

The problem is that Popper sometimes formulated his views on induction and demarcation in ways that suggest that we can justify our knowledge, and indeed that we must justify it, in order for it to be regarded as rational—despite his explicit claims to the contrary. This has not only confused philosophers as to how his views about induction and demarcation constitute solutions to these problems, it has also obscured the real nature of the problems themselves, and the ways in which Popper's solutions to them are related to each other. The purpose of this paper is to explain these problems and Popper's solutions to them in a way that avoids these confusions.

II

In order to understand Popper's solutions to the problems of induction and demarcation, it is necessary to understand his problem situation. It is necessary, in other words, to understand why Popper regarded induction and demarcation as the two fundamental problems of epistemology.

This, I suggest, can best be understood as a result of the collapse of foundationalism, which can in turn be best understood as posing a problem regarding the rational authority for our beliefs.

Traditional 'bedrock' foundationalism said that knowledge must be justified in order to be rational, and it attempted to justify our knowledge by deriving it from an indubitable and infallible source. Descartes, it is well known, declared that the God-given intellect is such a source, and that whatever we clearly and distinctly perceive with it must be true. But by the eighteenth century, many philosophers had grown sceptical of attempts to ground rational knowledge upon a priori intuition. These philosophers regarded sense experience as the only criterion of truth. They said that our general theories must be inferred inductively from experience. And they demanded that we eliminate beliefs that could not be grounded upon sense experience alone.

But Hume then argued that the attempt to ground our scientific knowledge upon sense experience leads to irrationalism. Hume pointed out that there is no 'middle term' that allows us to validly infer future events from past experiences, and that such inductive inferences provide only *psychological*, as opposed to rational, justification through custom and habit. Hume thought that our knowledge was, in fact, psychologically justified in just this way, and he said that reason is and ought to be the slave of the passions. But Kant rejected Hume's irrationalism, and, thinking that Hume was right to think that empiricism entailed it, proclaimed that there must be a priori knowledge after all. Kant pointed to Euclidean Geometry and Newtonian Mechanics as examples of what he called a priori synthetic knowledge. And he tried to explain how a priori synthetic knowledge was possible by saying that the mind imposes its laws upon nature in order to understand it, and that all rational beings impose the same laws.

This, as Popper understood it, was the situation in epistemology before Einstein.

Kant's attempt to salvage the rationality of science collapsed when Einstein imposed a non-Euclidean geometry and a non-Newtonian physics upon nature. Einstein described a natural world that rational beings before him had never conceived. And his descriptions were then corroborated by the results of the experiments that he conceived in order to test them.

The success of Einstein's theory shattered all hopes of explaining the rationality of science in terms of a priori foundations. If Kant could be wrong about the a priori certainty of Newtonian Mechanics and Euclidean Geometry, then how could anyone ever claim to be a priori certain again? But it did not quite shatter the hopes of foundationalists, who, forgetting about Hume's irrationalism, once again tried to explain the rationality of science as a by-product of its justification by sense experience. Wittgenstein and the logical positivists in particular, argued, as Hume had argued before them, that the meaning of a term is reducible to sense impressions, and that empirical verifiability is what distinguishes science from metaphysics, and sense from nonsense.

It was in this context that induction and demarcation emerged for Popper as the two fundamental problems of epistemology.

Popper realized that the attempt to explain the rationality of science as a byproduct of its justification had failed. We cannot rationally ground science upon a priori cognition because a priori cognition is unreliable, and we cannot rationally ground science upon sense experience because inductive inference is invalid. If we want to avoid Hume's conclusion that science is *irrationally* grounded in custom and habit, then we have to explain how scientific knowledge can be rational *given* the fact that it cannot be rationally justified.

This, in a nutshell, was Popper's problem. In order to solve it, Popper had to first offer an alternative to the view that science is distinguished from non-science by its inductive method, and then an alternative to the view that the rationality of a belief depends upon its justification. He had, in other words, to offer an alternative to the view that science is both science and rational because it justifies its theories through sense experience.

III

Popper's problem, in a nutshell, was to explain how the growth of scientific knowledge can be both empirical and rational. Here, Popper agreed with Hume that the attempt to justify our knowledge by inductive inferences from experience leads to irrationalism—but he denied that scientists generally reason inductively at all. He agreed with Kant that experience and observation presuppose a priori ideas—but he denied that our a priori ideas are certainly true. And he agreed with the positivists that it is no longer possible to appeal to a priori valid principles in our attempts to justify natural science—but he argued that metaphysical theories need not be meaningless and that verifiability, in any event, cannot be the demarcation between science and metaphysics, because it fails to account for the scientific character of scientific laws, which cannot be verified through inductive arguments from experience.

But where Hume, Kant, Wittgenstein, and the positivists all agreed that our knowledge must be justified in order to be rational, Popper cut the Gordian knot by arguing that scientific knowledge cannot, and need not, be justified at all—and by saying that it is rational not because we have justified it, but because we can criticize it. Popper argued that any attempt to justify our knowledge must, in order to avoid infinite regress, ultimately accept the truth (or reliability) of some statement (or faculty, or person) without justification. But the fact that the truth (or reliability) of this statement (or faculty, or person) is accepted without justification, means that we attribute to it an authority that we deny to others. Thus, where Wittgenstein and the positivists appealed to experience to justify our knowledge, Popper argued that 'the main problem of philosophy is the critical analysis of the appeal to the authority of "experience"—precisely that "experience" which every latest discoverer of positivism is, as ever, artlessly taking for granted.'[2]

The observation statements that report our experience never entail the truth of a strictly universal statement (or theory). So universal statements (or theories) cannot be justified (or verified) by experience. But it takes only one genuine counter-example to show that a universal statement is *false*. So some universal statements (or theories) can be criticized (or falsified) by experience—or, at least, by the acceptance of observation statements that contradict them. Popper concluded that it is falsifiability, and not verifiability, that distinguishes empirical science from metaphysics. And then, by pointing out that there is a logical asymmetry between universal and singular statements—so that universal statements can be falsified, but not verified; and singular statements can be verified, but not falsified—he showed that the distinction between science and metaphysics cannot coincide with the distinction between meaningful and meaningless statements, because if a statement is meaningful then its negation must be meaningful as well.

This is the logical part of Popper's solution to the problems of induction and demarcation. But Popper also denied that scientific theories are typically *discovered* through inductive reasoning. Scientists, according to Popper, do not usually discover their theories by making repeated observations and then generalizing them. They typically *invent* their theories as speculative solutions to their problems—and they typically appeal to observations and experience in order to *test* these solutions, and not in order to justify them.

In this way, Popper argued that the growth of science is both empirical and rational. It is empirical because we *test* our solutions to scientific problems against our observations and experience. And it is rational, because we make use of the valid argument forms of deductive logic, especially the *modus tollens*, to criticize theories that contradict the observation statements that we think are true—and because we never conclude from the fact that a theory has survived our tests that it has been shown to be true.

Popper's alternative is easily misunderstood, in part, because it offers a real alternative. In order to understand it, we must think of knowledge and of rationality in a way that does not presuppose that our knowledge must be justified in order to be rational, and is also misunderstood due to the way in which Popper himself presented it.

IV

In *Objective Knowledge*, Popper credits his solution to the problem of induction to his reformulation of the problem. 'The traditional philosophical problem of induction,' according to Popper, was:

> *Tr* What is the justification for the belief that the future will be (largely) like the past? Or, perhaps, What is the justification for inductive inferences?[3]

Popper argued that formulations like this are 'wrongly put.' They beg the question by presuming that inductive inferences, or the belief that the future will be (largely) like the past, are in fact justified.[4] The problem thus becomes one of providing a justification that is already presumed to exist.

Popper reformulated the logical problem of induction as:

> L_1 Can the claim that an explanatory universal theory is true be justified by 'empirical reasons'; that is, by assuming the truth of certain test statements or observation statements (which, it may be said, are 'based on experience')?[5]

This is clearly an improvement. Instead of presupposing that inductive inferences are justified, it allows us to say that they are not.

But L_1 still construes the problem of induction as a problem of justification. And this not only obscures the real problem with inductive inferences, it also obscures the relationship between Popper's solution to the problem of induction and his falsifiability criterion of demarcation.

In what follows, I will first try to clarify the real problem with inductive inferences, and I will then try to show how Popper's solution to the problem of demarcation is related to it.

V

Philosophers typically present the problem of induction as a problem of justification: as the problem, namely, of whether the premises of an inductive argument justify its conclusion—or, at least, our *belief* in its conclusion. But the conclusion of an argument and our belief in it are two different things. Later I will suggest that the failure to distinguish these two different things is responsible for the widespread belief that inductive arguments justify their conclusions. But this is not the focus of my discussion. For I do not believe that the real problem with inductive arguments has anything to do with justification at all. And this is what I want to explain here.

I can begin by saying that if the problem of induction were a problem about justification, then there should also be a problem of *deduction*. For it is well known that valid deductive arguments may have both false premises and false conclusions.

So it is clear, if justifying the conclusion means showing it to be true,[6] that deductive arguments never justify their conclusions.

Popper knew this, but tended to obscure it. For after answering L_1 in the negative, he 'generalized' the question as:

> L_2 Can the claim that an explanatory universal theory is true or that it is false be justified by 'empirical reasons'; that is, can the assumption of the truth of test statements justify either the claim that a universal theory is true or the claim that it is false?[7]

Here, part of the problem is that L_2 mixes inductive and deductive forms. Popper knew full well that the *modus tollens*, the argument form through which he would 'justify' the claim that a universal theory is false, is deductively valid. Nevertheless, he characterized it as 'the only strictly deductive kind of inference that proceeds, as it were, in the inductive direction; that is, from singular to universal statements.'[8]

I do not know what Popper meant by 'as it were.' But his claim that the *modus tollens* proceeds from singular to universal statements is simply false. It is possible, as Popper says, to use *modus tollens* 'to argue from the truth of singular statements to the falsity of universal statements.' But when we do so, we argue from the *negation* of a conditional's consequent to the *negation* of its antecedent. Here, the antecedent would be a theory, or a universal statement, and the consequent either a singular or existential statement. But the negation of a universal statement is an existential statement, and vice versa. So the *modus tollens* would proceed in the 'deductive direction' from universal to particular statements after all.[9]

But the real problem is that the *assumption* of the truth of a statement cannot justify anything. If you have to assume the truth of your premises in order to justify your conclusion, then you might as well assume the conclusion itself.

Neither inductive nor deductive arguments can show that their conclusions are true. If this is what it means to justify a conclusion, then neither inductive nor deductive arguments justify their conclusions. Here, someone might regard inductive arguments as worse in this respect. For valid deductive arguments *would* justify their conclusions, if we could be certain that their premises were true. Inductive arguments, on the other hand, are not even valid. Their conclusions may be false even if their premises are true.

There is nothing in this that I want to deny. But putting it like this obscures the problem. If the premises of a deductively valid argument are true, then its conclusion must also be true. But this does not mean that the premises of deductive arguments are true. It simply means that deductive arguments entail their conclusions. And this fact may be equally expressed by saying that if the conclusion of a deductively valid argument is false, then one or more of its premises must be false as well.

Deductive arguments entail their conclusions and inductive arguments do not. And entailment, I agree, is crucial. But entailment is not enough for justification. It pertains, instead, to validity, or formal implication, which is an entirely different thing. A valid deductive argument entails its conclusion. But it cannot justify its conclusion unless we are certain that its premises are true. Popper, however, thinks that we are fallible. And this, I presume, is what leads him to ask whether the *assumption* of the truth of a test statement can justify the claim that a universal theory is false.

In my view, the problem with inductive arguments pertains not to their utility for justification, but to their utility for criticism. Were I to follow Popper's example and reformulate the logical problem of induction, I would do so as follows:

L_3 Can our belief that the conclusion of an inductive argument is false ever force us to question the truth of its premises?[10]

The answer to L_3 is 'No.' Inductive arguments are one and all invalid. The falsity of their conclusions is entirely consistent with the truth of their premises. And this means that inductive arguments, unlike their deductive counterparts, could not justify their conclusions *even if* we were certain that their premises were true.

But this also obscures the problem. For it tends to suggest that deductive arguments can in some way justify their conclusions after all. And it tends to camouflage the fact that the invalidity of an inductive argument makes it entirely useless for criticism.

This, I suggest, is the real problem with induction inferences, and the real relationship between the problem of induction and the problem of demarcation.

Deductive arguments force us to choose between the truth of their conclusions and the falsity of (one or more) of their premises. Inductive arguments do not. This, in and of itself, does not show that anything is true or false. But if an argument is deductively valid, then we simply cannot, without contradicting ourselves, deny its conclusion unless we also deny (one or more of) its premises. In this way, deductive arguments enable us to exercise critical control over our scientific debates.

Far from enabling us to exercise critical control, inductive arguments deprive us of it. Since their premises do not entail their conclusions, the falsity of their conclusions gives us no reason even to question, let alone to deny, the truth of their premises.

Consider the situation. We assume the premises that we do because they seem to be obviously true. But their truth may suddenly seem doubtful if they are shown to entail statements that seem more obviously false. If a statement is a deductive consequence of premises, then it cannot be false without (one or more of) those premises being false. But this is not true of inductive arguments. And this is why they are useless for criticism.

The premises of an inductive argument seem obviously true—otherwise they would not be assumed as premises. And the conclusion of an inductive argument is not entailed by them—otherwise it would not be inductive. The argument itself says that its conclusion is true because its premises are true—or, at the very least, that you should believe that its conclusion is true because you believe that its premises are true. But the conclusion of an inductive argument does not *follow* from its premises.

So there is no reason at all for our confidence in the truth of those premises to change if we should think that the conclusion that is 'derived' from them is false.

It is not just that the falsity of the conclusion of an inductive argument does not force us to *deny* (one or more of) its premises. It is that the falsity of the conclusion gives us no reason to even *question* the truth of its premises. We believed those premises to be true before the 'conclusion' that we think is false was 'derived' from them. And there is nothing in the logical relationship between that conclusion and those premises to prevent the premises from being true and the conclusion false. So why should we now question whether the premises are true?

If this is true, then the problem with inductive arguments is not that they never justify their conclusions. It is that they never give us reason to question their premises. Since their conclusions do not follow from their premises, they never place us in a position in which we have to choose between accepting their conclusions and denying their premises.

Here I want to emphasize that neither L_3 nor its answer have anything to do with justification. We are not, as in L_1 and L_2, asking whether we can justify something on the strength of an assumption. And we are not, as in Popper's answer to L_2, claiming that we can.

VI

Popper's solution to his reformulated logical problem of induction, L_1, was the same as Hume's: 'no number of true test statements would justify the claim that an explanatory universal theory is true.'[11] But his answer to its 'generalization,' L_2, was 'Yes, *the assumption of the truth of test statements sometimes allows us to justify the claim that an explanatory universal theory is false.*'[12]

I have already cited two ways in which this obscures the problem. *Modus tollens* is a deductive argument form that proceeds in the deductive direction, regardless of what Popper claims. And if we need to assume premises in order to justify conclusions, then we might as well assume the conclusions themselves. There is, however, a third way in which L_2, and Popper's answer to it, obscures the problem.

To say that we can justify the claim that an explanatory universal theory is false is to say that we can falsify or refute our theories. Popper, while saying that scientific theories are falsifiable, has always denied that *conclusive* falsification is possible.[13] But by likening criticism to refutation, he seems to suggest that conclusive falsification is possible, and that the difference between inductive and deductive arguments is that deductive arguments can, but inductive arguments cannot, justify their conclusions.

If I am right, then the problem of induction pertains entirely to the *criticism* of our assumptions. But in order to explain this properly, I need to explain how criticism differs from refutation.

Most people regard refutation as proof that a theory is false. In this sense, 'refutation' is synonymous with 'falsification.' It is what we would do were it possible to justify the claim that an explanatory theory is false. Popper has characterized the method of science both as conjecture and refutation, and as the criticism of our tentative solutions to problems. In doing so, he has identified refutation with criticism, and has described the scientific attitude as the critical attitude. But he has always qualified this by denying that anything like conclusive refutations or disproofs are possible. And it is this, I think, that has always confused people.

If justification is impossible, then criticism is not the refutation of theories. It is the setting of problems for them. We set problems for a theory by showing that it contradicts other statements that we believe to be true. Since contradictory statements cannot both be true, we can force ourselves, in this way, to choose between a theory and our other beliefs. If our criticism is effective, then we may, at the minimum, have to refine our theory in some way so as to remove the contradiction. But the criticism itself never proves that our theories are false. And if this is what is meant by 'refutation,' then it never refutes them. The problems that we set may sometimes seem overwhelming, and they may even lead us to think that our theories have been shown to be false. But if they do, then we should remember that we are fallible human beings, and that our fallibility means that what seems overwhelming at one moment may seem easy to deal with the next. We may, for example, learn something new that makes what once seemed obviously true seem obviously false.

VII

But what is the relationship between Popper's solution to the problem of induction and his solution to the problem of demarcation?

Popper says that he solved the problem of induction seven years after he formulated and solved the problem of demarcation, and that only then did he notice a relationship between the two. The relationship is that many philosophers believe that inductive arguments can justify their conclusions because they believe that induction is the method of science. In this way, a mistaken belief about the method of science—and hence about the demarcation between science and non-science—provides psychological support for a mistaken belief about induction. 'Inductive inferences must

somehow be valid, because science is impossible without them.'
Popper, however, hoped to undermine belief in induction by
showing that science does not require it after all.

I have no doubt that many philosophers believe in induction because they believe that science is impossible without it. But this is
not the best way to explain the relationship between Popper's solution to the problem of demarcation and his solution to the problem of induction.

Falsifiability is the advice that we should be aware of our fallibility and critical of our theories. But we move from an awareness of
our fallibility to criticism of our theories only if we are looking for
truth.

This is where logic, or the science of truth,[14] enters the picture.
*But logical arguments can assist us in criticizing our theories only if those
arguments are valid.*

Why is this?

Because the point of criticism is to force someone to question
his assumptions, and because an argument can force someone to
question his assumptions only if it is deductively valid—and even
then only if he recognizes its validity, and only if he is looking for
truth.

Compare, for example, the valid *modus tollens*:

$$P \to Q$$
$$\sim Q$$
$$\therefore \quad \sim P$$

with the invalid *affirmation of the consequent*:

$$P \to Q$$
$$Q$$
$$\therefore \quad P$$

Each of these arguments has a corresponding conditional, namely:

$$[(P \to Q) \ \& \ \sim Q] \to \sim P$$

and

$$[(P \to Q) \ \& \ Q] \to P$$

respectively. It is well known that an argument is valid if-and-only-if its corresponding conditional is a tautology. But $(P \to Q)$ is equivalent to $(\sim P \lor Q)$. So each of the above corresponding conditionals has an equivalent 'corresponding disjunction,' namely:

$$\sim[(P \to Q) \ \& \ \sim Q] \lor \sim P$$

and

$$\sim[(P \to Q) \ \& \ Q] \lor P.$$

By putting things in this way, we clarify the fact that an argument presents us with a *choice* instead of a justification. An argument asks us to choose between asserting its conclusion and denying (the conjunction of) its premises. The argument cannot make the choice for us. It is up to us to decide.

But the disjunctions that correspond to the valid *modus tollens* are tautologies, whereas the disjunctions that correspond to the invalid *affirmation of the consequent* are not. And this is crucial. For it means that we are free to deny both of the alternatives offered by the *affirmation of the consequent*—but that we are *not* free to deny both of the alternatives offered by the *modus tollens*.

What 'free to deny' means here is free to deny *without contradicting ourselves*. If we do not care about whether or not we contradict ourselves, then we are free to assert and deny anything we please.

Suppose that I want to deny the 'conclusion' of the *modus tollens* and assert that $\sim P$ is false. I will find, simply by looking at Truth Table 1 below, that in each of the cases in which $\sim P$ is false, the statement $\sim[(P \to Q) \ \& \ \sim Q]$ is true.

This means that I cannot assert that $\sim P$ is false without implying that $\sim[(P \to Q) \ \& \ \sim Q]$ is true.

Suppose, on the other hand, that I want to assert that $\sim[(P \to Q) \ \& \ \sim Q]$ is false. I will find, again by looking at Truth Table 1 below, that in the only case in which $\sim[(P \to Q) \ \& \ \sim Q]$ is false $\sim P$ is true.

Truth Table 1:

P	Q	~[(P → Q) & ~Q]	~P
T	T	T	F
T	F	T	F
F	T	T	T
F	F	F	T

This means that there is a *logical* relationship between the alternatives that the *modus tollens* offers. We are free to assert both statements. But we are not free to deny both statements. For if we deny either of them, we imply that the other is true.

Things are different with the *affirmation of the consequent*.

Suppose that I want to assert that its 'conclusion' P is false. ~[(P → Q) & Q] V P is not a tautology. I find, simply by looking at Truth Table 2 below, that there is a case in which P is false and ~[(P → Q) & Q] is true, and a case in which both statements are false.

Suppose, on the other hand, that I want to assert that ~[(P → Q) & Q] is false. I can find, again by looking at Truth Table 2 below, that there is a case in which ~[(P → Q) & Q] is false and P is true, and a case in which ~[(P → Q) & Q] is false and P is false.

Truth Table 2:

P	Q	~[(P → Q) & Q]	P
T	T	F	T
T	F	T	T
F	T	F	F
F	F	T	F

This means that, contrary to what we saw with the *modus tollens*, we are free to assert *and* deny both of the alternatives offered by the *affirmation of the consequent*.

What does it all mean?

It means that the *affirmation of the consequent* is as useless for criticism as it is for proof. It is useless for criticism because denying its 'conclusion' in no way forces us to rethink its premises. This, of course, is true of all invalid arguments. I have, however, focused upon the *affirmation of the consequent* because it mirrors most closely the general form of inductive arguments as they are supposed to be used in science.

But if inductive arguments do not justify their conclusions and do not give us critical control, then what do they do? They give us the appearance of justification, and the appearance of critical control. They *induce* us to believe, by giving us these appearances, that our guesses are somehow better than guesses, and that they are somehow sanctioned by logic—even though we know that the 'proofs' that sanction them do not entail their truth.

This, I suggest, is the real problem with inductive arguments, and the real connection between the problem of induction and the problem of demarcation.

VIII

Here it is easy to see why the problem of induction has nothing whatsoever to do with a 'principle of induction.' Some people think that inductive inferences would be all right if we could only rely on a 'principle of causality' or on a 'principle of the uniformity of nature.' But the problem of induction is a problem regarding *inference*. It is not about what our premises are, or how we get them, or even whether or not they are true. It is about how they are related to our conclusions. The great difference between deductive and inductive inferences is that the conclusions of inductive inferences *may be false even if all of their premises are true*. This is why Popper said that they are useless for justification. And it is why I say that they are useless for criticism.

I do not deny that things would be different if we could rely upon a principle of induction. But this is not because inductive inferences would then be valid. It is because our inferences would then not be inductive. They would, in that case, be deductive after all.

IX

Popper regarded a theory as scientific if it stands in contradiction to a singular or existential statement that describes a state of affairs that is possible to observe. He called such theories 'falsifiable' because we cannot say that the singular statements that contradict them are true without implying that the theories themselves are false.

Popper thought that falsifiability was best understood through the logic of *modus tollens*. But he repeatedly denied that it is possible to conclusively falsify a theory.

There are, however, widespread confusions regarding this[15] and other aspects of falsifiability.[16] And I believe that many of these confusions are due to the fact that most people believe that the purpose of a logical argument is to justify, or prove, its conclusion.

If the purpose of an argument is to prove its conclusion, then it is difficult to see the point of falsifiability. For deductive arguments cannot prove their conclusions any more than inductive ones can.

But if the purpose of the argument is to force us to choose, then the point of falsifiability becomes clear.

Deductive arguments force us to question, and to reexamine, and, ultimately, to deny their premises if we want to deny their conclusions. Inductive arguments simply do not.

This is the real meaning of Popper's *Logic of Scientific Discovery*— and it is the reason, perhaps, why so many readers have misunderstood its title and its intent. The logic of discovery is not the logic of discovering theories, and it is not the logic of discovering that they are true.

Neither deduction nor induction can serve as a logic for that.

The logic of discovery is the logic of discovering our errors.[17] We simply cannot deny the conclusion of a deductive argument without discovering that we were in error about its premises. *Modus tollens* can help us to do this if we use it to set problems for our theories. But while inductive arguments may persuade or induce us to believe things, they cannot help us to discover that we are in error about their premises.

X

Earlier I said that the failure to distinguish between the conclusion of an argument and our belief in that conclusion is responsible for the widespread belief that inductive arguments justify their conclusions. I would now like to explain what I mean.

Most philosophers still believe that scientific knowledge is justified true belief, and that a belief is rational to the extent to which it has been justified as true. For this reason, most of the methodological debates in the philosophy of science ultimately concern the justification of belief and the nature of truth. But here, a good deal of confusion is generated by the fact that 'belief' may refer either to our act of believing a statement or to the statement that we actually believe. There is nothing wrong with either of these meanings.

But conflating them is largely responsible for the belief that inductive arguments can justify their conclusions.

The ambiguity of 'belief' has, in fact, led many philosophers to conflate two very different justified true belief theories of knowledge. The one, which I call 'objective,' concerns itself with the justification of the statements, or objects, that we believe. The other, which I call 'subjective,' concerns itself with the justification of the people, or subjects, who believe them.

How does this pertain to induction?

Most philosophers agree that a finite number of singular statements does not entail that a universal statement is true. But they also believe that they, themselves, would be justified by such 'evidence' in believing it. Since they fail to distinguish the conclusion of an argument from their belief in it, they tend to believe that the universal statement that they believe must somehow be justified by this 'evidence' too.

We cannot help but to encourage such misunderstandings so long as we present the problem of induction as a problem about justification (or proof, or certainty), as opposed to a problem about validity (or entailment, or implication).

XI

But I also qualified my criticism that Popper's use of terms like 'justification' and 'refutation' tend to obscure his solutions to the problems of demarcation and induction. I said '*if* this is what it means to justify a conclusion' and '*if* this is what is meant by "refutation".'

But what else could be meant by 'justification' and 'refutation'?

I do not agree with the inductivists that we can justify our beliefs in the sense of showing that they are supported or confirmed by the evidence. But I do think that these words have senses that, while perhaps not as common as 'to show or prove to be true' and 'to show or prove to be false,' are fully consistent with the way in which Popper uses them and with the way in which I have tried to explain his positions here.

There are senses of 'refutation,' for example, in which someone refutes a statement not by proving that it is false, but by contradicting it, or simply by denying that it is true. And there are senses of 'justification' in which someone justifies a statement not by proving that it is true, but by showing that it is a logical consequence of other things that he asserts.

Indeed, there is even a sense in which to prove a statement is simply to *test* whether or not it is true.[18]

I say this, because I do not want to be misunderstood as saying that Popper's use of these terms was mistaken or wrong. I am saying only that it is easily misunderstood, and that it was in fact misunderstood in a way that obscured his solutions to the problems of induction and demarcation.

Modus tollens is another matter. Popper knew that *modus tollens* proceeded in the deductive direction. But he thought that it was better, for 'strategic reasons,' to present things as he did. He thought, no doubt, that he might have a better chance of convincing inductivists and verificationists if he tried to meet them halfway.

It is difficult to know how Popper's views would have been received had he presented them in the way in which I have presented them here. It is very possible that many will regard my attempt to clarify his views as obscuring them even further. But the fact that so many philosophers have misunderstood Popper's views on induction and demarcation has convinced me it is worth the attempt to put strategy aside and to try to explain his views as I have.

XII

But do Popper's solutions to the problems of induction and demarcation still have relevance today?

I believe that they do, and that they are, in fact, more important today than ever. This is the reason why I have tried to clarify these problems and the ways in which Popper's views on induction and demarcation relate to each other. Simply put, I believe that contemporary philosophy has, by misunderstanding Popper's contribution, ignored a possible solution to one of its most pressing problems. I also believe that the solution that it has adopted will, despite good intentions, end up by turning philosophy and science, once again, into an authoritarian and oppressive affair. But in order to explain all of this, I will need to return to the problem of rationality, and to put things in a broader context.

The fundamental epistemological fact of the twentieth century was the collapse of 'bedrock' foundationalism. The fundamental epistemological problem of the twentieth century has been how best to respond to it. Some philosophers have concluded that scientific knowledge is unjustified and hence irrational after all. But the most popular response, by far, has been to retain the idea that scientific knowledge is justified, but to weaken either the idea that truth is correspondence to the facts or the idea that justification shows that a statement is true—and pretend that nothing else has changed. Each of these responses retains the foundationalist theory of rationality, according to which it is irrational to accept a belief that has not been justified. But I call the latter 'floating foundationalism,' since it retains the foundationalist's belief that scientific knowledge is justified and his belief that this is what makes it rational, while leaving the 'justification' itself irrationally floating in midair.

Floating foundationalism is a widespread phenomenon. It can be seen in Wittgenstein's idea that science is grounded in a form of life, in Carnap's idea that it is grounded in the external questions of a linguistic framework, in Kuhn's idea that it is grounded in the acceptance of a scientific paradigm, and in Rorty's idea that it is grounded in the solidarity of a community.

Each of these is a return to Hume's idea that our knowledge of matters of fact is ultimately grounded upon custom and habit—though each seems to forget about Hume's irrationalism.

The fundamental idea in each of these theories is that our knowledge *is grounded*, and that it must be grounded if we are to regard it as rational.

In my view, floating foundationalism, in each of its forms, is but a pretence of rationalism. It pretends to 'justify' our knowledge with statements that are not themselves justified—so that our 'rational' knowledge, and the idea that it is justified, must ultimately be accepted on the basis of authority alone.

But rationalism is the idea that we ought not regard our beliefs as justified if we can 'justify' them only by appealing to authority.

All of this would be sad enough. But the real problem with floating foundationalism is that it postulates a point beyond which rational discussion is no longer possible. We may allow our 'foundations' to float, but we must not subject them to criticism. We must, on the contrary, commit ourselves to them. In this way, floating foundationalism encourages us to relinquish critical control over our theories and beliefs—at least at the foundational level—and to accept our most fundamental philosophical beliefs, and the beliefs upon which everything else is supposedly based, without ever really thinking about them at all.

Is Popper's critical rationalism really any better?

I think that it is—if only because it does not pretend to do something it can not. Popper's suggestion was to acknowledge that justification is impossible and to focus upon criticism instead. If we think of criticism as conclusive disproof, as many philosophers have, then critical rationalism will seem to be just the other side of the justificationist's coin. But if we regard it as I have tried to present it here, then we can recognize it as clarifying the alternatives between which we must choose.

Popper, like the floating foundationalists, says that science is rational. But unlike the floating foundationalists, he says that it has no rational authority. Like the irrationalists, Popper says that scientific knowledge cannot be justified. But unlike the irrationalists, he says that our choice between competing views can be influenced by logical arguments.

Like both the floating foundationalists and the irrationalists, Popper believed that we must, in science, ultimately make some sort of unjustified decision. And some have called him an 'irrational rationalist' for this fact. But unlike the floating foundationalists and the real irrationalists, Popper believed that we could always argue about our decisions; and that we could do so with deductive arguments; and that while these deductive arguments could not prove anything, they could present us with problems, and force us to choose between accepting their conclusions and denying their premises; and that we could use them, in this way, to exert some sort of critical control over our decisions and over science itself.

What we are left with is a consistent account of the rationality of science that involves neither its justification nor its rational authority.

This is the great significance that Popper's philosophy has for our time. It is that there are no authorities to whom we can or must look to for the truth. It is that we are, as fallible human beings, inherently subject to error; and, as rational human beings, each responsible for our own beliefs and for our own decisions. It is that we can, if we think they are bad, struggle against our customs and habits, against our forms of life, and our linguistic frameworks, paradigms, communal solidarities, and the like. And it is that we can struggle against them, and also against the ruling scientific theories of our day, without having to feel that we are irrational for doing so. It is that we can, if we think it is best, continue to examine life in the way that Socrates thought made life worth living. And it is that our rationality and our responsibility for our own beliefs and for our own lives is something that we may each decide for ourselves to relinquish, but that no one else has the authority or power to take away from us.

It offers us, at a time when so many others are advising us to join up with the pack and howl with the wolves, one of the very few philosophies that is still worthy of the name.

Notes

1 This is a revised version of a paper that was written at the invitation of *Časopis za kritiko znanosti*, the Slovenian journal for the criticism of science, for a special issue intended as a first attempt to present Karl Popper's philosophy in the Slovene language. The article was translated into Slovenian and published in *Časopis za kritiko znanosti*, letnik XXV, 1997, številka 186–187. The English original was later presented at the Romanian-Finnish Logic Colloquium in Predeal, Romania on 19 October 1997; and published in the Romanian journal *Krisis*, no 6/1998. The motto is from Karl R. Popper, *The Logic of Scientific Discovery*, 1959. Reprinted by Routledge, London, 1995, p. 281.

2 Popper, *The Logic of Scientific Discovery*, pp. 51–52.

3 Karl R. Popper, 'Conjectural Knowledge: My Solution to the Problem of Induction' in Karl R. Popper, *Objective Knowledge*, Oxford University Press, London, 1972, p. 2.

4 Kant also made this mistake. He asked 'How is a priori synthetic knowledge possible?' instead of 'Is a priori synthetic knowledge possible?'

5 Popper, 'Conjectural Knowledge: My Solution to the Problem of Induction,' p. 7.

6 Of course, 'justifying the conclusion' may mean something else. But we ultimately want to judge whether or not the statement that we are arguing about is true. And arguments alone cannot tell us this.

7 Popper, 'Conjectural Knowledge: My Solution to the Problem of Induction,' p. 7.

8 Popper, *The Logic of Scientific Discovery*, p. 41.

9 Popper told me, after I pointed this out to him (see M.A. Notturno, *Objectivity, Rationality, and the Third Realm*, Martinus Nijhof, Dordrecht, 1985, p. 121, fn 25), that I was right about the logic, but that it was better *strategically* to characterize *modus tollens* as proceeding in the inductive direction.

10 This question and its answer have nothing whatsoever to do with justification. We are not, as in L_1 and L_2, asking whether we can justify something on the strength of an assumption. And we are not, as in Popper's answer to L_2, claiming that we can.

11 Popper, 'Conjectural Knowledge: My Solution to the Problem of Induction,' p. 7.

12 Popper, 'Conjectural Knowledge: My Solution to the Problem of Induction,' p. 7.

13 In his *Logic of Scientific Discovery*, (p. 50) for example, Popper writes:

> A system such as classical mechanics may be 'scientific' to any degree you like, but those who uphold it dogmatically—believing, perhaps, that it is their business to defend such a successful system against criticism as long as it is not *conclusively disproved*—are adopting the very reverse of that critical attitude which in my view is the proper one for the scientist. In point of fact, no conclusive disproof of a theory can ever be produced; for it is always possible to say that the experimental results are not reliable or that the discrepancies which are asserted to exist between the experimental results and the theory are only apparent and that they will disappear with the advance of our understanding. If you insist on strict proof (or strict disproof) in the empirical sciences, you will never benefit from experience, and never learn from it how wrong you are.

14 The term 'science of truth' comes from Frege. See Gottlob Frege, 'The Thought: A Logical Inquiry,' translated by A.M. and Marcelle Quinton, *Mind* 65, 1956.

15 Thomas Kuhn, for example, expressed what many philosophers had in mind when he pointedly asked 'What is falsification if it is not conclusive disproof?' (Thomas Kuhn, 'Logic of Discovery or Psychology of Research?' in *Criticism and the Growth of Knowledge*, edited by Imre Lakatos and Alan Musgrave, Cambridge University Press, Cambridge, 1970, p. 15.)

16 Many philosophers today understand that Popper did not intend falsifiability as a criterion of meaning, and that he was very critical of the positivists' idea that non-scientific statements are meaningless. And many of these also no longer regard the fact that the falsifiability criterion is not itself falsifiable as a problem. There is, nonetheless, still a widespread belief that falsifiability means that *each and every* statement in a theory must be *individually* falsifiable in order for it to be scientific. This confusion is a holdover from the mistaken belief that falsifiability is a criterion of meaning. For Popper, it is a theory as a whole that is falsifiable. And the theory, as a whole, is falsifiable if, taken as a whole, it entails at least one observation statement that contradicts it.

17 That Popper had this in mind (*The Logic of Scientific Discovery*, p. 14) is clear from his motto, in which he quotes Lord Acton:

> There is nothing more necessary to the man of science than its history, and the logic of discovery ... : the way error is detected, the use of hypotheses, of imagination, the mode of testing.

18 There is a tradition that the verb 'to prove'—in the 12th century—meant to try or to test. I do not object to the idea that a function of logic is to prove the truth of statements, so long as 'to prove' is understood in this sense. But already by the 13th century 'to prove' was being used in the sense of 'to demonstrate' or 'to show good,' which is, apparently, the original use of the term 'proof' in English. I submit that today the sense of 'to prove' as to test or to try is all but forgotten in epistemology. Today, when we say that something has been proved, we usually mean not that it has been tested, but that it has been shown to be true. And today, when we ask for a proof, we are usually asking for a demonstration that the item in question is true.

6 Inference and Deference: Authority and the Goals of Critical Thinking[1]

> *Today, the appeal to the authority of experts is sometimes excused by the immensity of our specialized knowledge. And it is sometimes defended by philosophical theories that speak of science and rationality in terms of specializations, experts, and authority. But in my view, the appeal to the authority of experts should be neither excused nor defended. It should, on the contrary, be recognized for what it is—an intellectual fashion.*
>
> Karl R. Popper

I

I should preface these remarks by saying that I approach these issues—arguments from authority and the goals of critical thinking—from a Popperian perspective, according to which there is no such thing as inductive logic, the best of our knowledge is inherently fallible, and no statement can ever be justified or shown to be true. Much of what I have to say can be understood as explaining the roles that logical arguments, critical thinking, and authority play in science and in our intellectual life at large if the Popperian perspective is correct.

II

Let me begin by pointing out some inconsistencies in a few of the contemporary treatments of arguments from authority.

In his *Introduction to Logic* Irving Copi writes that:

An argument ... is generally constructed to prove that its conclusion is true... An argument whose premises do not imply its conclusion is one whose conclusion *could* be false *even if* all its premises were true. In cases of this kind, the reasoning is bad, and the argument is said to be *fallacious*, or to be a *fallacy*.[2]

An invalid argument, according to Copi, is a fallacy, though Copi goes on to say that 'It is customary in the study of logic to reserve the term 'fallacy' for arguments which, although incorrect, are psychologically persuasive.'[3]

So far so good. But when it comes to the *argumentum ad verecundiam* Copi writes:

> When we argue that a given conclusion is correct on the ground that an expert authority has come to that judgment we commit no fallacy. Indeed, such recourse to authority is necessary for most of us on very many matters. Of course, an expert's judgment is not conclusive proof; experts disagree, and even in agreement they may err; but expert opinion is surely one reasonable way to support a conclusion.
>
> The fallacy *ad verecundiam* arises when the appeal is made to parties having no legitimate claim to authority in the matter at hand.[4]

So an appeal to authority is fallacious only when the authority in question is not *really* an authority in the field about which he is speaking. An appeal to 'appropriate' authority, on the other hand, is no fallacy at all, and surely one reasonable way to support a conclusion.

Surely?

I understand why an appeal to authority is fallacious when the 'authority' appealed to is not really an authority. But if a fallacy is a psychologically persuasive argument in which the conclusion may be false even if all of its premises are true, and real experts may err even when they agree with each other—then why isn't an argument from 'appropriate' authority fallacious as well?

Arguments from authority are clearly invalid. For as Copi himself points out, 'an expert's judgment is not conclusive proof.' But arguments from 'appropriate' authority are also psychologically persuasive—so psychologically persuasive that an expert on fallacies may fail to see that they are fallacious according to his own definition.

Copi is not alone.

III

David Kelley writes in *The Art of Reasoning* that:

> It is perfectly appropriate to rely on the testimony of authorities if the conditions of credibility are satisfied. If they are not satisfied, however, appealing to authority is fallacious.
>
> The first condition is that the alleged authority be competent—an expert on the subject matter in question...
>
> The second ... is that the alleged authority be objective.[5]

Kelley does not offer as explicit a definition of 'fallacy' as Copi, saying only that fallacies are 'arguments so weak that the premises do not support the conclusion at all.'[6] But he does say that an *ad hominem* argument:

> ... is a fallacy because the truth or falsity of a statement, or the strength of an argument for it, has nothing to do with the character, motives, or any other trait of the person who makes the statement or argument.[7]

And what is bad for an *ad hominem* is, or at least ought to be, bad for an *ad verecundiam*. If arguments against the man are fallacious because the truth or falsity of a statement has nothing to do with the character traits of the person who asserts it, then appeals to 'appropriate' authority should be fallacious as well.

But why regard arguments from authority as invalid? Aren't they better treated as enthymemes, as arguments whose validity is revealed once we supply their hidden premise—namely, that the statements that competent and objective experts make about matters within their areas of expertise are true? Perhaps. But neither Copi nor Kelley are willing to say that the statements of even the most competent and objective of experts are always true.

IV

Still, one might think that if legitimate authorities are not *always* 'correct' when they speak about issues in the areas of their expertise, then they are at least *usually* 'correct'—and that being usually 'correct' ought to count for something. Merrilee Salmon takes this approach in her *Introduction to Logic and Critical Thinking*. Salmon says both that 'it is a serious intellectual mistake to fail to distinguish between non-evidential persuasion and evidence that supports an assertion,' and that 'this mistake is called committing a fallacy.'[8] But she also says that:

> Sometimes ... we appeal to what experts have said on the matter instead of presenting any direct evidence to support the claim we are making. Such reliance on experts is not opposed to critical thinking, for—under certain restrictions—it may be justified as a type of strong statistical syllogism. After all, experts or authorities are almost always, or usually, correct when they make statements about the subject in which they are experts.[9]

After all?

Salmon requires consensus amongst experts in addition to the previously mentioned criteria in order to make an appeal to authority legitimate. But her claim that experts are usually correct when they make statements within their expertise is either tautologous or false.

It is tautologous if the criteria for expertise include being usually correct about one's subject. For then, being wrong more often than not would constitute someone's *not* being an expert—regardless of the consensus of expert opinion, and regardless of the training, study, and experience that might otherwise be thought to indicate expertise. Here it would be true that experts are usually 'correct' about subjects within their expertise. But now the problem would be to *recognize* the experts, something that could no longer be done with reference to training and study and, indeed, not at all without already knowing the truth of what the expert says—a knowledge that, if available, would vitiate the very point of appealing to his authority.

But if Salmon's claim is not tautologous, then it is clearly false. One might, on the contrary, say that experts have usually been *mistaken* about subjects within their expertise. Indeed, one might characterize the history of science to date as a steady and continual process of showing that what the experts had said is wrong. And if this is not clear at once, then simply recall that every major science, in which someone could possibly claim expertise, has undergone revolution within the past century alone. It is not entirely clear how one should describe this state of affairs. But it seems as wrong to say that Galileo was not an expert in physics as it does to say that his physics were 'correct.' Better we face the fact that the expertise that comes with training, study, thought, and experience bears a tenuous relationship to truth, that expertise is neither predicated upon nor a guarantee of being right, and that it is to be valued for entirely different reasons.

V

I have been assuming that what Copi means by saying that a statement is 'correct' is that it is true, and that what Salmon means in saying that the experts are usually 'correct' is that the statements that they assert are usually true. But if this is not what they mean, then they owe us an explanation of what 'correct' does mean. And it will not do to say that being correct means saying what the experts say!

But even authors who are wary of our increasing reliance upon experts find it difficult to repudiate arguments from authority altogether. In *Asking the Right Questions: A Guide to Critical Thinking*, M. Neil Browne and Stuart M. Keeley say that they were motivated to write because they:

> ... were dismayed at the degree to which students and acquaintances showed an increasing dependence on 'experts' ... As the complexity of the world seems to grow at an accelerating rate, there is a greater tendency to become passive absorbers of information, uncritically accepting what is seen and heard.[10]

But there is uncritical acceptance and uncritical acceptance. And when it comes time to treat arguments from authority, Browne and Keeley say that:

> We should treat an appeal to authority as *good evidence* when the authority is
> *any* of the following:
> 1. In a position to have especially good access to pertinent facts.
> 2. Qualified by training to make these kinds of inferences,
> *or*
> 3. *Relatively free* of vested interests and biases.[11]

The irony here is worth noting. For despite their dismay, Browne
and Keeley propose the weakest criteria for the 'validity' of an argument from authority of those that we have yet surveyed. Indeed, one
might think that a primary cause of our reliance upon experts is that
we use books that purport to be guides to critical thinking to teach
our students—in large numbers—that 'reliance on experts is not opposed to critical thinking,' that it is (on the contrary?) 'necessary for
most of us,' and is (thus?) 'no fallacy,' but (so?) 'good evidence'—the
'correct,' 'appropriate,' and 'reasonable' thing to do.

With guides like these, who needs critical thinking?

But even were we to agree with Copi, Kelley, Salmon, and all
the others who recognize conditions under which arguments from
authority are non-fallacious, the question remains whether these
conditions could ever be satisfied.

VI

My appeal to authority is non-fallacious only if I do not have independent knowledge of the matter in question, only if my expert is
competent and objective, and only if he agrees with the other experts in the field. But this last condition only casts the difficulty
into high relief. For what looks like consensus to laymen seldom
looks like consensus to the experts themselves. And one need only
point to the law of the excluded middle to realize that even the
most basic truths in the most certain of fields can seem controversial to thinkers with some claim to expertise.

And this is just the tip of the iceberg. For if I do not have independent knowledge of the matter in question, then how could I
possibly be in any position to judge whether an alleged expert
really *is* an expert? How could I, who am not an expert, know

whether or not he agrees with the experts in his field—let alone evaluate his objectivity and competence?

Well, I could do what we ordinarily do. I could check his credentials, letters of recommendation, and list of publications. But I cannot do this without involving myself in yet another argument from authority. I check his credentials, letters of recommendation, and list of publications because I want to appeal to his authority, and because I need to know that he is an objective and competent expert in his field in order to do so. But in checking his credentials, letters of recommendation, and list of publications, I appeal to the authority of the institutions and individuals that certified them. How do I know that *their* judgment that he is objective and competent is itself objective and competent?

If the legitimacy of my appeal to one authority depends upon the legitimacy of my appeal to another, then how can any appeal to authority be legitimate at all?

So we are confronted with a paradox of authority much like the paradox of the *Meno*. Either we are authorities or we are not. If we are authorities, then we cannot rightfully appeal to authorities. And if we are not authorities, then we cannot rightfully recognize those who are. In either case, it is difficult to see how an argument from authority could be anything but fallacious.

VII

The texts we have surveyed offer accounts of the *argumentum ad verecundiam* that are *inconsistent*—sometimes with their own definition of fallacy, sometimes with their treatment of other fallacies, sometimes with what we know about expert opinion, and sometimes with their authors' own intentions to combat our reliance upon authority. These inconsistencies are ironic. For when all is said and done, the ability to recognize inconsistencies is the only real tool that a critical thinker has. In my view, arguments from authority are always fallacious and appeals to authority are never consistent with the goals of critical thinking. And in the rest of this paper I will argue that thinking otherwise results partly from a tendency to confuse critical thinking with two non-critical uses of logic, and partly from a confusion about what an argument can and cannot do.

VIII

Critical thinking, in my view, is first and foremost an attempt to make judgments of our own. It is inspired by a scepticism that is opposed to the deference that one shows in appealing to authority. And it is characterized by a reluctance to accept what you are told *without first examining for yourself exactly what it means and whether or not it is true*. Logical argument is no doubt a necessary component of critical thinking. But not every use of logical argument is critical. And I want, for this reason, to distinguish critical thinking from two non-critical uses of logic that I call 'defensive thinking,' on the one hand, and 'political thinking' on the other.

Defensive thinking is motivated by a need to feel secure. Defensive thinkers do not *ask* whether their beliefs are true, they give reasons to show that they are *justified*—or, at the very least, that *they themselves* are justified in believing them. Defensive thinking can be confused with critical thinking, if its demand for justification is mistaken for a concern with truth. But defensive thinkers are not inspired by the search for truth. They are inspired by a need to vindicate themselves from error, to show that they themselves are not to blame for their beliefs. Their concern for justification, however, often leads them to focus upon evidence that supports their beliefs, and to disregard evidence that presents problems.

Political thinking, on the other hand, is motivated by a need to be accepted, or to get ahead. To think politically is to forget about what *you* think is true and to voice opinions that you think are likely to win approval from your friends. It is to say what your *friends* would say, or at least what you think they would like to hear. It is sometimes confused with critical thinking, since it is said to be the 'smart thing to do'—especially if your friends are powerful—and since it sometimes takes a bit of critical thinking to figure out who your friends are and what they would like to hear. But the questions that critical thinkers ask—'What does this really mean?' and 'Is it really true?'—are the very questions that political thinkers try to duck.

Arguments from authority are usually exercises in defensive thinking. But they are, due to the power and prestige of The Scientific Institution, often used by political thinkers as well. Offered with the naïveté that expertise guarantees truth, defensive appeals to authority are uncritical testaments of faith. But they become more sophisticated, and also more cynical, when they are offered with the understanding that experts often err. For they then attempt to garner whatever benefits might accrue from voicing a 'justified' opinion, while simultaneously erecting a defense against blame should that opinion turn out to be false. Political appeals to authority are obviously even more cynical. But it often takes courage to say what you think is true. And if the proponents of The Scientific Institution are correct, young scientists who show such courage inevitably do so at the risk of their careers.

IX

Not every argument from authority is an instance of defensive or political thinking. But every such argument is an attempt to justify a belief. And each of the authors we have mentioned believes that the primary goal of logical argument is to prove, or to support, or, as Kelley puts it, 'to show *that* some proposition is true.'[12]

But this misconstrues what we actually do with arguments. For as often as not, we construct arguments with no intent whatsoever to show that their conclusions are true. Oftentimes we draw inferences from statements in order to see what those statements mean—to see what other statements must be true if the statements in question are true. Oftentimes we use arguments as explanations, to help us to understand *why* a statement is true by showing how it is related to others that we think may also be true. And oftentimes our arguments are designed to show that certain statements are inconsistent with each other and *cannot*, for that reason, possibly all be true.[13]

Still, the idea that the primary goal of logic is to justify our beliefs is widespread and well-entrenched. And it has given rise to critical thinking courses that introduce logical arguments as methods for justifying our beliefs, as opposed to methods for criticizing them. Such courses might be better described as courses in defensive thinking. But their primary fault is not that they have little if anything to do with critical thinking. Their primary fault is that they unwittingly lead students to become misologues and irrationalists—first by suggesting that logical arguments can do more than they really can, and then by obscuring the more modest but still nonetheless very important power they actually have.

We have already seen that arguments from authority cannot show that their conclusions are true: that they are either invalid or have premises that are obviously false. But even were we to regard such arguments as sound, we would still regard them as opposed to the spirit and goals of critical thinking. It is not simply that arguments from authority are fallacious attempts to justify our beliefs. It is that they are arguments from *authority*. They may, perhaps, help us to assert statements that are true. But they do not, as far as I can see, help us to understand them—let alone to make judgments of our own.

X

We begin to think critically about a proposition when we begin to question whether or not it is true. But a critical thinker does not simply want to know *that* it is true. He also wants to understand *what* it means and *why* it is true. He wants to be able to *explain* its meaning and its truth to himself and to others in words that both he and they can understand. And he wants, perhaps most of all, to develop the ability and confidence to make a *judgment of his own* regarding it.

Here it is easy to see how and why deference to authority conflicts with the goals of critical thinking. For we defer to the opinions of experts only when we want to voice an opinion, but are unable or unwilling to risk voicing an opinion of our own. And regardless of whether or not their conclusions are true, arguments from authority do nothing whatsoever either to further our understanding of what their conclusions mean and why they are true, or to develop our ability and confidence to make judgments of our own concerning them.

But what does it mean to make a judgment of our own? What do such judgments have to do with logical argument? And what, in any event, does logical argument have to do with critical thinking?

To construe justification as the primary goal of logic is to seriously misconstrue what logical arguments can and cannot do. For logic, with the exception of tautologies, simply cannot show that a statement is true. A valid argument shows only that its conclusion is true *provided that its premises are*. Validity, we might say, is a *disjunction*.

The validity of an argument means only that it is logically impossible for its premises to be true and its conclusion false. And this means only that it is logically necessary that *either* one or more it its premises are false *or* its conclusion is true. There is nothing at all new in this. It is the very definition of validity. But if we take it seriously, then it means that valid arguments are really double-edged swords that may be taken to show *either* that their conclusions are true, *or* that one or more of their premises are false, *or* nothing whatsoever. And if the very best of our arguments are double-edged swords, then it is at the very least misleading to speak of them as showing that their conclusions are true, or that they are justified, or that we are somehow justified in believing them.

But if the best of our logical arguments cannot justify their conclusions or our belief in their conclusions, then what exactly can they do? And why should critical thinkers take them seriously?

A valid argument is not so much a proof as a choice. It presents the critical thinker with a set of mutually exclusive alternatives between which he must choose. He can choose either to accept the premises of the argument, in which case he must also accept its conclusion; or to reject the conclusion of the argument, in which case he must also reject one or more of its premises; or to reject (or suspend judgment concerning) the premises of the argument, in which case he need do nothing at all vis-à-vis its conclusion. The critical thinker can decide to do any of these things. But the work of the argument is to show him that he cannot, without contradicting himself, choose to *both* accept its premises *and* reject its conclusion.

The alternatives between which a critical thinker must choose and the decisions that he can make are, in this way, restricted by logical necessity. And the work of the argument is to clarify this restriction—as well as the critical thinker's options—by showing that the possibility that its conclusion is false while its premises are true is, well, not a possibility. Such an elucidation is neither a justification nor a judgment. But it is a powerful aid to a critical thinker, precisely because the display of a statement's logical consequences may help him to understand what that statement means, and what restrictions he is under in judging that it is true or false.

This, I submit, is the very best that an argument can do. But lest we think it worthless, we should remember that *invalid* arguments—including arguments from authority and inductive arguments—cannot do even this.

Invalid arguments never force us to reexamine our beliefs, let alone to choose between them. And this is the primary reason why they are worthless for critical thinking.

XI

The reason that Copi, Kelley, and Salmon give for regarding inductive arguments and the argument from appropriate authority as non-fallacious is that they are necessary components of scientific inquiry and everyday life.

But if what I have been saying is true, then it is judgments of our own that are really necessary. Valid arguments play the extremely important role of clarifying our options. But they cannot make our judgments for us. And the very idea that critical thinkers must justify their beliefs is really a recipe for defensive thinking.

Critical thinkers do not justify their beliefs; they *criticize* them. They *question* and *test* the beliefs that others take for granted. In doing so, they oftentimes clarify how some of their beliefs are based upon others. But this basing of beliefs one upon another must ultimately end. And if you are a critical thinker, then you will, somewhere in the course of your tests, inevitably come upon statements that you believe for no other reason than that they seem true—*to you*.

In such a case, it would be more accurate to say not that such statements are justified, but that they seem, *in your judgment*, to be true. But if this is true, then the very least that a critical thinker should do is to say so.

XII

But isn't the idea that we can get by without experts untenable? And isn't my ideal of making judgments of our own really a caricature of critical thinking—a caricature that is quixotic in a world in which knowledge has become so specialized that even the best of our thinkers have difficulty transcending their narrow specializations? Given the number of different fields, the number of claims that are made in each, the number of claims that are pertinent to their evaluation, and the differences in background knowledge they all presuppose, wouldn't the critical thinker's attempt to judge each claim for himself be at best impractical—if not a downright counterproductive waste of time?

Isn't the aim of critical thinking proposed in this paper an impossible dream?

I agree that there will be times—very many times—when we will be unable to make judgments of our own. And I agree that deferring to the judgments of experts may, at such times, be the best that we can do. But I also think that we should not confuse it with critical thinking.

I would be the last to suggest that critical thinking is easy, or that it is possible to think critically about everything. I am, on the contrary, almost amazed that anyone these days can think critically about anything. But I see no reason in this to think that critical thinking is compatible with deference to authority, or that it is anything other than what I have described.

Yes, it will often be impossible to make judgments of our own. And yes, it may be best at such times to defer to expert opinion. But instead of saying that deferring to expert opinion is compatible with critical thinking, we would do better to say that there will be times when we will be unable or unwilling to think critically. We would do better to say this, because saying otherwise inevitably impedes the efforts of those who try to think critically, and who are willing to challenge the expert opinion of their day.

But shouldn't an expert's authority count for something? And isn't there *some* appropriate use of authority in critical thinking?

If what I have been saying is true, then courses in critical thinking should teach our students how to criticize authority instead of teaching them how to defer to it. But if this is true, then a statement by an 'appropriate' authority should be the *first* word in a critical inquiry instead of the *last*. It should be the word that we listen to in order to discover how things stand in a field, what its major problems are, and which of the solutions that have been proposed seem most promising. And it should be the word that we then examine and question and put to the test as we begin to think critically about the field ourselves. I have no doubt whatsoever that *this* use of authority is very often necessary, appropriate, and reasonable. But it is not an *argument* from authority. It does not pretend to be good evidence. And it is not presented as a justification of any claim. It would, however, be one that is fully consistent with the goals of critical thinking.

Notes

1 This is a revised version of a paper that was first presented at the Third ISSA Conference on Argumentation, which was held in Amsterdam, Holland from 21–24 June 1994; and later at Kiev State University in Kiev, Ukraine on 6 November 1996. It was first published in *Analysis and Evaluation: Volume II of the Proceedings of the Third ISSA Conference on Argumentation (University of Amsterdam, June 21–24, 1994)*, edited by Frans H. van Eemeren, Rob Grootendorst, J. Anthony Blair, and Charles A. Willard, Amsterdam: Sic Sat, 1995. A Ukrainian translation was later published in *Vichnik Universitety Vnytrishnih Sprav*, No. 2, 1997. The motto is from Karl R. Popper, *The Myth of the Framework*, edited by M.A. Notturno, Routledge, London, 1994, pp. ix–x.

2 Irving Copi and Carl Cohen, *Introduction to Logic*, eighth edition, Macmillan, New York, 1990, pp. 91–92.

3 Copi and Cohen, p. 92.

4 Copi and Cohen, p. 92.

5 David Kelley, *The Art of Reasoning*, W.W. Norton, New York, 1988, pp. 118–119.

6 Kelley, p. 109.

7 Kelley, p. 120.

8 Merrilee H. Salmon, *Introduction to Logic and Critical Thinking*, second edition, Harcourt Brace Javanovitch, New York, 1989, p. 5.

9 Salmon, p. 71.

10 M. Neil Browne and Stuart M. Keeley, *Asking the Right Questions: A Guide to Critical Thinking*, third edition, Prentice Hall, Englewood Cliffs, N.J., 1990, 'Preface.'

11 Browne and Keeley, p. 125. My italics.

12 Kelley, p. 344. Copi (p. 6) writes that 'An argument, in the logician's sense, is any group of propositions of which one is claimed to follow from the others, which are regarded as providing support or grounds for the truth of that one.' And Salmon (p. 40) underscores the importance of support by writing that 'Arguments can be *classified* in terms of whether their premises (if true) would provide (1) conclusive support; (2) partial support; or (3) only the appearance of support (that is, little or no support at all).' (My italics.)

13 And one can, of course, show this without having any idea as to which of the statements is false.

7 The Meaning of World 3, or Why Wittgenstein Walked Out[1]

> *The correct method in philosophy would really be the following: to say nothing except what can be said—i.e. something that has nothing to do with philosophy—and then, whenever someone else wanted to say something metaphysical, to demonstrate to him that he had failed to give a meaning to certain signs in his propositions.*
>
> Ludwig Wittgenstein

> *The controversial question whether philosophy exists, or has any right to exist, is almost as old as philosophy itself. Time and again an entirely new philosophical movement arises which finally unmasks the old philosophical problems as pseudo-problems, and which confronts the wicked nonsense of philosophy with the good sense of meaningful, positive, empirical science.*
>
> Karl R. Popper

I

Most contemporary philosophers regard World 3 as an unfortunate product of Popper's old age: as incoherent, irrelevant, and perhaps, if the truth be told, a bit ridiculous. Even those who have followed Sir Karl down the path of critical rationalism—past the garden of fallibilism and the eternal spring of conjecture and refutation—usually stop when they get to World 3. For this, they say, is a ripe old swamp, and decidedly more of a problem than even a *tentative* solution.[2]

In what follows, I will argue that none of this is true. I will argue that World 3 is one of the few serious attempts in this anti-philosophical century to solve an ancient, but still very much alive, and very real, philosophical problem. I will argue that it is no aberration of Popper's old age, but the very key to his critical rationalism. But more than that, I will argue that those who reject World 3 do so as a result of prejudices that simply do not bear critical scrutiny.

Whether or not the theory of World 3 is true is another question. But it is a question that cannot be critically discussed until we understand why Popper proposed it, and until we rid ourselves of the prejudices that encourage us to dismiss it out of hand.

My subtitle, 'Why Wittgenstein Walked Out,' deserves an explanation. Popper was a student in Vienna when Wittgenstein published his *Tractatus Logico-Philosophicus*. Wittgenstein claimed in this book that that there are no such things as real philosophical problems and that philosophical theories are nonsensical. Popper disagreed with these claims, and developed his own philosophy largely in response to them. And this disagreement, years later, led to a famous confrontation between the two Viennese philosophers:

> Early in the academic year 1946–47 I received an invitation from the Secretary of the Moral Sciences Club at Cambridge to read a paper about some 'philosophical puzzle.' It was of course clear that this was Wittgenstein's formulation, and that behind it was Wittgenstein's philosophical thesis that there are no genuine problems in philosophy, only linguistic puzzles. Since this thesis was among my pet aversions, I decided to speak on 'Are there Philosophical Problems?' I began my paper (read on October 26, 1946, in R.B. Braithwaite's room in King's College) by expressing my surprise at being invited by the Secretary to read a paper 'stating some philosophical puzzle;' and I pointed out that, by implicitly denying that philosophical problems exist, whoever wrote the invitation took sides, perhaps unwittingly, in an issue created by a genuine philosophical problem.[3]

Popper says that he intended this as a challenging and somewhat light-hearted introduction to his talk, but that Wittgenstein jumped up saying loudly and angrily 'The Secretary did exactly as he was told to do. He acted on my own instruction.' Popper tried to continue, saying that he would not be a philosopher if he thought that there were no real philosophical problems, and that the fact that many people uncritically adopt solutions to philosophical problems was the only justification for being a philosopher. But Wittgenstein jumped up again and began to explain his theory that there are no real philosophical problems:

> At a moment which appeared to me appropriate, I interrupted him, giving a list I had prepared of philosophical problems, such as: Do we know things

through our senses?, Do we obtain our knowledge by induction? These Wittgenstein dismissed as being logical rather than philosophical. I then referred to the problem whether potential or perhaps even actual infinities exist, a problem he dismissed as mathematical. (This dismissal got into the minutes.) I then mentioned moral problems and the problem of the validity of moral rules. At that point Wittgenstein, who was sitting near the fire and had been nervously playing with the poker, which he sometimes used like a conductor's baton to emphasize his assertions, challenged me: 'Give an example of a moral rule!' I replied: 'Not to threaten visiting lecturers with pokers.' Whereupon Wittgenstein, in a rage, threw the poker down and stormed out of the room, banging the door behind him.[4]

This confrontation was more than a clash between strong Viennese personalities. It reflects deep philosophical differences that are themselves reflected in the use of argument, and in the conflict between reason and authority. I have told you about it because it provides a subtext for my discussion of the theory of World 3. In what follows, I will try to explain Popper's theory of World 3 and the reasons why he proposed it. I will then try to explain why it is the key to his critical rationalism, and why so many philosophers reject it out of hand. I will argue, in the bulk of my paper, that it is the empiricist and materialist biases that lead philosophers to reject the theory of World 3 out of hand—and not the theory itself—that ought to be rejected. And I will, in addition to all this, try to explain why Wittgenstein walked out.

II

Popper's theory of World 3 says that we can distinguish at least three different worlds of our experience.[5] There is, first of all, the material world of tables and chairs, trees and plants, planets and stars. This is Popper's World 1. It is objective in the sense that it can be experienced by others, and autonomous in the sense that its existence does not depend upon our own. Then, there is the mental world of pleasures and pains, loves and hates, beliefs and dispositions. This is what Popper called World 2. It is subjective in the sense that the mental states of one mind cannot be experienced by another, and non-autonomous in the sense that their existence depends upon the existence of the mind that actually experiences them. There are, however, other things that we experience that do not fit easily into either of these worlds.

There are, for example, words and statements, books and symphonies, states and laws, numbers and triangles. These things are immaterial,[6] unlike the objects of World 1. But they are also objective, unlike the mental states of World 2. And when it comes to autonomy, their status seems entirely different. For they are, according to Popper, all products of the human mind. But they also give rise, once they are created, to consequences that their creators neither intended nor foresaw. These are the objects of World 3.

The objects in Worlds 1, 2, and 3 not only exist, they also interact. This is already implicit in the idea that World 3 objects are products of the human mind. We *create* a World 3 object when we take one of our World 2 thoughts and articulate it in a medium, such as language or music or film, that others can understand. We are able, in this way, to treat our thought as an object. We are able to throw it out onto the table, like a radio or a wristwatch, and take it apart to see how it works. More important, we are able to see how and why it does not work, or how it could work better. And we are able to work on improving it until it does. I know that many contemporary philosophers attribute all sorts of 'alienations' to this process of reification. But it is, to my mind, one of the most attractive and inspirational features of Popper's philosophy. It means that we not only can contribute to World 3, but that we can also work toward improving both our contributions and the contributions that others make.

This, in fact, is what I was doing when I wrote this paper. I had a thought in mind. But so long as I kept it only in mind, you could not know what it is, let alone whether or not it is true. So I wrote it down. And I read it over carefully. In many cases I decided that what I had written was not really what I wanted to say. So I changed it, and started the whole process all over again. And even now, when I think that what I have written expresses more or less what I want to say, I am sure that someone, either myself or someone else, might still convince me otherwise.

So our minds can act upon World 3, and World 3 can act upon our minds. And in this way, our conscious selves can develop and become what they become by contributing to World 3 and by learning from the contributions that others make. And isn't this what really happens? None of us were born into this world knowing about Wittgenstein and Popper. But the interesting thing is that we can decide, knowing virtually nothing more than their names, to learn something about these men and their philosophies—and, by doing so, to transform ourselves into something other than what we are. We can, in this way, even talk about our conscious selves—which Popper regards as the highest stage of development in World 2—as being products of World 3.

Thus far I have talked about interaction between Worlds 2 and 3. But these worlds also interact directly and indirectly with World 1. Popper thought that our World 2 states, and especially our conscious selves, act as a sort of control system for the body—and that our World 3 creations, especially our scientific theories, act as a sort of control system for the mind. When someone feels a pain, and moves away from whatever he thinks is causing it, the movement involved results from an interaction between Worlds 1 and 2. And when someone reads a book, and accepts or rejects what it says, the movement involved results from an interaction between Worlds 2 and 3. But when someone reads a book and, accepting what it says, fills the volume inside a wire coil with iron and runs an electric current through it, the movement involved results from an interaction between Worlds 1, 2, and 3. In this way, all three of the worlds interact with each other through the medium of the human mind.

There is nothing so mundane as following a recipe to bake a cake. But this mundane process illustrates the way in which a World 2 mind can use a World 3 theory, which may or may not have been its own product, to produce a change upon material objects in World 1. And it also shows how World 1 can exercise critical control over Worlds 2 and 3. For we might, depending upon how that cake turns out, well decide to see whether and how it can be improved.

Earlier I said that a human mind creates a World 3 object when it takes one of its thoughts and articulates it in a medium that others can understand. This articulation no doubt involves the 'embodiment' of the thought in material objects. And this has led empiricists and materialists to try to reduce thoughts to the material medium in which they are expressed. But a book is much more than the matter in which it is embodied. It is not the *paper* that we understand when we understand what it says. It is, on the contrary, the thought itself that we must grasp, and understand, if we are to use it to effect changes in the material world.[7] And it is, despite the fashionable idea that thought is determined by language, quite easy to see that it must be something different from the language in which it is expressed. For it very often happens that we say or write something that does not say what we wanted it to say. But this simple thing—writing a sentence and then realizing that it does not say what we thought it did—would be impossible if thought were really determined by language.

Every serious theory is proposed as a solution to some problem, and Popper's theory of the three worlds is no exception. It is, in fact, proposed to solve *two* problems at once: the problem of objective knowledge on the one hand, and the problem of the relationship between the body and the mind on the other. Popper thought that these two problems are interrelated, and that 'in order to understand the relationship between the body and the mind, we must first recognize the existence of objective knowledge as an objective and autonomous product of the human mind, and, in particular, the ways in which we use such knowledge as a control system for critical problem-solving.'[8]

This is Popper's theory of World 3. I will say more about the problems that it was meant to solve in a moment. But first let me explain why I think that it is the key to critical rationalism.

III

Critical rationalism can be understood, in Popper's own words, as an attitude of admitting that '*I may be wrong and you may be right,*' and that '*by an effort, we may get nearer to the truth.*' Here, the effort that Popper had in mind is the effort of critical discussion. It is the effort by which we discover some problem, propose a theory as its tentative solution, eliminate any errors that we might find in it, and, through the elimination of such errors, progress to the discovery of a new problem. But here, the very possibility of critical discussion—at least as Popper envisioned it—depends upon the possibility of contradiction. It depends, in other words, upon there being statements that are related in such a way that they cannot all be true and they cannot all be false. Criticism depends entirely upon the existence of contradictions. *But there are no statements, and hence no contradictions, in Worlds 1 & 2.* Statements are neither material objects nor mental entities. They are not the material media—the sound waves through which we talk or the paper upon which we write—that we use to express them. They are objective enough to be experienced by different minds. And they are autonomous in the sense that they very often have consequences, both logical and otherwise, that their creators neither intended nor foresaw. Statements, in other words, belong to the immaterial but objective World 3. And this, in a nutshell, is why World 3 is the key to critical rationalism.

IV

So why have people denied this?

Most philosophers who reject Popper's theory of World 3 simply do not understand it. This, in part, is because they confuse it with Plato's theory of ideas or with Frege's theory of the *dritte Reich*. In doing so, they quickly come to the conclusion that World 3 contradicts Popper's own fallibilism—and then, even more quickly, to the further conclusion that Popper's theory as a whole is contradictory. And then, thinking that they must reject something, they come to the final conclusion that it is not the fallibilism but World 3 that should go—without, apparently, ever stopping to ask how conclusions and contradictions might be possible without it. They come to these conclusions because they realize that Plato's theory of eternal and immutable ideas and Frege's theory of eternal and immutable thoughts were introduced, in part, to supply metaphysical scaffolding *for scientific claims to objective certainty*.[9] But they apparently never think it far enough to see that there is no reason why World 3 must be used in this way, or that this is not the way in which Popper in fact uses it.

Popper, like Plato and Frege, introduced World 3 in order to solve the problem of objective knowledge. But Popper, unlike Plato and Frege, did not regard scientific knowledge as certain. The problem, for Popper, was not to explain how objective knowledge could be certain. It was to explain how fallible knowledge could be objective. His solution was that the objectivity of scientific knowledge consists in its susceptibility to criticism. Far from supplying support for scientific claims to certainty, World 3 is introduced to supply the means for rationally criticizing them. And far from being eternal and immutable, World 3 is described as an evolutionary product of the human mind that is itself subject to further evolution.

But this already gives these misunderstandings far more credit than they really deserve. For the fact of the matter is that most philosophers do not even think it this far. Most philosophers simply reject World 3 out of hand—which means that they do not think it far enough to possibly understand it. They reject it out of hand because their empiricist and materialist biases are so well-entrenched that they cannot even recognize them as biases. They regard them, instead, as part of what is known and as part of what no acceptable theory can possibly deny. In this way, a problem like 'How is objective knowledge possible?' is understood as 'How is objective knowledge possible—*given that the only things that exist are those that can be known through the senses.*' And being understood in this way, it then becomes entirely rational to dismiss any theory that attempts to solve the problem through the introduction of immaterial objects. No such theory could *possibly* be a solution to the problem, because the *problem* is to explain how objective knowledge is possible *without* introducing immaterial objects.

But why should we understand the problem in this way?

Well, why shouldn't we?

I once taught at a Catholic university where, whenever someone came to give a talk, the philosophers would huddle together and ask each other whether or not they could agree with what the speaker had said—not whether or not it was true, but whether or not it was consistent with their faith. They regarded this as a necessary condition for the acceptability of any thesis. And this made perfect sense, given their faith that the doctrines of the Church are infallibly true. If something is regarded as infallibly true, then any inconsistency that might exist between it and something else speaks against that something else and not against what is regarded as infallibly true. But empiricism and materialism are not religious dogmas—or if they are religious dogmas, philosophers, at least, should not treat them as infallibly true.

The problem 'How is objective knowledge possible—*given that the only things that exist are those that can be known through the senses*' is an empiricist's problem.

'Given that the only things that exist are those that can be known through the senses' means given empiricism.

It may be well and good for an empiricist to give himself empiricism, and for a materialist to give himself materialism. But the reason why philosophers should not understand the problem of objective knowledge in this way is that empiricism and materialism are *theories*—which means that they are not at all certain, and very possibly false. Since empiricism and materialism are theories, they should be tested instead of given. And one way of testing them is by asking whether or not they can explain how objective knowledge is possible without appealing to immaterial objects.

Here I want to be perfectly clear that I have no objection whatsoever to someone trying to solve this problem. But if we make empiricism and materialism *conditions* for the acceptability of a solution—if we reject out of hand any theory that postulates the existence of immaterial objects that cannot be perceived through the senses—then we rob ourselves of the very possibility of testing them by treating them as infallible dogmas instead. And while this may be well and good for an empiricist, or for a materialist, or for anyone else who wants to treat empiricism and materialism as infallible dogmas, it is not so well and good for someone who wants to know how objective knowledge is possible.

What I want to suggest is that there is *no* reason—despite these empiricist and materialist dogmas—to believe that World 3 does not exist. I cannot, however, show that a reason does *not* exist. But what I can do is to show that the reasons that are typically given by empiricists and materialists do not bear criticism.

V

One reason why philosophers reject World 3 is that it violates the principle of parsimony, or, as it is more often called, Ockham's Razor.

Ockham's Razor is a methodological caution against introducing more theoretical entities than are necessary to explain a phenomenon.[10] But it is usually[11] interpreted by empiricists as forbidding the introduction of *any* theoretical entities at all—or, at least, as forbidding those that are not reducible to sense perception. This advice, if taken seriously, would be impossible to follow—which is, perhaps, the reason why nobody really follows it. But this does not prevent empiricists from muttering the words 'Ockham's Razor' when they are confronted with non-empirical theories that they oppose but cannot otherwise refute. And this, in any event, is the way in which Ockham's Razor is typically used in arguments against World 3.

I do not think that Ockham's Razor, as interpreted by empiricists, makes good methodological sense, or that there is any good reason to think that the world is necessarily parsimonious. But it is interesting to note that neither Plato, nor Frege, nor Popper began with a theory of World 3. Each of them was *led* to it, and led to it reluctantly, as a response to repeated failures to explain the objectivity of knowledge without it. This, as I have already said, was a different problem for Popper than it was for Plato and Frege. But it was a problem that was, at least for Frege and for Popper, closely related to the problem of how communication is possible. And *this*, we should remember, was a problem because the empiricist doctrine that meanings are mental entities would seem to make communication impossible.

It may sound strange to hear the idea that meanings are mental entities described as an *empiricist* doctrine. Today's empiricists are typically content with the slogan that 'meaning is use.' But we should remember that the theory that 'meaning is use' was an empiricist's attempt to solve the private language problem that follows almost immediately from his earlier empiricist theory that meanings are mental entities. And we should also remember that the use theory of meaning, in this context, is an utter failure. The fact of the matter is that it is simply impossible to explain how a word or a sentence is being used without appealing to intentions that are every bit as mental as the meanings that the use theory is supposed to replace.

This can be argued at length, but I think the point has been made. To appeal to Ockham's Razor as a reason for rejecting World 3 is simply to beg the question. For whether or not World 3 is necessary to explain the objectivity of knowledge is precisely the question at issue. And the repeated failures of empiricism to explain objectivity without smuggling in World 3 objects somewhere along the line has made it an interesting one. But do not misunderstand. Even if we could somehow explain objectivity without appealing to World 3, it would not mean that World 3 does not exist—any more than a principle of parsimony means that the world is parsimonious. But invoking Ockham's Razor against it would, in that case, at least make sense.

VI

A second reason why philosophers reject World 3 is that its very description violates the principle of materialism. This is the metaphysical theory that everything that exists consists of matter, and must, for that reason, be explained in terms of matter. But here, the interesting thing is that materialism, in the sense in which it was originally conceived, does not even hold for the theory of matter—which is, perhaps, the one place in which one might think it should.

Matter, according to the original materialists, was something extended in space. And materialism, as originally conceived, meant that everything that exists consists of, and must be explained in terms of, things that are extended in space. But today's physics is more apt to think of matter as space filled by electromagnetic forces. And this makes matter seem more like monads than extended substance.

But if this is true, then it constitutes a refutation of material-ism.[12] For it means that matter does not consist of matter and must be explained by forces that are not themselves material.

Here I do not want to be misunderstood. We can, of course, al-ways *call* these forces 'material.' If the word 'material' is really *that* important, then we can simply resolve to use it as a name for what-ever is necessary for an explanation. And this, in fact, is what many materialists seem to have done. But they have done so only by transforming a substantive metaphysical theory into a tautology.

Whereas materialists once began with the idea that matter is extension and the hypothesis that everything that exists is ex-tended, they now begin with the axiom that everything that exists is matter and use it to interpret everything that exists, whether ex-tended or not, as material.[13]

We can, of course, use this example to illustrate the evolution of concepts—to say that 'materialism used to mean such-and-such, but now it means this-and-that.' But we can also use it to illustrate the refutation of theories. And my own sense is that it is the latter use, and not the former, that is more conducive to clarity.

VII

A third reason why philosophers reject World 3 is that Popper's talk about interaction between the three worlds seems to violate the principle of causality. Here, the problem is that we simply do not understand how an immaterial object—like a mind or a proposition—can cause a material one to change.

The problem of how bodies and minds can interact was one of the primary problems with Cartesian dualism. And far from solving it, Popper's introduction of World 3 seems only to have reminded people of it.

I do not really have a solution to this problem, other than to say that immaterial selves somehow do have the power to initiate action and that they often use it under the influence of theories. But this says nothing more than that such interaction can occur because it can occur. And that does not really say much at all. So I acknowledge that there is an unsolved problem here. But I do not see why it is a problem that should make us doubt that interaction takes place—as if our inability to solve a problem somehow means that there is no problem there to be solved.[14]

But it is more than this. I really do not see why *this* objection should be raised at all. Those who raise it apparently think that we have a perfectly clear understanding of how material bodies interact with each other, and that this understanding is then muddied when we begin to talk about their interactions with a self. But the fact of the matter is that we do not understand how causality works at all. And the fact of the matter is that we have known that we do not understand how it works at least since Hume.

Here it would be tempting to say that if we do not understand causality it is only because we have uncritically followed Hume's empiricist advice—only, that is, because we have insisted that an explanation of causality must be given exclusively in terms of things that can be sensed, and because we have, in doing so, deprived ourselves of the conceptual apparatus necessary for understanding it.[15]

The problem with understanding causality is *not* that we cannot distinguish empirically between constant conjunction and causality. The real problem, I think, is much deeper. It is that we simply do not understand how material bodies are able to move in the first place. Once we get the first material body to move, we can begin to talk about push and pull. And while push and pull will not really take us that far, we can at least begin to argue about whether or not we are entitled to mean anything more by 'causality' than constant conjunction.

But how do we get a material body to move in the first place?

I have no answer for this. But I do think that it should be reasonably clear that the Newtonian idea that it is the *nature* of material bodies to move—so that it is not really motion, but *change* of motion, and rest, that need to be explained—says nothing more than that material bodies can move because they can move. And this, I submit, is not so different from saying that immaterial selves can cause changes in material bodies because they have the power to do so.

Here there is another tendency among materialists and empiricists to beg the question, namely, by interpreting the principle of materialism in terms of the principle of causality. It is easy, in this way, to regard as material anything that has causal effects upon the material world. Why else would anyone regard electrons and nuclei—which are not, after all, extended in the way in which the original materialists demanded—as material objects, if not for the fact that they have causal effects upon the material world? But this would mean nothing, were it not for the hidden premise that only material objects can have effects upon the material world. And that, once again, is the very point at issue.

So while our inability to explain how the three worlds interact is an unsolved problem, it is not really a special problem. The fact of the matter is that we cannot explain how material bodies interact—we can only assume that they do, and try to describe it. And if this is what we do in physics, then I see no reason why we cannot do it in philosophy too.

VIII

This brings me to the fourth, and perhaps the most common, reason why philosophers reject World 3. It is that the theory of World 3 is a *philosophical* theory designed to solve philosophical problems—and that philosophical theories or problems do not, for one reason or another, really exist.

This theory, which is perhaps the most influential philosophical theory of the twentieth century, is usually associated with Wittgenstein, who held it, in one form or another, throughout his adult life. And this, perhaps, is the most remarkable thing about it. For it means that he continued to hold it despite his rejection of the 'picture' theory of meaning, from which it was originally supposed to follow, and his adoption of the 'use' theory of meaning, from which it was also supposed to follow—a fact which might lead someone to wonder exactly which theory was supposed to follow from which.

It is useful when thinking of Wittgenstein to remember David Hume. For Hume wrote—nearly two hundred years before Wittgenstein, but for *exactly* the same reasons—that books dealing exclusively with metaphysics and theology can contain nothing but sophistry and illusion and should, for that reason, be committed to the flames.[16] Most people who remember Hume in this connection also remember his empiricist reductions of our ideas of causality, necessary connection, force, and the self to the sense impressions from which he claimed they are derived. But this, I think, is to remember the wrong thing. Hume based these reductions upon a theory of meaning that held that the meaning of a term is an idea, and that a term is meaningful only if that idea is a copy of an impression or a combination of impressions. And here, the most interesting thing about Hume's empiricism, and the thing that is most useful to remember when discussing Wittgenstein, is that it can be interesting only if it is wrong.

Hume's empiricism is best expressed in his theory of the origins of ideas, which says that 'all of our ideas or more feeble perceptions are copies of our impressions or more lively ones.'[17] In his famous attempt to 'clarify' our ideas *in accordance with this principle*, Hume argued that our idea of causality is derived from our feeling of expectation that one event will follow another. And this feeling, according to Hume, is developed after we have repeatedly witnessed the conjunction of two events. Here it is important to understand that Hume thought this because he thought that 'every idea is copied from some preceding impression or sentiment; and where we cannot find any impression, we can be certain that there is no idea'[18]—*and* because he recognized both that we have an idea of causality, and that any other analysis of its origins would involve ideas that are not reducible to impressions.[19] But here it is also important to remember that Hume introduced his theory of ideas not as an epistemology, but as an empirical psychology. His claim that all of our ideas are reducible to impressions was supposed to be a matter of fact and not simply a criterion for their acceptance.

But if all of this is true, then the problem that Hume has with the ideas of causality, force, and the self is not that they are false. The problem is that we cannot, as a matter of psychological fact, *have* them.

But if we really cannot have ideas of causality, force, and the self, then why do Hume's analyses of these terms come as such a surprise? Why are they controversial? And why should they seem to be such deflations?

If Hume had presented his theory of ideas as an epistemology, then the answers to these questions would be clear. For he could, in that case, say that we can and do have full-blooded ideas of causality, force, and the self, but that we have no *right* to have them because they are not copies of preceding impressions. If Hume's theory of ideas were an epistemology, then there could actually be a point to his saying that we *ought* not have full-blooded ideas of causality, force, and the self—precisely because it would then be possible for us to have them. And if Hume's theory of ideas were an epistemology, then we could legitimately regard his analyses as deflations of our full-blooded ideas, we could be legitimately surprised by these deflations, and we could legitimately regard them as controversial. 'My God,' we could say, 'I thought that my idea of cause and effect was well-founded. But now I see that it is not, and that I am really entitled only to an expectation of constant conjunction.'

But Hume's theory of ideas is *not* presented as an epistemology. It is presented as an empirical psychology. It does not say that we *should not* have such full-blooded ideas of causality, force, and the self. It says that we *do not* have them and that we really have other ideas instead. And this is why Hume's empiricism can be interesting only if it is wrong. For if his theory of ideas were true and we really could not have full-blooded ideas of causality, force, and the self, then we would not be able to think the thoughts that we must be able to think in order for us to think that his reductions of these ideas are interesting.

If Hume's theory of ideas were true, then we simply could not have any idea of causality other than the expectation that one event would follow another. And in that case, no one could possibly be surprised by Hume's analysis, or regard it as controversial, because no one could, quite literally, think of what else causality could possibly be.

But the fact of the matter is that we *are* surprised by Hume's analyses. And this means that we *do* have a full-blooded idea of causality that is not reducible to the expectation that one event will follow another. That is why we find it so interesting when Hume says that 'causality' means nothing more than an expectation that one event will follow another. We find it interesting, because we thought 'causality' meant something else. And this means that Hume's psychological theory of ideas must be false—because it would simply be impossible to think this were his theory true.

Now I mention all of this partly because I believe that Wittgenstein's philosophy is very similar to Hume's and partly because the very same criticism that I have just leveled against Hume applies equally well to Wittgenstein. My criticism is not that Hume's theory is unjustified, or uninteresting, or inappropriate. It is that Hume's theory is false. And my reason for saying that Hume's theory is false is not that it is too naturalistic, or too psychologistic, or too metaphysical. My reason for saying that it is false is that it is *self-contradictory*.

There are, insofar as this is concerned, three glaring contradictions in Wittgenstein's work that should always be borne in mind in any discussion of his work. The first is already apparent in the very idea of a philosophical theory that there can be no philosophical theories. Wittgenstein wanted to attribute to his own philosophical theories a status that he denied to others. He thus says in his 'Preface' to the *Tractatus* that his book deals with 'the problems of philosophy,' that 'the *truth* of the thoughts that are here communicated seems to me unassailable and definitive,' and that 'I therefore believe myself to have found, on all essential points, the final solution of the problems.'[20] But he later writes, as its penultimate point, that 'my propositions serve as elucidations in the following way: anyone who understands me eventually recognizes them as nonsensical, when he has used them—as steps—to climb up beyond them.'[21]

But if Wittgenstein's propositions are truly nonsensical, then they can neither express thoughts nor be true—for *that* is what his picture theory of meaning and its doctrine of nonsense was all about.[22] Nor can they serve as the solution to problems. For if they are literally nonsensical, then they cannot be put meaningfully into words. And if they cannot be put meaningfully into words, then the 'problems' that they are supposed to solve cannot, according to Wittgenstein, be put meaningfully into words either.[23]

Here, my point is *not* that Wittgenstein's theory is philosophical and hence in violation of his own theory of language. For *that* is simply what Wittgenstein himself acknowledged in that penultimate point. My point is that what Wittgenstein says in his 'Preface' *contradicts* both what he says in the *Tractatus* about philosophical theories and what he says in its penultimate point about the non-sensical character of his propositions. Either Wittgenstein's philosophical theory is the kind of theory that can be true or false—in which case it is difficult to see how it could possibly be true,[24] let alone why *other* philosophical theories could not then also be true or false—or Wittgenstein's philosophical theory *is* nonsense—in which case it is difficult to see how it could possibly serve as an elucidation of anything,[25] let alone why anyone would be well advised to follow him up the tractarian ladder.

When Wittgensteinians are confronted with this type of criticism, they usually respond with the Wittgensteinian stare. They then begin to talk—either about Wittgenstein's sense of the mystical or about his *Philosophical Investigations*. But while the *Philosophical Investigations* may have replaced the picture theory of meaning with talk about language games and forms of life, this very shift is itself the second of the three glaring contradictions in Wittgenstein's work. And it is not just that the use theory of meaning contradicts the picture theory. We must, on the contrary, remember the role that linguistic analysis was supposed to play in Wittgenstein's philosophy. For Wittgenstein, in each of his books, attributed the widespread but (according to Wittgenstein) mistaken idea that there *are* real philosophical problems to a misunderstanding of the logic of our language. And if there is one thing that is clear about Wittgenstein, it is that even he eventually recognized that he had, at least in his *Tractatus*, misunderstood the logic of his language. But Wittgenstein's second attempt to put an end to philosophy is really no better. Based now upon a linguistic analysis that identifies the meaning(s) of a sentence with the move(s) that it is used to make in a 'language game,' this attempt is a failure because philosophy *should*—but somehow does not—emerge from the analysis, if the analysis were consistent at all, as but another language game and another form of life. But it emerges instead as a kind of disease. And this is the third great contradiction in Wittgenstein's work. For in reducing natural science to but one language game among many, Wittgenstein somehow failed to notice that what we call 'philosophy' is a language game too. And in his continued zeal to put an end to philosophy, Wittgenstein also failed to notice—despite his own injunction to 'Look and see'—that it is a language game that has been played, right alongside the game of natural science, since time immemorial. Indeed, if Wittgenstein had only followed his own advice, he would have seen that none of the great philosophers ever thought that philosophical theories could be justified empirically, and that none of the great scientists ever thought that they could do without them.

IX

I think that the theory that there cannot be any philosophical theories would have easily been seen for what it is, had it not been for the mystique of authority associated with Wittgenstein. Part of this mystique was no doubt due to Russell, who early on proclaimed Wittgenstein as the next great philosophical genius.[26] Another part of it is no doubt due to the seriousness with which Wittgenstein took himself, and to the lack of seriousness that he attributed to others.[27]

And I am sure that a part of it is due to other things as well.

But I think that the greatest part of this mystique is due to the fact that Wittgenstein, for whatever reason, consistently held himself above the fray. His attempt to avoid criticism is already implicit in the very idea that we have all misunderstood the logic of our language.

I mean, how do you really *argue* with it?

But it is also apparent in the fact that he wrote in aphorisms; that he published, aside from the *Tractatus*, only one short article during his lifetime; that he did not tolerate criticism,[28] and that he chose to communicate with certain philosophers and not with others.[29] All of this contributed to his mystique of genius. And the upshot of it all is that instead of recognizing Wittgenstein's critique of philosophy for what it is, three generations of philosophers have now practiced his stare, along with his technique of explaining why philosophical problems are not really problems after all.

X

And this somehow brings me back to Popper and to World 3. For there is, as I said earlier, a good deal more in this incident than a confrontation between strong Viennese personalities. We cannot, try as we might, really avoid philosophical problems. And Wittgenstein, judging from his penultimate tractarian point, apparently knew it as well. But what we can avoid is the philosopher's task of thinking about them critically. We can, in this way, beg philosophical questions instead of arguing about them—though the very best way to beg a question is not to ask it at all. And even a *philosopher* can do this, if he can get others to accept his authority.

This is what that poker represented when Wittgenstein waved it in his hand like a conductor's baton while challenging Popper to 'Give an example of a moral rule!' And this is what Popper challenged, and indeed what he ridiculed, when he replied 'Not to threaten visiting lecturers with pokers.' It was this challenge to his authority, delivered in the form of a joke, that enraged Wittgenstein. And this, I think, is why Wittgenstein walked out. What was at stake then, and what still is at stake today—indeed what will *always* be at stake—is whether we will submit to the authoritarian stare and its attempt to intimidate, or go with Popper to that ripe old swamp in an effort to get closer to the truth.

Notes

1 This is a revised version of a paper first presented at a conference on Karl Popper's philosophy that was held at the London School of Economics on 11 March 1995. It was later presented, among other places, at the Department of Philosophy at Charles University in Prague, Czech Republic on 27 April 1995; at the Center for Analytic Philosophy in Tallinn, Estonia on 17 April 1997; and at the International Conference on Logic and Ontology in Timisoara, Romania on 22 May 1998. A Croatian translation was later published in *Filozofska Istraživanja*, 61, God. 16, Sv. 2, 1996. The mottoes are from Ludwig Wittgenstein, *Tractatus Logico-Philosophicus*, translation D.F. Pears & B.F. McGuinness, Routledge & Kegan Paul, London, 1922, 6.54; and Karl R. Popper, *The Logic of Scientific Discovery*, 1959. Reprinted by Routledge, London, 1995, p. 51.

2 See, for example, Ernest Gellner, 'The Rational Mystic' in *The New Republic*, April 19, 1993.

3 Karl Popper, *Unended Quest*, 1974. Reprinted by Routledge, London, 1992, p. 122.

4 Popper, *Unended Quest*, p. 123. Peter Munz, a student of both Popper and Wittgenstein, was present at the event and tells a different version (*Our Knowledge and the Growth of Knowledge: Popper or Wittgenstein?*, Routledge & Kegan Paul, London, 1985, pp. 1–2):

> After Popper's declaration that he did not believe in puzzle-solving and his affirmation that there were genuine philosophical problems, Wittgenstein started to challenge him to name a 'philosophical' problem. I cannot now recall the precise sequence of events, but after Popper tried to name one or two philosophical problems and Wittgenstein kept countering by saying that he did not know what he could 'mean' by his statements, the drama occurred. Popper was sitting on one side of the fireplace, and Wittgenstein on the other. Both were facing the audience. In the middle, in a big armchair, facing the fireplace with his back to the audience, there was Bertrand Russell. Suddenly Wittgenstein, who had been playing and fidgeting with the poker in the fire, took the red-hot poker out of the fire and gesticulated with it angrily in front of Popper's face. Thereupon, Russell—who so far had not spoken a word—took the pipe out of his mouth and said very firmly in his high-pitched, somewhat scratchy voice: 'Wittgenstein, put down that poker at once!' Wittgenstein complied and soon after got up and walked out, slamming the door.

5 This is a rough-grained distinction. We could, if we liked, distinguish between many more worlds than three. But we cannot, without stretching our concepts beyond recognition and any useful function, say that only matter exists.

6 Though some of them, e.g., books, are embodied in material objects.

7 This is Popper's main argument ('Indeterminism Is Not Enough' in *Encounter* 40, 1973, pp. 20–26) for the existence of the mental world:

> My main argument for the existence of the world 2 of subjective experiences is that we must normally grasp or understand a world 3 theory before we can use it to act upon world 1; but grasping or understanding a theory is a mental affair, a world 2 process: my view is that world 3 usually interacts with world 1 *via* the mental world 2.

8 Karl R. Popper, *Knowledge and the Body-Mind Problem*, edited by M.A. Notturno, Routledge, London, 1994, p. ix.

9 This is how Plato used his theory of ideas in the fourth century B.C., and it is how Frege used his theory of *'der dritte Reich'* at the beginning of our own. Rightly impressed by the subjectivity and fallibility of sense-experience, but still believing in objectively certain knowledge, Plato and Frege each introduced a third realm of eternal and immutable objects, and then insisted that true knowledge involves the apprehension of these objects through an act of the intellect that carries its justification within itself.

10 Ockham himself seems not to have used this formulation, but instead warned against assuming plurality without necessity, and against multiplying explanatory assumptions without necessity.

11 Perhaps due to Ockham's own empiricist biases.

12 See, in this connection, Karl R. Popper, 'Philosophy and Physics' in Karl R. Popper, *The Myth of the Framework*, edited by M.A. Notturno, Routledge, London, 1994.

13 These remarks apply equally to 'naturalism.' Whereas naturalists originally began with a concept of nature and used it to argue that whatever exists, exists in and can be explained by nature, they now begin with the axiom that whatever exists, exists in nature and use it to conceive as natural anything of whose existence they become convinced.

14 But this, of course, is precisely what Wittgenstein meant when he said that 'When the answer cannot be put into words, neither can the question be put into words' and that 'If a question can be framed at all, it is also *possible* to answer it.' (Wittgenstein, *Tractatus Logico-Philosophicus*, 6.5.)

15 It is as if someone asked us to explain baseball without referring at all to bats and balls and bases, and then complained triumphantly when we were unable to do so.

16 See David Hume, *An Enquiry Concerning Human Understanding*, edited by Eric Steinberg, Hackett, Indianapolis, 1977, especially §II.

17 Hume, *An Enquiry Concerning Human Understanding*, p. 11.

18 Hume, *An Enquiry Concerning Human Understanding*, p. 52. Hume himself argued that there was at least one exception to this rule, and allowed that we might, under certain circumstances, be able to form an idea of a certain shade of the color blue without having had a prior impression of it. But since there is, I as-

sume, nothing in his example so special about the color *blue*, one might conclude that in recognizing this *'one contradictory phenomenon'* Hume was in fact recognizing a potential infinity of ideas that are not copies of preceding impressions.

19 Hume concludes that our idea of causality is copied from our *internal* impression of expectation only after eliminating all possibilities that it is copied from other internal impressions or our impressions of *external* objects. (See Hume, *An Enquiry Concerning Human Understanding*, pp. 49–53.)

20 Wittgenstein, *Tractatus Logico-Philosophicus*, p. 5.

21 Wittgenstein, *Tractatus Logico-Philosophicus*, 6.54.

22 This criticism circumvents any attempt to salvage Wittgenstein's position from contradiction via talk about *cognitive* meaning. According to such attempts, the propositions in Wittgenstein's book could have some sort of meaning that would allow us to understand them as elucidations while still being nonsensical, since 'nonsense,' for Wittgenstein, means 'neither true nor false.' I do not want to deny that this is what 'nonsense' means for Wittgenstein. I only want to assert that there is a contradiction between Wittgenstein's calling his propositions nonsense and saying that they are true.

23 See Wittgenstein, *Tractatus Logico-Philosophicus*, 6.5.

24 This, of course, is because Wittgenstein says that philosophical theories cannot be true or false.

25 Or are we now to suppose that nonsense is the road to clarification and, if so, that only Wittgensteinian nonsense is of the sort that clarifies?

26 Russell, of course, later came to regret this assessment.

27 Ernest Nagel, for example, told me that he had once, while visiting Cambridge, asked Wittgenstein for permission to sit in on his seminar, only to be told abruptly, 'I don't like philosophical tourists!' And this picture is corroborated in Julian Bell's satiric poem 'An Epistle On the Subject of the Ethical and Aesthetic Beliefs of Herr Ludwig Wittgenstein' (first published in the Cambridge student magazine *The Venture*, No. 5, February 1930, pp. 208–215). Bell writes:

... who, on any issue, ever saw
Ludwig refrain from laying down the law?
In every company he shouts us down,
And stops our sentence stuttering his own;
Unceasing argues, harsh, irate and loud,
Sure that he's right, and of his rightness proud ...

Bell, incidentally, also writes that Wittgenstein:

... talks nonsense, numerous statements makes,
Forever his own vow of silence breaks:
Ethics, aesthetics, talks of day and night,
And calls things good or bad, and wrong or right.

So there seems to be little chance that Wittgenstein would have appreciated the scene toward the end of Derek Jarman's biographical film *Wittgenstein*, where he is made to remark to Keynes while on his death-bed, 'I always wanted to write a book on jokes.' When Keynes is made to ask why he did not, Wittgenstein is made to reply, 'As things turned out, I didn't have a sense of humor.'

28 Wittgenstein's refusal to hear criticism of his views from others has been well documented. Carnap ('Intellectual Autobiography' in *The Philosophy of Rudolf Carnap*, edited by P.A. Schilpp, Open Court, LaSalle, 1963, p. 26), for example, writes:

> Wittgenstein, on the other hand, tolerated no critical examination by others, once the insight had been gained by an act of inspiration. I sometimes had the impression that the deliberately rational and unemotional attitude of the scientist and likewise any ideas which had the flavor of 'enlightenment' were repugnant to Wittgenstein.

29 Carnap, for example, reports that 'From the beginning of 1929 on, Wittgenstein wished to meet only with Schlick and Waismann, no longer with me or Feigl,' and that Wittgenstein had 'said to Schlick that he could talk only with somebody who "holds his hand" '. (Carnap, 'Intellectual Autobiography,' p. 27.)

8 Popper's Critique of Scientific Socialism, or Carnap and His Co-Workers[1]

> The individual no longer undertakes to erect in one bold stroke an entire system of philosophy. Rather, each works at his special place within the one unified science... Each collaborator contributes only what he can endorse and justify before the whole body of his co-workers. Thus stone will be carefully added to stone and a safe building will be erected at which each following generation can continue to work.
>
> Rudolf Carnap

> The more we try to return to the heroic age of tribalism, the more surely do we arrive at the Inquisition, at the Secret Police, and at a romanticized gangsterism.
>
> Karl R. Popper

I

I should begin by saying that it is entirely unlikely that a paper entitled 'Popper's Critique of Scientific Socialism' could have been published openly in Moscow only a few short years ago. This is because scientific socialism, throughout most of the history of the USSR, was not so much a *scientific* theory as a *state* ideology. It was not a hypothetically proposed solution of problems, but an all-embracing world view that was held in such a way that no real criticism of it was allowed. I know that I do not need to inform you of this. But it is, nonetheless, ironic. For it was, after all, called *scientific* socialism. And the attitudes and concerns that motivate science are decidedly at odds with those that motivate ideology. It is, however, doubly ironic that at the very moment when the people of Russia are struggling to free their minds from ideologies, philosophers in the West are encouraging us to embrace them.

Today, the prevailing philosophical fashion in America is to denigrate truth, objectivity, and rationality in favor of irony, subjectivity, and solidarity. Today, the fashion is not to reason critically in an effort to discover truth, but to embrace a paradigm, or a form of life, or a linguistic framework, or an ideology—and to commit ourselves dogmatically to its beliefs. Today, we are told that a rational comparison of competing theories is not so much difficult as impossible. And today, we are drowning in philosophical 'arguments' that are riddled with linguistic impressions, appeals to authority, veiled threats, and *ad hominem* critique.

Such methods will not help us to discover truth. But they may help to forge solidarity. Solidarity is clearly not truth. But it is, or so the fashionable philosophers assure us, a reasonable facsimile.

I can well imagine that solidarity *could* be innocuous—if through the free exchange of ideas we all just happened to agree. But solidarity can be downright frightening when it is forged through the power politics of communalism. For when communal solidarity becomes too powerful, it can easily impede the freedom of thought and the growth of knowledge. And if we are truly concerned with the freedom of thought and the growth of knowledge, then it may even be our philosophical duty to oppose solidarity and communalism when they threaten to become powerful enough to do so.

But we all know that fashions can be very powerful, that opposing them may have undesirable consequences, and that it often requires courage to do so. So I find it inspiring to have known at least one philosopher who had the courage to oppose prevailing fashions and to defend enlightenment ideals against communalism and solidarity. And I find it inspiring even though his views have been virtually excluded from rational discussion by academic philosophers in the United States. I am, of course, referring to Karl Popper. And it is truly ironic, if not a preview to what solidarity and communalism have in store, that Popper's philosophy has been so excluded. For Popper was the twentieth century's greatest proponent of open society. And exclusion from rational discussion is what closed society is all about.

I say that Popper's thought has been excluded, because it would be too naive to think that it has been neglected or ignored. Almost every graduate student that I knew in America had a negative impression of Popper's philosophy. But not one that I knew had ever spent very much time reading it. So where, one might ask, did they get their impressions? If their experience was anything like mine, then they got them from their teachers. They got them from the undergraduate instructor, fresh out of Princeton, who after a cursory mention of Popper's critique of Carnap assigns a paper on the topic 'Why Carnap is correct'—or from the graduate professor who simply refuses to speak with students who defend Popper's views.

This exclusion of Popper's philosophy from academic philosophy in America is just one of the reasons why so much of academic philosophy in America has become *merely* academic. And it is part of the reason why professional philosophy in America now borders upon ideology. Bill Bartley has described the situation in his *Unfathomed Knowledge, Unmeasured Wealth*.[2] I will not add to his description here, except to note, this time without irony, that there is really nothing new here to explain. This kind of exclusion is business as usual in a society that aims at solidarity and communalism.

But why the hostility?

Some say it is because Popper was a difficult man. And there is no doubt some truth to this. Popper was so persistent in his criticism of logical positivism that members of the Vienna Circle called him 'The Official Opposition.' And his manner in argument was so aggressive that members of the Alpbach Forum called him *'Der Mittelstürmer.'* And this is just the tip of the iceberg. Popper characterized Plato and Hegel as totalitarians, and Judaism and Catholicism as 'tribal' religions. He claimed that 'traditional epistemology ... led students of epistemology into irrelevancies.'[3] He had a famous confrontation with Wittgenstein over the reality of philosophical problems. And he utterly refused, at a time when most philosophers practiced some form of linguistic analysis, to argue about the meanings of words. He called the popular Copenhagen Interpretation of Quantum Mechanics a 'muddle.' And, as if all of this were not enough, he claimed to have solved the problem of induction—a claim about which one very influential American philosopher told me, 'Well even if it *is* true, there are some things one just doesn't say!'

Do not be afraid if you suddenly feel strange vibrations beneath your feet. It is only old Socrates spinning in his grave. For twenty-four hundred years after he drank the hemlock, we now have professional 'lovers of wisdom' in 'the land of the free and the brave' who openly prefer tact over truth. I admit that I am no longer surprised by this. It is just another little taste of what solidarity and communalism have in store. But it is, given this context, at least interesting that when I asked Popper himself why American philosophers are so hostile to his work, he answered with a mischievous smile but without a moment's hesitation, 'It is because I am on the right.'

He was, of course, referring to his famous critique of Marxism. And there is at least circumstantial evidence for thinking that he is right. Marxism may or may not be dead here and in other parts of the world. But the American academy is one place in which it is clearly alive.

Still, my own sense is that Popper's political explanation may require its own explanation. For the terms 'right' and 'left' are notoriously vague. And they mean different things in different parts of the world. And the world, in any event, is a sphere. And this means that someone is bound to wind up on the right if he travels far enough to the left.

I say this, in part, because it is well known that Popper was a member of the *sozialistische Mittelschüler* during his student years in Vienna, that he considered himself a communist for a short period in 1919, and that he continued to support the socialists for a long time after his disavowal of communism. But I also say it because Popper retained many ideas and ideals from his socialist youth even in his old age.[4] I want, in fact, to emphasize that, despite his rejection of communism and his subsequent critique of scientific socialism, Popper never abandoned the *moral* vision that motivated Marx's work[5]—and that he praised Marx's 'moral radicalism' in the very midst of criticizing his historicism.

Popper thought that Marx's criticism of capitalism was effective mainly as a moral criticism. And he also thought that the love of freedom and the sense of social responsibility that fueled Marx's moral radicalism were things that are still alive and that 'must survive.' Indeed, Popper said that it is our *task*—and by this, I take it, he meant the task of open society—to keep them alive and to make sure that they do not die with his political radicalism.[6] Popper described Marx's historicism as a superstition, and Marx as a false prophet.[7] But he continued to respect Marx as a thinker and as a person. He wrote that:

> One cannot do justice to Marx without recognizing his sincerity. His open-mindedness, his sense of facts, his distrust of verbiage, and especially of moralizing verbiage, made him one of the world's most influential fighters against hypocrisy and pharisaism. He had a burning desire to help the oppressed, and was fully conscious of the need for proving himself in deeds, and not only in words. His main talents being theoretical, he devoted immense labour to forging what he believed to be scientific weapons for the fight to improve the lot of the vast majority of men. His sincerity in his search for truth and his intellectual honesty distinguish him, I believe, from many of his followers.[8]

I say all of this because I want to discuss Popper's critique of scientific socialism: to say what it is and what it is not. There can be no doubt that Popper was a critic of scientific socialism. But the targets of his critique are in no way peculiar to Marx's economic and political programs. They are, on the contrary, deeply embedded *ethical* attitudes that are frequently found among socialists and played an important role in their acceptance of Marx's philosophy. But the same ethical attitudes can be found among proponents of virtually *every* economic and political system that we know.

It is important, for this reason, to identify these attitudes and to keep them clearly in view. And I want, insofar as this is concerned, to relate Popper's critique of scientific socialism to his defense of enlightenment values and to the dangers that I see in the contemporary rise of communalism and solidarity. For if I am right, then we are today at risk of replacing one instance of closed society with another. Indeed, if the advocates of solidarity and communalism are correct, then we may have already done so.

II

The *locus classicus* of Popper's critique of socialism is *The Open Society and Its Enemies*—a two-volume work that Isaiah Berlin once called 'the most scrupulous and formidable criticism of the philosophical and historical doctrines of Marxism by any living writer."[9] I have already referred to *The Open Society and Its Enemies* in my opening remarks, and I will undoubtedly refer to it again. But I want to base my discussion upon a far more personal and less formidable text. I want to base it upon an exchange of letters between Popper and his one-time friend and long-time positivist rival in the philosophy of science, Rudolf Carnap. These letters have yet to be published. But I want to base my discussion on them for a number of reasons.

First of all, Popper's explanation of his attitude toward socialism is in these letters informal, candid, and concise. It contains none of the detailed arguments and references of *The Open Society and Its Enemies*, but only a list of the points upon which he agrees and disagrees. This allows us to see more clearly how Popper himself understood his critique. Secondly, logical positivism was and, despite Popper's claim to have killed it,[10] remains one of the most influential philosophical movements of the twentieth century. Any philosophical exchange between its chief proponent and its primary critic is bound to be of scholarly interest. But this particular exchange provides us with a rare opportunity. For it is an exchange regarding social issues between philosophers whose published differences almost exclusively concern problems in the philosophy of science. Finally, several of Carnap's remarks in these letters seem to corroborate Popper's idea that socialism has tendencies toward closed society—and, perhaps, also Popper's political explanation as to why some philosophers have reacted to his work with such hostility. In doing so, they also reveal some of the dangers for scientific inquiry that I regard as the legacy of logical positivism.[11]

III

The Carnap correspondence file in The Karl Popper Archives contains thirty-eight letters written over a period of forty years. But the exchange that I want to focus upon involves three letters written between 1946 and 1947. So I should, perhaps, put this exchange into some sort of context.

Carnap was eleven years Popper's senior and completed his doctorate at Jena in 1921 with a dissertation on the concept of space. He devoted several years to private research in logic and the foundations of physics, and had already established himself as one of the most influential proponents of logical positivism and its Unified Science Movement while Popper was still a graduate student in Vienna. Carnap joined the faculty of the University of Vienna in 1926 and published *Der Logische Aufbau der Welt* and *Scheinprobleme in der Philosophie* in 1928. He founded the positivist journal *Erkenntnis* with Hans Reichenbach in 1930, and spent the next four years as professor of natural philosophy at the German University in Prague. He published *Logische Syntax der Sprache* in 1934 and *Philosophy and Logical Syntax* in 1935. He then emigrated to the United States in 1935 and received a permanent appointment as a research professor at the University of Chicago in 1936. Carnap published *Testability and Meaning* in 1936–37, *Logical Syntax of Language* in 1937, *Foundations of Logic and Mathematics* in 1939, *Introduction to Semantics* in 1942, *Formalization of Logic* in 1943, and *Meaning and Necessity* in 1947. He also co-edited the *International Encyclopedia of Unified Science* with Otto Neurath and Charles Morris.

All of this made Carnap one of the most powerful figures of his time in American academic philosophy. And it is apparent from his correspondence with Neurath and Morris in the Archives of the Unity of Science Movement at the University of Chicago that Carnap often used this power to find jobs for, and to further the interests of, positivist philosophers at universities in America and Europe.

Popper, on the other hand, earned his doctorate from the University of Vienna in 1928 with a dissertation in the psychology of thinking. He was interested in methodological problems and continued to write philosophy after he graduated. But he was also interested in practical social work and did not intend to become a university professor. So instead of devoting his time to full-time research, he earned a teaching certificate in 1929 and spent the next eight years teaching mathematics and physical science in a secondary school in Vienna. Popper grew increasingly critical of logical positivism during this period. He met and discussed his views with several members of the Vienna Circle, including Carnap. Schlick did not want him present at their meetings, but they were impressed with his arguments and encouraged him to publish them in book form. Popper, however, was still teaching secondary school when *Logik der Forschung* was published in 1934. And despite its international success, he did not receive a university position until 1937 when, leaving Vienna in anticipation of the *Anschluss*, he accepted a lectureship at Canterbury University College in New Zealand.[12] But this lectureship was not a research position. Popper had limited library resources and heavy teaching loads. And he had to deal with superiors who 'advised' him not to publish anything while in New Zealand since 'any time spent on research was a theft from the working time as a lecturer for which [he] was being paid.'[13]

Popper wrote long letters to Carnap during this period regarding logic, probability theory, and semantics. Many of these letters reveal the intellectual and cultural isolation that he suffered in New Zealand, and it is important to understand that he was very often a supplicant during this period. He asked Carnap to send him offprints of articles and back issues of journals that were unavailable in New Zealand. He also asked Carnap for job recommendations, references to publishers, and, repeatedly, for Tarski's address.

But Popper, despite his isolation, his heavy teaching load, and the 'advice' of his superiors, continued to write philosophy. He had, before the war, already conceived of a book that would trace the philosophical roots of authoritarianism and totalitarianism to the problem of change. And toward the end of the war, he was actively seeking both a publisher for his book and a better position for himself.

The letters that I want to focus upon were written after Popper left New Zealand for London. They were, in fact, written shortly after the publication of *The Open Society and Its Enemies* and his subsequent appointment at the London School of Economics. The exchange begins when Carnap, in a letter dated 17 November 1946, asks Popper whether or not he is still a socialist. But the ensuing discussion of socialism has its roots in letters written while Popper was still in New Zealand. So I should, perhaps, turn to those earlier letters first.[14]

IV

Popper first wrote to Carnap about *The Open Society and Its Enemies* in 1942. He was then calling his book *False Prophets: Plato—Hegel—Marx,* and he described it, in a letter to Carnap dated 15 October, as his 'war effort.' He went on to say that his book was 'an attack on a kind of superstition introduced into the field of social investigation by Plato and further developed by Hegel and Marx.'[15] He also told Carnap that he was sending the book to some American publishers and that he had given his name as a possible reference.

Carnap replied to Popper in a letter dated 29 January 1943, saying that, 'If a publisher writes to me I shall be very glad to do what I can to help by recommending it.' But he apparently had some reservations, for he went on to caution Popper against criticizing Marx:

> I hope you are cautious in your criticism of Marx in order not to furnish arguments to those who do not only differ with his views but also reject his goal. A careful separation of what is right and what is wrong in his views is necessary, such as you did in your article on 'Dialectics,' which I liked very much. Perhaps this article or something similar is now a chapter of the book? If the book has the same careful, objective, critical attitude then it will be very useful.

There may be a bit of irony in Carnap's advice to be critical, but not *too* critical of Marx. But Popper was sensitive to his worries and responded two months later, writing:

> Concerning your questions regarding my treatment of Marx: The book does, I believe, full justice to Marx, both to his intentions and to his theoretical achievements. But it criticizes him. We do not need a Great System of social philosophy. My criticism of Marx is careful and detailed, and if you

found my article 'objective,' then you will certainly say the same of the book. I of course cannot say of myself that I am 'objective'; I can only say that in spite of my critical attitude, I have a weakness for Marx, and I admire him as a thinker. I also clearly express in the book that I owe very much to Marx's influence. At the same time, I try to show that Marx's 'historicism,' i.e. his fundamental belief in a predetermined course of history, must lead to mysticism, and that it stands in the way of a cool and rational 'piecemeal social engineering,' of a technological approach to social problems.

Popper, however, was trying to solicit Carnap's help. And he immediately continues:

> I say all this because I wish to re-assure you in this matter, considering that you have so kindly expressed your readiness to help. The publication-issue does not look too good...
>
> It is terribly difficult to organize anything from this distance...
>
> If you could give me further advice, or help, I should be very grateful indeed. (Do you know Harry D. Gideonse, editor of the Public Policy Pamphlets, Chicago University Press: I think he might be interested in a book like that.)

I do not know whether Carnap ever contacted anyone at Chicago University Press—or, for that matter, whether any publishers ever contacted Carnap regarding Popper's book. Popper, in any event, did not receive a reply to this letter, or to his next—and Carnap apparently did not write to Popper again until after he had learned, nearly a year and a half later, that *The Open Society and Its Enemies* had been accepted for publication.

Indeed, the next letter from Carnap that appears in the Popper archives is dated 30 May 1945 (over two years later). It was sent with a testimonial Carnap had written to support Popper's application for a chair in philosophy at Dunedin—a testimonial that may have arrived too late to be used, since applications for the position had closed in Dunedin on May 1 and in London on June 1.

But Popper did not really need Carnap's help—either to publish his book or to find a position. The great Austrian economist Friedrich von Hayek had immediately recognized the importance of *The Open Society and Its Enemies*. And it is apparent from other documents in the Popper archives that Hayek went to extraordinary lengths to find both a publisher for Popper's book and (unbeknownst to Popper at the time) a position for Popper himself. So Popper was able to make light of Carnap's late testimonial, writing in a letter to Carnap dated 23 June 1945 that the chair in Dunedin was no longer important to him, since he had been offered a readership in logic and scientific method at the London School of Economics.

But this connection with Hayek is important for another reason.

Popper acknowledged his debt to Hayek in *The Open Society and Its Enemies*, saying that the book would not have been published without his interest and support. This acknowledgement apparently aroused Carnap's interest in Popper's political position. And it set the stage for the exchange that I want to focus upon now.

When Popper sent Carnap a copy of his book, Carnap replied with cautious praise for the book and prying curiosity regarding his relationship with Hayek:

> I thank you most cordially for sending me the two volumes of your great work 'The Open Society and its Enemies.' I find it extremely interesting and many parts quite fascinating. I cannot of course judge the details of your historical and philosophical analysis of Plato, but your fight for reducing his all too high authority is very welcome at the present time. The same holds also for Hegel, although his influence is, at least in this country, by far not as large as that of Plato. Your analysis of Marx' method is very illuminating, and I am sure that many people, whether followers or opponents or neutral scholars, will learn much from it, no matter whether they agree or not in all details. In many of the points which you discuss, I am not in a position to make a definitive judgment. But ... I was somewhat surprised to see your acknowledgement to von Hayek. I have not read his book [*The Road to Serfdom*] myself; it is much read and discussed in this country, but praised mostly by the protagonists of free enterprise and unrestricted capitalism, while all leftists regard him as a reactionary. I wonder what you think about his book.[16]

Carnap's interest in *The Road to Serfdom* is ironic in light of his earlier 'advice' about Marx. Carnap had urged Popper to be cautious in his criticism of Marx 'in order not to furnish arguments to those who do not only differ with his views but also reject his goal."[17] But Hayek had written in *The Road to Serfdom* that 'many people ... who value the ultimate ends of socialism no less than the socialists refuse to support socialism because of the dangers to other values they see in the methods proposed by the socialists.'[18] Carnap, however, had not read *The Road to Serfdom,* and was thus in no position to appreciate the irony when Popper replied:

> One remark in your letter I must answer specially; this is the remark on Hayek, and his 'reactionary' reputation. Hayek is certainly trying to show the dangers of 'Socialism' and especially the Utopian attempt to run a society without a market. But he is certainly not a protagonist of unrestricted capitalism. On the contrary, he insists on the need of a system of 'Social Security,' on anti-cycle-policy, etc. That all, or rather most, leftists regard him as reactionary is, unfortunately, only too true. But most leftists are only too willing to sacrifice all democratic control of the rulers if only those rulers are sufficiently left. That they are outraged by anybody who points out that political democracy is the only known way of preventing rulers, benevolent and otherwise, from doing whatever they wish, is one of the sad things of our anti-rationalistic time.

But I would imagine that he may have sensed the irony when Popper went on to say:

> I should like to mention that I did not know Hayek's book ('The Road to Serfdom') when I wrote mine; in fact, my book was finished about six months before his. All I knew was a little pamphlet 'Freedom and the Economic System,' in which he advocates 'Planning for Freedom.' But he happened to read my Manuscript and was so struck by it that he did everything in his power to find a publisher for me; and it is mainly due to him (and Herbert Read) that Routledges in the end accepted my book. The acknowledgement in my book refers to his practical help rather than to his influence; but since I wrote my book, I have read Hayek's book (and several excellent articles), and I can only say that I have learned a *very* great deal from it. A few leftists here in England are in the same position, for example Barbara Wootton who has answered Hayek in a very serious way, acknowledging how much she has profited from his arguments. Hayek, who I had seen only four or five times before, has been really wonderful to me in his many repeated approaches to various publishers, and I understand from the people here in the School that he is always so. His interest in my book was mainly due to the fact that he too is hoping for a common basis of discussion for socialists and liberals.[19]

V

I do not intend to draw any conclusions from the material that I have just quoted. I have, on the contrary, presented it to provide a context for the material that I will present now—and entertainment for those of you who are still interested in irony, subjectivity, and solidarity. I hope that I have succeeded in doing both. We have, in any event, already learned a great deal about Popper's critique of socialism. We have seen that it is *not* a critique of Marx's moral vision, and that Popper believed that Marx's feeling of social responsibility and his love of freedom are things that 'must survive.' We have seen that it is primarily a critique of Marx's historicism, which Popper regarded as a superstition that leads to mysticism and ultimately to fascism. And we have seen that Popper regarded socialists as closed-minded and naïve, as unwilling to listen to criticism and too willing to relinquish democratic control over their rulers. These three points are, no doubt, interrelated. But we have yet to come to the heart of the matter. So I would now like to return to Carnap's letter of 17 November 1946.

When Carnap wrote this letter, he had read both *The Open Society and Its Enemies* and the articles that would later form *The Poverty of Historicism*. He seems, however, to have been more interested in Popper's own political position than in his philosophical arguments. And he turns the discussion, after a few polite remarks, directly to the question whether Popper still considers himself a socialist:

> Well, this brings us just back to the question of socialism versus capitalism. I read with very great interest your articles on historicism. And I now circulate them among friends who are interested in these problems too. However, in one point, which interests me very much, I could not see your position quite clearly from these articles any more than from the books: whether or to what extent you still regard yourself as a socialist. From some formulations in the articles, it might seem as if you had given up socialism, but it is not quite clear. In your letter you speak of the hope for a common basis of discussion for socialists and liberals. To which of the two groups do you count yourself? I have seen Hayek himself in the meantime, because he came here last spring. Since I do not know his book, I did not speak with

him directly about those problems, but I asked him about you personally and also about your political position. He seemed quite surprised that you had been a social-democrat in Vienna; he did not seem to think that you regarded yourself as a socialist now. I realize, of course, that you may find it difficult to characterize your position adequately in terms of an inexact concept like 'socialism.' Therefore, let me put the question in these terms: would you agree with me in the belief that it is necessary to transfer at least the bulk of the means of production from private into public hands? I think that such a transfer would by no means be incompatible with what you call social engineering.

Popper replied to Carnap on 6 January 1947 saying:

You ask me whether I am still a socialist.

Answer: I prefer not to use such terms as 'socialism' or 'capitalism' or anything of the sort for characterizing a serious and responsible political position.

But Popper was not trying to deflect the question. He simply did not want to be drawn into Carnap's 'with us or against us' trap. It is clear from his reply that Popper saw both good and bad elements in each of these systems. But it is also clear that he thought that their tendency to polarize the issues was one of the socialists' greatest flaws.

Popper, in any event, immediately laid out his views for Carnap—explicitly detailing the points upon which he agreed with the socialists:

The following beliefs I share, presumably, with most socialists:

(1) There is a need for a much greater equalization of incomes than it is realized in any state I know of ...

(2) There is a need for reasonably bold, but *critical* experimentation in the political and economical sphere.

(3) I do not see why such experiments should stop short of experimenting with 'socialisation of means of production,' *provided* (a) the considerable and serious dangers raised by such experiments are frankly faced, and means are adopted to meet these dangers; (b) the mystical and naive belief is given up that socialisation is a kind of cure-all...

(4) I further believe, with most socialists, that certain business-interests are liable to interfere in a very dangerous way with politics, and that strong means should be adopted (possibly not falling short of socialisation, if this

should prove otherwise desirable) to curb these instances. And I believe, further, in the need to do something drastic about monopolies. (In the case of monopolies which cannot be broken up, I am even rather strongly in favour of some kind of socialisation.)

And also the points—or perhaps I should say the point—upon which he disagreed:

> Now here are the points in which I *disagree* with most socialists:
> (1) I do not believe that there is a cure-all in politics. I believe that, in a socialized economy, (a) there *could be* worse differences of income than there are now; (b) there could be, accordingly, worse exploitation than there is now, for exploitation is misuse of economic power, and socialization means accumulation of economic power; (c) there could be very easily more undue interference of the economically powerful people in politics than there is now; (d) there could be a greater amount of control of *thought* by the economically and politically powerful people than there is now.

Popper recognized that socialization *might* make things better. But he also recognized that it *might* make things worse:

> In other words, I am neither pro-socialisation nor against it. I realize that socialisation might improve certain matters, but I also realize that it might make matters worse. It all depends on how one goes about these things. Socialists, I am afraid, don't, as a rule, realize these dangers, and they therefore go about these things in a way which invites disaster.

Popper, moreover, was convinced that making things worse was not just an abstract possibility but a very real danger. And here, he thought that the main danger lay in the uncritical 'aesthetic-Utopianist-Messianist' attitude with which most of the socialists whom he knew approached the question of reform:

> I feel that it is our task to become less prejudiced in these serious matters, i.e. less religious and more sober. Socialism as it exists to-day is very largely a religious and Messianistic movement—the dream of heaven on earth, a consequence of the strain of civilisation and the lost paradise of tribalism. But it has very good things in it: I mean the belief that things *must* be improved and that they *can* be improved, and the will to experimentation and to science—although the scientific readiness to give up cherished beliefs is hardly ever understood by socialists. (Their belief in science is, as a rule,

nothing but a naive, vulgar-Darwinist progressivism or evolutionism.) It is this aesthetic-Utopianist-Messianist element in socialism which is its main danger, and which drives it so easily into a totalitarian direction.

He drew upon his own experience with the *Kinderfreunde Bewegung* in Vienna to illustrate his point:

> There was something very valuable in this movement; good social work, and a religious pride, raised the people to a higher view of their lives. But it *was* indoctrination, in no way distinct from the religious indoctrination of little children in schools and in Church, or from the Nazi-indoctrination. The Viennese social democrats did more in the direction of making the whole life of the workers part of a collective movement than perhaps anybody between Plato and Hitler. There is something great and attractive about such a totalitarian movement, but we must not allow ourselves to become the victims of this attraction.

And he then summed up his position by saying:

> I believe that the political philosophies of socialism and of liberalism which we have inherited from the 19th century are both just a little too simple and too naive. I fully share (as you know from my book) the conviction of the liberals that freedom is the most important thing in the political field. But I am convinced that freedom cannot be saved without improving distributive justice, i.e., without increasing economic equality.
>
> This is why I believe that we must give up dogmatic and semi-religious beliefs in this field and must try to reach a more rational attitude. And this could be shared by liberals and socialists.

Earlier I said that Carnap was more interested in Popper's political position than in his philosophical arguments. Carnap never asked *why* Popper believed that socialism leads to totalitarianism, but only whether or not he was still a socialist. And it is ironic, for this reason, that Popper ends his letter by saying that 'we must give up dogmatic and semi-religious beliefs in this field and must try to reach a more rational attitude.' For he had, already in *The Open Society and Its Enemies*, traced such an interest in a thinker, as opposed to his thought, to an abandonment of the rationalist attitude.

But here, the point to be made is that Popper had no a priori objections to *any* of the economic or political proposals of socialism.

He agreed with the socialists that there was a need for much greater equalization of incomes, that there was also a need for bold political and economic experimentation, that such experimentation might include socialization of the means of production, that certain business interests interfered perniciously with politics, and that 'strong means' should be adopted to curb those influences.

So what is his critique of socialism?

His critique is that socialists tend to abandon the rational attitude—that they tend to adopt their socialism uncritically, remaining insensitive to its problems, and believing with a kind of religious fervor that socialism will be a cure for all their social ills.[20]

Popper, contrary to this, recognized that things could easily be worse under socialism—that the accumulation of economic power in the hands of the state inevitably poses a threat to freedom, and that there *could* easily be wider gaps in income, worse exploitation of workers, greater corruption in government, and more *thought control* under socialism. Popper regarded none of this as *necessary*. 'It all depends on how one goes about these things.' But his experience was that socialists were too naïve, too emotional, and too dogmatic to do it well. His experience was that they were driven by an irrational 'aesthetic-Utopianist-Messianist' attitude that blinded them to the dangers of socialism, made them unwilling to give up their cherished beliefs, and eventually drove them too easily towards totalitarianism.

There is, again, nothing a priori or necessary in this. It is a matter of experience. But this was Popper's experience. And lest anyone think that support for such religious fervor comes only from right wing fanatics, I should note that this point about the importance of a religious attitude for political action is the one point in Popper's analysis of socialism with which Carnap *qualitatively* disagreed. As Carnap put it:

> I entirely agree with you that political thinking and political activity should be based on sober and scientific thinking. On the other hand, however, I believe that it is hardly possible to base a political movement which tries to be a mass movement, merely on rational arguments. I think emotional appeal and what you correctly describe as a kind of religious attitude is psychologically necessary.[21]

But if political thinking and political activity should be based on sober and scientific thinking, then why is it hardly possible to base a mass political movement merely on rational arguments? Why are emotional appeals and a religious attitude psychologically necessary for its success?

Carnap does not say why he believes that emotional appeals and religious fervor are necessary for the success of a mass movement.[22] But it is easy to see in his remark a germ of the anti-democratic sentiments that Popper wrote *The Open Society and Its Enemies* to expose. For Carnap apparently believed that there is something about a *mass* political movement that requires these things. And it is easy to see in this the Platonic idea that the masses are driven by their emotions, that they are unable to act upon reason alone, and that they therefore need to be controlled, for justice's sake, by a philosopher king and his co-workers.[23]

If this is what motivates Carnap's remark, then the tension entirely disappears. Plato also believed that political thinking and political activity *should* be based upon sober and scientific thinking. But he believed that such sober and scientific thinking can be done only by the philosopher kings, who must then appeal to the *emotions* of the masses in order to incite them to action.

But if this is what is necessary for the success of a mass political movement, then it is difficult to see how it could fail to be both authoritarian and totalitarian.

Earlier I said that Popper never abandoned the moral vision that motivated Marx's work. This, I think, is why he resisted the charms of solidarity and communalism. It is why he retained his intellectual honesty, and continued to praise Marx for his commitment to freedom and distributive justice while criticizing him for his blindness to the dangers of accumulating economic power in a state. Popper thought that the possibilities that things could be worse under socialism were 'very real,' and that they were made even more real by the irrational attitudes of the socialists whom he knew, as manifested in their belief that socialism was inevitable and that they had nothing to learn from others.

The adoption of such an irrational attitude was in no way necessary. But it was not accidental either. It was, ironically enough, nourished by Marx's historicism and by his claim that socialism is 'scientific.'

The idea that there are laws of history by which we can predict our future economic and political development was the primary basis for Marx's claim that socialism is scientific and inevitable. And the idea that socialism is scientific and inevitable is what encouraged socialists to believe that they have nothing to learn from others. The subjective certainty that resulted from this, combined with the beauty of Marx's moral vision, led them to divide the world into friends and foes and to seek solidarity of belief instead of truth.

Popper never abandoned Marx's love of freedom. But he never accepted his understanding of science. Popper did not say that socialism *cannot* be scientific. He said that no *science* can be 'scientific' in the way Marx thought. Science, on Popper's account, is not a set of a priori certain or even empirically justified true beliefs. It is an ever-fallible, never-justified, and frequently changing process of conjecture and refutation—a process of proposing hypotheses to solve our problems, testing them against experience, and readjusting the one in light of the other in an effort to make the two of them fit. *This* kind of scientific knowledge is possible only if we already possess at least two different kinds of freedom that Marxism ultimately denied.

We must be free to recognize, criticize, and correct the errors that exist in the hypotheses we currently hold. And we must be free to alter the future through our own thoughts and actions. We must, in a nutshell, be free to think and free to change.

The trouble with scientific socialism, according to Popper, is that it is not scientific enough.

VI

I would like to end my paper with a few thoughts about the consequences that logical positivism's emphasis upon solidarity and communalism have had for the philosophy of science, and a few thoughts about how solidarity and communalism may pose problems for society at large.

Popper, in his autobiography, recalls how he and Carnap spent a vacation together in 1932 during which Carnap read the first volume of Popper's then unpublished *Die beiden Grundprobleme der Erkenntnistheorie*,[24] and the two had daily discussions regarding epistemology.[25]

Carnap published an article[26] shortly after this vacation that gave a detailed account of Popper's deductive method for testing statements in physics and that recommended Popper's account of protocol statements over Neurath's as the best procedure thus far available in the field. Four years later, after the publication of *Logik der Forschung*, Carnap would again acknowledge Popper's influence in 'Testability and Meaning.'[27]

Many philosophers have taken these acknowledgements as an indication that Popper was also a logical positivist. But Popper himself devotes a chapter of his autobiography to the question 'Who killed Logical Positivism?'—and, during the course of the chapter, claims to have done it himself.[28]

Popper rejected not only the positivists' idea that verifiability is the criterion of meaning. He denied that philosophy should be concerned with meaning at all. He rejected not only their idea that scientific theories are justified through induction, but also the idea that they can and need to be justified at all.

Popper argued that scientific laws can be neither verified nor confirmed, and that metaphysical presuppositions are both meaningful and a necessary component of any science. Carnap continued, all the while, to talk about the elimination of metaphysics through the analysis of language. But he weakened his concept of justification, and then even his concept of truth. And this finally resulted in a transformation of his original proud bedrock foundationalism into what might be called 'floating foundationalism'—a philosophy that retained the structure and function of foundationalism, but left the foundations themselves floating in midair.

But despite all this, A.J. Ayer attributes the death of logical positivism, at least in part, to the death of Otto Neurath.[29] And anyone who has ever seen Neurath's letters in the archives of the Unity of Science Movement at the University of Chicago can understand why. These letters, typed in single-spaced lines that cover the paper top to bottom and side to side, went on for pages informing the members of the movement of the latest positivist news. But what is, perhaps, most amazing is that Neurath often wrote—and apparently typed—*several* of these letters in the same day, a fact that at once attests to his great energy, and explains why the positivist movement lost its cohesion when the energy that fueled it died out.

Otto Neurath was a Marxist. And while most of the positivists were socialists,[30] it was Neurath, more than any of the others, who expressed in his publications their dream that the goals of Marxism could somehow be achieved through the development of unified science.

Neurath wrote that 'unified science is the outgrowth of comprehensive *collective labor*,'[31] and he cast doubt upon the ability of 'isolated individuals' to achieve anything resembling it. His Marxism may seem at odds with his claim that logical positivism was not 'seeking to oppose a new "Weltanschauung" to an old one' and that 'the opposition, rather, is between all world-views and science which is "free of any world-view".'[32] But these claims are consistent with his view that Marxism is not a philosophy, or a world-view, but 'to a higher degree than any other present-day sociological theory, a system of empirical sociology.'[33]

These claims seem incredibly naïve today, and they seemed naïve to Popper even in 1931. But Neurath continually stressed the collaborative aspect of scientific inquiry, writing that 'unified science, alongside of which there exists no "philosophy" or "metaphysics," is not the achievement of isolated individuals, but of a generation.'[34] Neurath was not alone in his idea that science is a collective labor. Carnap held it too and tells us in his 'Intellectual Autobiography' how he would rely upon Reichenbach for information in physics and how he would, in turn, explain to Reichenbach the developments in problems related to logic and mathematics.[35]

This reliance sometimes went beyond matters of exposition. And Carnap, in the second edition of *Logical Foundations of Probability*, would reject Popper's claim that his system contained a contradiction, writing simply that Bar-Hillel, Kemeny, and Jeffrey reject it too. But the idea that science is a collective labor among co-workers was present from the very beginning. It can, in fact, be found in a famous passage from Carnap's preface to the *Logische Aufbau der Welt*:

> If we allot to the individual in philosophical work, as in the special sciences, only a partial task, then we can look with more confidence into the future: in slow careful construction insight after insight will be won. Each collaborator contributes only what he can endorse and justify before the whole body of his co-workers. Thus stone will be carefully added to stone and a safe building will be erected at which each following generation can continue to work.[36]

I regard the idea that science is a collective labor as part of the legacy of logical positivism. It is an idea that has led many contemporary philosophers to characterize the scientific community as collectively underwriting the authority of scientific knowledge—and to define scientific knowledge, if not truth itself, as the consensus of belief within the scientific community itself.

Neurath's commitment to the idea of science as a collective labor may explain his dislike for the admiration that so many of the members of the Vienna Circle felt for Wittgenstein and Popper, each of whom, in very different ways,[37] resisted the positivists' attempts to co-opt their views. Neurath regarded this admiration as dangerous. And he recalls, in a letter written to Carnap dated 16 June 1945,[38] how he warned the positivists first against Wittgenstein's mysticism:

> I behaved sometimes noisily and intensely, when speaking of Wittgenstein. I regarded him from the start as a mystic and metaphysician of the refined type, as an antiscientific person through and through and I dared to say so as the admiration of Wittgenstein was the fashion in the Vienna Circle.

And then against Popper's rationalism:

> I remember, how I disliked the Popper admiration, whom I thought as an antiempiricist man with many empiricist arguments, full of clever ideas, but not reliable, when empiricism of the unified science is at stake, he with his ONE WORLD SCHEME AS THE BEST etc. Antipluralist through and through. The defects of his probability arguments I felt strongly, but not

being able to reach a real judgment on that, I behaved with restrictions there. I cannot deny, that I did not give way in the case of Popper, in spite of the friendly judgment you and Hempel found appropriate.

It is, in a way, ironic that Neurath believed that his vigorous and vocal opposition to Wittgenstein and Popper was what led Carnap to complain that he reacted emotionally and violently to criticism.[39] And it is, perhaps, doubly ironic that Neurath, who seems from the tone of his letter to Carnap to have been deeply offended by Carnap's charge, responded by saying that Carnap was 'mixing up totally different things, criticism and offence.'

Neurath eventually gave way in the case of Wittgenstein. He did not accept the positivists' suggestions that he look at Wittgenstein from a different angle. And he clearly stated his belief that they should not follow Wittgenstein all the way up the tractarian ladder.[40] But he nonetheless agreed, for the sake of solidarity and communalism, to add his name to Carnap's and Hahn's as one of the three editors of the *Wiener Kreis* pamphlet.

In doing so, he swallowed his own judgment and his strong distaste for Wittgenstein's philosophy and signed his name onto a document that singled out Wittgenstein and his *Tractatus* for special mention in tracing the intellectual debts of the Vienna Circle.[41] But Neurath refused to 'give way' in the case of Popper—despite the 'friendly judgment' that Carnap and Hempel thought appropriate.

It is difficult to know exactly what Neurath meant in saying that he 'did not give way in the case of Popper.' He may have been referring to his critical review of *Logik der Forschung*, which stood in contrast to the more sympathetic reviews written by Carnap and Hempel. And he may have been referring to something else. But these words were written in the summer of 1945, very shortly after Carnap had written that letter of recommendation that was mailed too late to do Popper any good. They occur in a context in which Neurath is recounting the history of his refusal to support certain job candidates who, while qualified in their fields, had political positions that differed from his own. Some of these people were Nazis. But it is at least ironic that Neurath calls Popper 'antipluralist through and through' in the very same breath in which he describes him as 'not reliable, when empiricism of the unified science is at stake.' But then, positivist pluralism seems to kick in only *after* you accept its basic dogmas.

Examples like these can be multiplied at length. But I think the point has been made. Science may or may not be a collective labor. But it is the inevitable character of communities to have both their insiders and their outsiders.

VII

Positivism, from its very beginning, stressed the communal nature of scientific inquiry over the freedom of thought. So it is *not* ironic that Auguste Comte, the original founder of positivism, attempted to establish a positivist church modeled upon Roman Catholicism, with holy days of obligation named for the famous scientists to replace holy days of obligation named for the saints.

The founders of logical positivism in the twentieth century also stressed the communal nature of science, which they conceived, now under the influence of Marx, as a 'collective labor' in which 'each collaborator contributes only what he can endorse and justify before the whole body of his co-workers.'

This conception of science as a community of co-workers is still alive today—though there is, today, a big difference.

In Carnap's original vision, the authority of the scientific community was supposed to follow from the justification of its theories, and not the justification of its theories from the authority of the community. This was a vision that Carnap, by retreating to induction as the logic of justification and to consensus as a criterion of truth, tried to maintain long after the theoretical grounds for it were gone. And it was a vision that eventually led to a strain in his relationship with Neurath.

Carnap was undoubtedly a socialist. But Carnap at least *tried* to keep his philosophical work separate from his political aims.[42]

My own sense, however, is that any philosopher who conceives of science as a community of co-workers, and who advocates induction as rational inference, and consensus as a criterion of truth, will eventually find himself in situations in which he will feel forced to 'give way.'

My own sense is that there will be times when he will sacrifice his own judgment, and perhaps even his integrity, to the solidarity of his community.

Earlier I said that I wanted to relate Popper's critique of socialism to the dangers of solidarity and communalism, and to his defense of enlightenment values. There can be little doubt that science is a social enterprise. But my own sense is that trying to base it upon solidarity and communalism is a big mistake. Solidarity and communalism undoubtedly have their charms. But they are still, as they have always been, the primary threat to the freedom of thought. And the freedom of thought, in my view, is what science and philosophy are really all about.

VIII

Popper did not regard socialism or capitalism or any economic system as an end in itself. He thought that such systems are to be valued—and evaluated—primarily as means toward freedom. The same holds true for political systems. Even democracy should be valued as a means to another end. It may well help us to preserve freedom, but it can never *create* freedom if we ourselves do not care for it. Indeed, Popper thought that it was especially important to understand that democracy is not a political cure-all or guarantee of freedom. But if this is true, then every citizen must constantly be on his guard against the charms of solidarity and communalism. For might not democrats and capitalists also become too religious, too emotional, and too uncritical of their beliefs? Might they not also develop an 'aesthetic-Utopianist-Messianist' attitude, become dogmatic about their capitalism, blind to its dangers, and willing to sacrifice or manipulate democratic control in order to insure that their rulers are sufficiently right? Might not democrats and capitalists also close their minds to criticism and seek solidarity and communalism instead?

Haven't many of them done so already?

Popper wrote to Carnap, 'Here are the points in which I *disagree* with most socialists: (1) I do not believe that there is a cure-all in politics.' But there is, interestingly enough, no number 2 on Popper's list.

On the contrary, Popper told me only shortly before he died that, 'If socialism were possible without the power problem, then I would still call myself a socialist.'

But there are no cure-alls in politics. And there are no democratic or capitalist cure-alls either. Regardless of our political and economic systems, we will always have to fight vigilantly to resist the temptations of solidarity and communalism, and to preserve our freedom to think. Now is no time for rest. And it does not matter whether you find yourself on the left, or on the right, or in the middle. Power still corrupts, and absolute power corrupts absolutely.

Notes

1 This is a revised version of a paper that was first presented before the editorial board of *Voprosy Filosofii* in Moscow on 17 January 1993. A Russian translation was published in *Voprosy Filosofii*, December, 1995. It has since been presented at the Institute on Nationalism at the Central European University in Prague, Czech Republic on 25 April 1995; at the Soros Foundation in Tashkent, Uzbekistan on 19 October 1998; and at the Soros Foundation in Shymkent, Kazakhstan on 23 October 1998. A revised version of the English original was published in *Philosophy of the Social Sciences*, Volume 29, No. 1, March, 1999. The mottoes are from Rudolf Carnap, *The Logical Structure of the World*, translated by Rolf A. George, in *The Logical Structure of the World & Pseudoproblems in Philosophy*, University of California Press, Berkeley, 1969, pp. xvi-xvii.; and Karl R. Popper, *The Open Society and Its Enemies*, 1945. Reprinted by Routledge, London, 1998, vol. 1, p. 200.
2 William Warren Bartley, III, *Unfathomed Knowledge, Unmeasured Wealth*, Open Court, La Salle, Illinois, 1990.
3 Karl R. Popper, 'Epistemology Without a Knowing Subject' in Karl R. Popper, *Objective Knowledge*, Clarendon Press, Oxford, 1972, p. 108.
4 See Karl Popper, *Unended Quest*, 1974. Reprinted by Routledge, London, 1992, p. 33. Popper (Karl Popper, 'Against Big Words' in Karl Popper, *In Search of a*

Better World, translated by Laura J. Bennett, Routledge, London, 1992, pp. 82–83) has more recently described his relationship with socialism as follows:

I started out as a socialist at secondary school, but did not find school very stimulating. I left school at sixteen and only returned to take the university entrance examination (*Reifeprüfung*). At seventeen (1919) I was still a socialist, but I had become an opponent of Marx (as a result of some encounters with Communists). Further experiences (of bureaucrats) led me to the insight, even prior to fascism, that the increasing power of the machine of the state constitutes the utmost danger for personal freedom, and that we must therefore keep on fighting the machine. My socialism was not just a theoretical stance: I learnt cabinetmaking (by contrast with my intellectual socialist friends) and took the journeyman's examination; I worked in children's homes; I became a primary school teacher; prior to the completion of my first book … I had no intention of becoming a professor of Philosophy…

I have retained many ideas and ideals from socialist youth in my old age. In particular:

Every intellectual has a very special responsibility. He has the privilege and the opportunity of studying. In return, he owes it to his fellow men (or 'to society') to represent the results of his study as simply, clearly and modestly as he can. The worst thing that intellectuals can do—the cardinal sin—is to try to set themselves up as great prophets vis-à-vis their fellow men and to impress them with puzzling philosophies. Anyone who cannot speak simply and clearly should say nothing and continue to work until he can do so.

5 Although Popper did come to question whether and to what extent Marx himself was the best representative of that vision. See, in this connection, Popper, *The Open Society and Its Enemies*, vol. 2, p. 396.

6 See Popper, *The Open Society and Its Enemies*, vol. 2, p. 211.

7 See Popper, *The Open Society and Its Enemies*, vol. 2, p. 82.

8 Popper, *The Open Society and Its Enemies*, vol. 2, p. 82.

9 Isaiah Berlin as quoted in Bryan Magee, *Popper*, Fontana, London, 1973, p. 9.

10 See Popper, *Unended Quest*, pp. 87–90.

11 See, in this connection, M.A. Notturno, 'Thomas Kuhn and the Legacy of Logical Positivism' in *History of the Human Sciences*, vol. 10, no. 1, February, 1997.

12 Popper told me that he became a university professor *only* because he was unable to work as a school teacher outside of Austria and had to seek employment on the basis of his published book.

13 Popper, *Unended Quest*, p. 119.

14 In what follows, all references to Popper's correspondence with Carnap, unless otherwise indicated, are to letters in The Karl Popper Archives, Box 282, file 24.

15 The superstition that Popper is referring to here is historicism—or the belief that the course of history is predetermined. Popper argued that historicism

was a reaction to the problem of change, and he regarded it as implicit in any theory which, like Marx's, tries to predict the course of future economic and political developments. (See Popper, *The Open Society and Its Enemies*, vol. 2, p. 83.)

16 Carnap to Popper, 9 February 1946.

17 Carnap to Popper, 29 January 1943.

18 F.A. Hayek, *The Road to Serfdom*, The University of Chicago Press, Chicago, 1944.

19 Popper to Carnap, 25 April 1946.

20 The assessment offered here corresponds with Popper's own. In his *Unended Quest* (p. 115), for example, Popper writes:

... these books [*The Poverty of Historicism* and *The Open Society and Its Enemies*] were meant as a defense of freedom against totalitarian and authoritarian ideas, and as a warning against the dangers of historicist superstitions...

In *The Open Society* I stressed that the critical method, though it will use tests wherever possible, and preferably practical tests, can be generalized into what I described as the critical or rational attitude. I argued that one of the best senses of 'reason' and 'reasonableness' was openness to criticsm—readiness to be criticized, and eagerness to criticize oneself; and I tried to argue that this critical attitude of reasonableness should be extended as far as possible...

Implicit in this attitude is the realization that we shall always have to live in an imperfect society.

21 Carnap to Popper, 27 May 1947. Carnap also sees a 'difference in emphasis' in their attitudes toward socialization, with Carnap estimating its usefulness 'in a certain given situation more highly' and Popper putting 'more weight ... on the danger involved.' Carnap also sees a difference in their views regarding 'the first aim of Socialism':

You seem to regard as the first aim of Socialism 'A greater equalization of incomes.' For me this point seems less important than the question of economic power. The situation seems to me to be analogous to the question of monarchy. I take it that our chief argument against monarchy is not our objection against the unusually high income of a king, which seems to me rather unimportant, but rather our objection against the concentration of more or less unlimited power in one person. Analogously, my main objection against capitalism is not directed so much against the high income of some capitalists, which again seems to me rather unimportant, but rather against the concentration of not sufficiently limited or regulated power concentrated in the hand of a private individual or group.

But Popper, insofar as this is concerned, agreed with Carnap's objection to the concentration of unregulated power in the hands of a private individual or group. He simply recognized that the concentration of unregulated power in the hands of the state or a public group would not necessarily solve the problem, and that it might even make things worse.

22 Though Carnap does say that he had the impression from Neurath 'that the Socialistic movement in Vienna was distinguished by being less dogmatic and based upon scientific analysis of the actual situation to a higher degree than most of the other Socialistic movements in European countries.' (Carnap to Popper, 27 May 1947.) And this, I think, is ironic. Carnap believes that emotional appeal and a religious attitude are necessary for the success of socialism. But he is trying to say that socialism need not be as dogmatic and unscientific as Popper suggests. Popper, however, had himself *experienced* the socialist movement in Vienna, and he found it too dogmatic and bureaucratic for his taste. So if socialism was really less dogmatic and more scientific in Vienna, then that only makes matters worse.

23 Correspondence between Carnap and Neurath in the University of Chicago's Archives of the Unity of Science Movement suggests that Carnap had ambivalent thoughts about democracy. While Neurath had hopes that the movement might play a role in democratizing Europe, Carnap worried 'whether democracy is actually incompatible with efficient planning and regulation.' (Carnap to Neurath, 24 June 1942.)

24 See Karl R. Popper, *Die beiden Grundprobleme der Erkenntnistheorie*, zweite, verbesserte Auflage, herausgegeben von Troels Eggers Hansen, J.C.B. Mohr (Paul Siebeck), Tübingen, 1979.

25 See Popper, *Unended Quest*, p. 89. Popper also refers to this vacation in Karl R. Popper, 'The Demarcation Between Science and Metaphysics' in *The Philosophy of Rudolf Carnap*, edited by P.A. Schilpp, Open Court, La Salle, 1963, p. 183.

26 See Rudolf Carnap, 'Über Protokollsätze' in *Erkenntnis*, 3, 1932.

27 But I do not wish to leave the wrong impression. Carnap, for whatever reason, did not always acknowledge Popper's influence, and in the end wrote that Popper's ideas did not play 'quite the central role in the development of my views which he ascribes to them.' (Rudolf Carnap, 'Replies and Systematic Expositions' in *The Philosophy of Rudolf Carnap*, p. 880.)

But Popper, as is clear from his correspondence with Carnap, thought that Carnap did not always remember exactly where his ideas came from—and did not always acknowledge their correct sources even when he did.

In 1942, for example, Carnap sent Popper a copy of his *Introduction to Semantics* (Harvard University Press, Cambridge, 1942) and later a letter, dated 17 June, asking for his comments. In the 'few remarks on the *Introduction to Semantics*' that he appended to his 15 October 1942 reply, Popper parenthetically writes:

(By the way: you mention on p. 151 Wittgenstein: 'For the assertive power of a sentence consists in its excluding certain states of affairs (Wittgenstein).' But I think you had here not W. in mind, but my book, esp. the last lines of p. 67 and many other passages. This, indeed, was just one of my fundamental ideas, and I do not think I got it from W. I have searched the *Tractatus*, and I could not find anything like it.)

Carnap later acknowledged Popper in this connection in his *Logical Foundations of Probability* (University of Chicago Press, Chicago, 1950, p. 406), saying 'my previous reference to Wittgenstein in this context ([Semantics]), p. 151) was due to an error of memory.' But twelve years later, Carnap sent Popper a copy of a 'Dear Friends' letter, dated January 1962, asking for comments on the first draft of a new preface to the second edition of his *Logical Foundations of Probability* (University of Chicago Press, Chicago, 1962), and 'especially on the terminological questions (about which I am rather uncertain) and on Popper's criticisms (to which I wish to do full justice).' In a letter dated 9 February 1962, Popper writes:

I now come to p. 8, and your remark 'Thus I recognize now...' starting in line 7 from the bottom of this page; and here I wish to say that I pointed this out for the last seven years—namely that your three concepts did not fit together. This I said in all the relevant publications. I feel that if you wish to do full justice to my criticism, this may well be mentioned.

28 See Popper, *Unended Quest*, pp. 88–90.
29 'With the outbreak of the war and Neurath's death in England some years later, the movement lost its cohesion.' (A.J. Ayer, ed., *Logical Positivism*, The Free Press, New York, 1959, p. 7.)
30 See Rudolf Carnap, 'Intellectual Autobiography' in *The Philosophy of Rudolf Carnap*, p. 23.
31 Otto Neurath, 'Sociology and Physicalism,' translated by Morton Magnus and Ralph Raico, in *Logical Positivism*, edited by A.J. Ayer, The Free Press, New York, 1959, p. 282.
32 Neurath, 'Sociology and Physicalism,' p. 283.
33 Neurath, 'Sociology and Physicalism,' p. 309.
34 According to Neurath ('Sociology and Physicalism,' pp. 282–283):

Unified science will be pursued in the same fashion as the individual sciences have been pursued hitherto. Thus, the 'thinker without a school' will have no more significance than he had when the sciences were disunited. The individual can here achieve just as much or just as little with isolated notions as he could before. Every proposed innovation must be so formulated that it may be expected to gain universal acceptance. Only through the cooperative effort of many thinkers do all its implications become clear. If it is false or meaningless, i.e., metaphysical, then, of course, it falls outside the range of unified science. Unified science, alongside of which there exists no 'philosophy' or 'metaphysics,' is not the achievement of isolated individuals, but of a generation.

35 So it is, perhaps, not too surprising that Reichenbach insists, *contra* Poincaré's claim that the geometry we use is a matter of convention and not of truth, that the question 'Which is the true geometry' is an *empirical* question and is to be decided by observation and measurement—*given*, of course, the conventional stipulation of a co-ordinating definition of the metric. (See Hans Reichenbach, 'The Philosophical Significance of the Theory of Relativity' in *Albert Einstein: Philosopher-Scientist*, edited by P.A. Schilpp, Open Court, La Salle, 1949, p. 297.) For what we have here is Carnap's distinction between the inside and the outside of the framework. (See Rudolf Carnap, 'Empiricism, Semantics, and Ontology' in *Revue Internationale de Philosophie*, IV, 1950.) And it is, in this light, at least interesting that Einstein, in response to the question 'Do you consider true what Reichenbach has here asserted?' writes: 'I can answer only with Pilate's famous question: "What is truth?"' (Albert Einstein, 'Reply to Criticisms' in *Albert Einstein: Philosopher-Scientist*, p. 676.)

36 Carnap, *The Logical Structure of the World & Pseudoproblems in Philosophy*, p. vii.

37 The difference here pertains to their appeal to argument. Whereas Popper piled argument upon argument in his criticism of positivism, Wittgenstein preferred to remain aloof.

38 References to Neurath's correspondence with Carnap, unless otherwise indicated, are to letters collected in the University of Chicago's Archives of the Unified Science Movement.

39 Carnap makes the charge in a letter to Charles Morris regarding Neurath's *Foundations of the Social Sciences*. And Neurath, in his 16 June 1945 letter to Carnap, quotes from Carnap's letter to Morris as follows:

I understand very well, that you, even if you felt likewise critical, hesitated to write to N. first because of the lack of time, and then also because of his sensitivity and violent emotional reactions to criticism and his obstinacy and unwillingness to accept suggestions for improvement from anybody ... I am convinced that the monograph will do more harm than good for the Encyclopedia and for the movement of empiricism in general. But I realize that to antagonize and offend N. now could possibly do still more harm. (Ellipsis in original.)

40 According to Neurath ('Sociology and Physicalism,' pp. 284–285):

The conclusion of the *Tractatus*, 'Whereof one cannot speak, thereof one must be silent,' is, at least grammatically, misleading. It sounds as if there were a 'something' of which one could not speak. We should rather say: if one really wishes to avoid the metaphysical attitude entirely, then one will 'be silent,' but not 'about something.'

We have no need of any metaphysical ladder of elucidation. We cannot follow Wittgenstein in this matter, although his great significance for logic is not, for that reason, to be less highly valued.

41 Neurath writes:

> I cannot deny that I did not give way to suggestions, I should look at Wittgenstein
> from a different angle etc. BUT NEVERTHELESS AS YOU CAN TESTIFY, I be-
> haved very collaboratively as we put together the WIENER KREIS pamphlet. Feigl,
> at that time fully occupied by Wittgenstein's greatness, and Waismann tried to put
> into that pamphlet an eulogy on Wittgenstein—and there it stands, supported by you
> and Hahn. Of course I am 'responsible' for that as one of the three editors, but on the
> other hand, I got the permission to put the 'EINHEITSWISSENSCHAFT' into the
> pamphlet, too.

42 See Carnap, 'Intellectual Autobiography,' pp. 22–24.

9 Is Freudian Psychoanalytic Theory *Really* Falsifiable? (and other political questions)[1]

> *We say that a dream is the fulfillment of a wish; but if you want to take these latter objections into account, you can say nevertheless that a dream is an attempt at the fulfillment of a wish. No one who can properly appreciate the dynamics of the mind will suppose that you have said anything different by this.*
>
> Sigmund Freud

> *I wish to criticize Freud's way of rejecting criticism.*
>
> Karl R. Popper

I

My paper has a story behind it that needs both a preface and a postscript. Its title, 'Is Freudian Psychoanalytic Theory *Really* Falsifiable?,' is meant to suggest that it is *not* falsifiable, and that someone else has said that it is. That someone else is Adolf Grünbaum, who, while President of the American Philosophical Association, published a book entitled *The Foundations of Psychoanalysis*. I do not know whether you have heard about this book. But it received a good deal of press in the United States, where it was widely praised for laying to rest Karl Popper's claim that psychoanalysis is a pseudo-science. Indeed, some of the newspapers in the States carried photos of both Grünbaum and Popper in their reviews, but *not* of Freud, which shows that even the journalists had realized that it was Popper, and not Freud, who was the real target of Grünbaum's critique.

I was spending a year as 'Lecturer in Psychiatry and Philosopher in Residence' at the Phipps Psychiatric Clinic of The John Hopkins Medical Institutions when Grünbaum's book appeared. I had not yet met Popper, and my own book about his anti-psychologism, *Objectivity, Rationality, and the Third Realm*, was still at press. But I had the fancy title since Paul McHugh, who was Chairman of the Department of Psychiatry, had invited me to Hopkins to teach his residents about Popper's philosophy.

McHugh and I were asked to review Grünbaum's book by different journals—by *Behavioral and Brain Sciences*, which devoted an entire issue to it, and by *Metaphilosophy*. Since we were already meeting on a regular basis and had formed the same general impression of Grünbaum's book, we decided to join forces and co-author our reviews.

What had impressed me most about *The Foundations of Psychoanalysis* was the triviality of its central claim. Grünbaum had argued that psychoanalysis *is* science, only to conclude, for many of the same reasons that led Popper to say that is unfalsifiable, that it is not very *good* science. But I was also struck by its willful misrepresentation of Popper's philosophy, and especially by its sneering and *ad hominem* tone. Grünbaum actually went so far as to question whether Popper had ever read Freud—and then, as if not noticing the inconsistency, to suggest that Popper had even doctored some of the passages that he quoted from Freud's texts while not reading them.

I did not really know what to think when I read this attack. But the little that I knew about Freud's concept of projection led me to check Grünbaum's own quotations. And this led me to the discovery that there may be a lot of truth in Freudian psychoanalysis, and especially in its idea of projection, even if it is ultimately unfalsifiable.

But the story that I have to tell is not about misquotation.

Behavioral and Brain Sciences had solicited about forty 'peer reviews' and their format called for Grünbaum to reply to each of them. But when he read our critique, the bulk of which I had written, Grünbaum immediately wrote to McHugh demanding that we withdraw it from publication. And when we refused to withdraw it, he wrote to the journal demanding that it not be published. And when the journal refused to suppress it, he said that he would not reply to it at all.

I remember that McHugh, at the time, suggested that I might want to drop my name as co-author, since I was then only beginning my career, and since 'things might get tough.' But I declined, thinking that there was nothing to worry about, and the review was published under both of our names. And when it was, we found that Grünbaum had devoted more space in his reply to it than to almost any other.

But none of what he said even came close to addressing my criticism that neither Popper nor Freud had said some of the things that he said they said. And when I later asked Grünbaum about it at a conference, he assured me that my criticism of his book would 'boomerang.'

I do not know exactly what he meant by this. But years later, when I was down on my luck, the chairman of a philosophy department in the States told me quite pointedly that young men who dare to reveal the intellectual *faux pas* of their elders are usually 'drummed out of the profession.'

This was not my first such experience, or my last. But when I look back at it now, I think that I have learned more from Grünbaum's book about how The Scientific Institution works than from anything else that I ever read.

II

With that as a preface, let me begin by saying that there is a lot in *The Foundations of Psychoanalysis* that needs to be sorted out. Grünbaum, on the surface, is arguing that psychoanalytic theory as conceived by Freud qualifies for scientific status, and is in need of empirical scrutiny; that the *clinical* observations claimed by Freud and others to provide the empirical evidence for it are 'remarkably weak' by inductivist standards;[2] and 'that the validation of Freud's cardinal hypotheses has to come, if at all, mainly from well designed extraclinical studies.'[3]

Grünbaum says that such extraclinical testing is largely a task for the future. But he also says that when such tests have been carefully performed their results tend to run counter to the predictions of psychoanalysis.[4] So his defense of the *scientific* status of psychoanalysis is *not* a defense of its *probative* status. Grünbaum acknowledges that 'it may perhaps still turn out that Freud's brilliant theoretical imagination was actually quite serendipitous for psychopathology or the understanding of some subclass of slips.'[5] But he concludes that 'while psychoanalysis may thus be said to be scientifically alive, it is currently hardly well, at least insofar as its clinical foundations are concerned.'[6]

Grünbaum's critique of the clinical evidence that is supposed to support psychoanalysis is rigorous, cogent, and generally on target. But it is not too surprising to anyone who is familiar with Popper's claim that psychoanalysis is unfalsifiable. And *this*, I think, *is* surprising. For his claim that psychoanalysis is falsifiable is explicitly presented as a critique of Popper's claim that it is not.

Grünbaum's critique of Popper is complicated, and it goes well beyond whether or not psychoanalysis is unfalsifiable. Grünbaum says that (a) Popper's critique of psychoanalysis is '*the centerpiece* of his castigation of *inductivism* qua method of scientific theory-validation and/or criterion of demarcation,'[7] and that (b) Popper's use of psychoanalysis as an example in his critique of induction is based upon a caricature of inductive standards that mistakes 'enumerative induction' as paradigmatic of inductive method.[8] He then says that (c) Popper has not proved that psychoanalytic theory is unfalsifiable,[9] and presents observational scenarios to show that (d) psychoanalytic theory is falsifiable after all.[10] And he finally tries to 'demonstrate' by textual citation that (e) Freud was open to the possibility of falsification and that he actively sought counterexamples to his theories.[11]

The truth of (b), according to Grünbaum, would vitiate any need for Popper's alternative to the inductivist criterion of demarcation by falsifying his claim that the 'confirmations' claimed by psychoanalysis are inductively sanctioned.[12] And the truth of any one of (c)-(e) would falsify Popper's claim that psychoanalytic theory is unfalsifiable and, contrary to Popper but in accordance with his own criterion of demarcation, establish the scientific character of psychoanalysis. Each of these points is logically independent of the others, but an important dialectical relationship emerges in the course of Grünbaum's critique. For if (a) is true, then the truth of any one of (b), (c), (d), or (e) would, according to Grünbaum, undercut Popper's more important attack on inductivism. And this, I think, is significant. For as (a) might suggest, it is inductivism, and not psychoanalysis, that Grünbaum is out to defend.

In my view, Grünbaum's claim that Popper's critique of inductivism is based upon a caricature of inductive standards is itself based upon a caricature of Popper's critique of inductivism. For it is based upon the idea that Popper's claim that psychoanalysis is unfalsifiable is the centerpiece of his critique. And this, I will try to show, is simply not true.

In what follows, I will argue that (a), (b), and (c) betray serious misunderstandings of Popper's philosophy of science. These misunderstandings have their root in the idea that Popper regarded scientific knowledge as a form of justified true belief—an idea that is common among inductivists who fail to take his denial of this idea seriously. (d) and (e), on the other hand, have been acknowledged by Popper. But I will argue that they are not really as compelling as Grünbaum suggests.

III

Psychoanalysis, according to Grünbaum, is *bad* science—or, at the very least, science not yet shown good. But it is, for Grünbaum and for all its faults, *science* nonetheless.

But how high is the wall that separates bad science from non-science?

Systematic explanatory theories that claim to be scientific but which, for one reason or another, are not are sometimes called 'pseudo-sciences.' Here, 'pseudo' refers not to the theory's claims about the truth of its subject matter, but to its metaclaim about itself. Popper, insofar as this is concerned, believed that pseudo-sciences should be carefully distinguished from false scientific theories. The latter are clearly false, but the former might well be true.[13] But he also believed that the distinction has nothing to do with justification, for *no* theory, according to Popper, can be justified or confirmed. Popper's distinction, on the contrary, is based upon testability. Scientific theories admit of severe and sincere empirical testing. Pseudo-sciences, for one reason or another, do not.[14]

This is Popper's criterion of demarcation. *In order to be scientific a theory must be falsifiable.* But here, there are different reasons why a theory might be regarded as *unfalsifiable.*[15] One reason is that the theory conflicts with no possible observations. But another and perhaps more common reason is that its proponents *refuse* to acknowledge the truth of anything that might falsify it. Popper, insofar as this is concerned, held that *no* theory can be *conclusively* falsified, because *any* theory can *immunize* itself against falsification through the assumption of *ad hoc* hypotheses or through other evasive tactics.[16] Marxism, according to Popper, thus *began* as an empirical science, but then, in its attempt to evade falsification, hopped the wall into pseudo-scientifica.[17]

But if this is true, then *any* universal generalization can be regarded as scientific *so long as its proponents are willing to acknowledge possible observations as falsifications.*

Popper, insofar as this is concerned, wrote that Freudian psychoanalysis is 'a programme for a psychological science, comparable to atomism or materialism, or the electromagnetic theory of matter, or Faraday's field theory, which were all programmes for physical science';[18] that he was 'convinced that Freud could have vastly improved his theory, had his attitude towards criticism been different';[19] and that 'much of what [Freud and Adler] say is of considerable importance, and may well play its part one day in a psychological science which is testable.'[20] He also wrote that his falsifiability criterion 'is vague, since it is a methodological rule, and since the demarcation between science and nonscience is vague.'[21]

Grünbaum for some reason deletes this line and leaves a quite different impression when he quotes Popper as saying:

> My criterion of demarcation ... is more than sharp enough to make a distinction between many physical theories on the one hand, and metaphysical theories, such as psychoanalysis, or Marxism (in its present [as distinct from the original] form), on the other. This is, of course, one of my main theses; and nobody who has not understood it can be said to have understood my theory.[22]

But this vagueness in the falsifiability criterion is important. For it means that scientific theories like Marx's can *become* pseudo-scientific due to a failure to acknowledge falsification, and that nonscientific theories like psychoanalysis can *become* scientific simply by specifying what would count as a falsification—*and sticking to it*.

Falsifiability depends in part upon logical form. Existential generalizations[23] may be verifiable, but they are not falsifiable since it is impossible to show that something does not exist. But universal generalizations[24] are usually falsifiable, since one genuine counter-example is enough to show that they are false. Falsifiability, however, also depends upon the critical attitude. And what Popper was criticizing when he claimed that *psychoanalysis* is unfalsifiable was not its logical form, but 'Freud's way of rejecting criticism.'[25] Thus, Popper writes that:

> Freud was by far the most lucid and persuasive of the expositors of the theories to which I am referring. But what was his method of argument? He gave examples; he analyzed them, and showed that they fitted his theory, or that his theory might be described as a generalization of the cases analyzed. He sometimes appealed to his readers to postpone their criticism, and he indicated that he would answer all reasonable criticism on a later occasion. But when I looked a little more closely at a number of important cases, I found that the answers never came.[26]

Scientific inquiry is oft-times likened to a mystery story. And Freud is oft-times more ingenious than Sherlock Holmes. Holmes begins with the facts, and the mystery is in finding a theory that explains them. Freud, on the other hand, begins with both a theory and the facts. This would not be bad if Freud used the facts to *test* his theory's truth. But in Freud's case, it is not so much the theory as the facts that are in doubt. *His* mystery more often consists in finding a way to *fit* the facts to the theory. And this is not always simple. In many cases, it requires 'deductions' that are breathtaking. Indeed, we will see that it was necessary in some cases for Freud to 'deduce' what the facts *really* were—to deduce, that is, what they *must* have been, assuming that his theory is true.[27] There can be little doubt these 'deductions' required ingenuity, or that Freud usually proved adequate to the task. But this, I take it, was the primary point of Popper's critique.

IV

But is it really true that Popper's critique of psychoanalysis is the centerpiece of his attack on inductivism?

In my view, that 'centerpiece' is more likely to be found in the detailed *arguments* against induction—both as logically valid inference and as psychological theory of learning—that Popper presents in *The Logic of Scientific Discovery*, *Objective Knowledge*, and *Realism and the Aim of Science*.

Popper rejects induction as the method of science in *The Logic of Scientific Discovery* and he introduces falsifiability as its criterion of demarcation, but he never mentions psychoanalysis or Freud at all. He explains his solution to the problem of induction in *Objective Knowledge* and he complains that philosophers have generally ignored it, but he mentions Freud only once in the entire book, and that is in a footnote regarding realism. And he discusses the problem of induction in *Realism and the Aim of Science* for one hundred forty-seven pages without ever mentioning Freud or psychoanalysis, and when he finally does mention them, it is again not in connection with the problem of induction. On the contrary, he writes that:

> In the present context, it hardly matters whether or not I am right concerning the irrefutability of any of these three theories [psychoanalysis, individual psychology, and Marxism]: here they serve merely as examples, as illustrations. For my purpose is to show that my 'problem of demarcation' was from the beginning the practical problem of assessing theories, and of judging their claims. It certainly was not a problem of classifying or distinguishing some subject matters called 'science' and 'metaphysics.' It was, rather, an urgent practical problem: under what conditions is a *critical appeal to experience* possible—one that could bear some fruit?[28]

Popper tries in each of these works to resolve the apparent tension between what he calls 'the principle of the invalidity of induction' ('there can be no valid reasoning from singular observation statements to universal laws of nature, and thus scientific theories') and 'the principle of empiricism' ('we demand that our adoption and our rejection of scientific theories should depend upon the results of observation and experiment, and thus upon singular observation statements').[29] But the problem, as he understood it, is not just that inductive arguments are invalid. It is also that the use of inductive arguments to 'justify' scientific theories presupposes that the singular observation statements that serve as their premises are, or can themselves, be justified. Inductivists say that such statements are justified by observations. But Popper rejected this approach as a form of psychologism that results in an irrationalist epistemology. And his move, in each of these works, is to abandon justification as a criterion of knowledge and to use singular observation statements to *criticize* theories instead of to justify them.

Now one would expect, if his critique of psychoanalysis were really supposed to be the centerpiece of his attack on inductivism, that Popper would focus upon psychoanalysis in these works, or at least mention it in connection with his critique of induction. But he simply does not. He *does* say in *The Logic of Scientific Discovery* that 'my main reason for rejecting inductive logic is precisely that *it does not provide a suitable distinguishing mark* of the empirical, non-metaphysical character of a theoretical system; or in other words, that *it does not provide a suitable "criterion of demarcation"*.'[30] But he also says that he discovered his falsifiability criterion of demarcation prior to his solution of the problem of induction. And he discusses the problem of demarcation in each of these works as a *consequence* of his critique of induction—for 'if you abandon induction, *how can you distinguish the theories of the empirical sciences from pseudo-scientific or non-scientific or metaphysical speculations?*'[31]

Grünbaum, however, does not refer to these books at all. He instead announces that:

> On turning to [*Conjectures and Refutations*] (chap.1, sections 1 and 2; pp. 156–157, 255–258), we find that not so much psychoanalysis itself (or present-day Marxism) is the prime target of [Popper's] charge of non-falsifiability, but rather its role as a *centerpiece* of his castigation of *inductivism* qua method of scientific theory-validation and/or criterion of demarcation.[32]

And once announced, Grünbaum's idea that psychoanalysis is the centerpiece of Popper's critique of inductivism becomes the centerpiece of his own critique of Popper. For when Peter Urbach complains that 'Popper was concerned to expose the *delusion* of the Freudians that the purported confirmations satisfy inductivist canons,'[33] Grünbaum responds that 'Urbach's reading boomerangs, for it completely undercuts Popper's avowed purpose to adduce psychoanalysis as a prime illustration of his thesis that the inductivist criterion of demarcation is unacceptably permissive, and that his falsificationist alternative is more stringent.'[34]

But is there any merit to Urbach's interpretation? Or, more simply, is Grünbaum's claim that Popper attacked a caricature of inductivism true?

This is more challenging. Popper often put 'confirmation' and 'verification' in quotes or italics when referring to psychoanalysis. And he also wrote that a nonscientific theory 'cannot claim to be backed by empirical evidence in the scientific sense—although it may easily be, in some genetic sense, the "result of observation".'[35] This may suggest that there are conditions under which theories may be regarded as confirmed after all. Indeed, at least two of the conclusions that he formulated in *Conjectures and Refutations* as a result of his reflections on Marxism and psychoanalysis state conditions under which confirmations should count:

> Confirmations should count only if they are the result of *risky predictions*; that is to say, if, unenlightened by the theory in question, we should have expected an event which was incompatible with the theory—an event which would have refuted the theory.[36]

and:

> Confirming evidence should not count *except when it is the result of a genuine test of the theory*; and this means that it can be presented as a serious but unsuccessful attempt to falsify the theory. (I now speak in such cases of 'corroborating evidence.')[37]

Each of these passages could be interpreted as promoting the sort of 'eliminative inductivism' that Grünbaum says Popper has ignored. But this would hardly resolve the problem. For if Popper's critique of psychoanalysis *is* the centerpiece of his critique of inductivism, and if that critique *is* based upon a caricature, then Popper would have simply replaced his own caricature with the more detailed portrait sketched by Bacon nearly four centuries ago. And *that* would be neither new nor a critique of inductivism. And if Urbach's interpretation is right, well, then what *is* Popper's critique of inductivism?

Here, Popper's parenthetical remark—I now speak in such cases of 'corroborating evidence'—provides a hint. But how does 'corroborating' evidence differ from 'confirming' evidence? And why did Popper *stop* speaking of confirmation and talk about corroboration instead?

Here, the difference between corroborating and confirming evidence is not so much in the nature of the evidence as it is in the interpretation of how the evidence supports the theory. Corroborating evidence supports a theory only in the sense that it *does not contradict* it—only, that is, in the sense that it is what we might expect if the theory in question is true. Corroboration, for this reason, is essentially concerned with a theory's past performance. A high degree of corroboration may lead us to prefer one theory over another, but it says nothing whatsoever about how the theory will perform in the future.[38]

Popper says that he used the term '*Bewährung*' in his *Logik der Forschung* because he wanted a word to describe how a hypothesis had stood up to severe tests that did not prejudge the question whether or not that hypothesis is 'more probable' as a result of having passed those tests. He says that he wanted such a term precisely so that he could discuss the problem whether or not 'degree of corroboration' could be identified with 'probability.' Carnap, however, translated '*Bewährung*' as 'confirmation' in 'Testability and Meaning.'[39] Popper says that he did not like this term because it suggests that theories with high degrees of confirmation have been 'firmly established' or 'put beyond doubt' or 'proved'—but he also began to use it, thinking that words do not matter, when Carnap declined his proposal to use 'corroboration' instead. He found, however, that Carnap and others were soon using 'confirmation' as an 'explicans' of 'probability,' and he eventually abandoned it entirely in favor of 'corroboration.'[40]

Here it is clear that Popper's critique of inductivism has less to do with a failure to use eliminative testing than with the inductivists' claim that such testing could, when used properly, *verify*, or *confirm*, or in some way *prove* the theory being tested. The argument is *not* that inductivists or psychoanalysts mistakenly construe psychoanalysis as verified or justified or confirmed. It is that inductivism is a form of verificationism, and that universal generalizations in general can be neither verified nor justified nor confirmed by empirical observations. So if inductive verification were the mark of the scientific, then scientific laws should not be regarded as scientific. But existential generalizations, on the other hand, *are* verifiable. So 'the arch-metaphysical assertion' that 'God exists' would, in that case, have to be regarded as scientific.[41] It was, simply put, a critique of the idea that inductive inference could be used as a means for *justifying* empirical theories.

Popper accepted Hume's idea that inductive inference is invalid, but he rejected justification as a criterion of knowledge. He then proposed falsifiability as a criterion of demarcation in order to show how epistemology could distinguish science from pseudo-science without appealing to justification or inductive inference. His critique of inductivism and his falsifiability criterion of demarcation are, nonetheless, logically distinct—which is why Carnap was able to use falsifiability (testability) as a criterion of demarcation while retaining the idea that scientific theories are and must be justified through induction. Popper, on the other hand, believed that no theory can be justified. And he also believed that theories do not need to be justified in order to count as scientific knowledge. This is his anti-justificationism. The *arguments* for it are found throughout *The Logic of Scientific Discovery*, *Objective Knowledge*, and *Realism and the Aim of Science*.[42]

This, I think, should also defuse Grünbaum's charge that Popper has not justified his claim that psychoanalysis is unfalsifiable. For if he really thought that justification is impossible, then it would hardly make sense for him to try to justify that claim. *No* theory, according to Popper, can be justified—not even the theory that psychoanalysis is unfalsifiable. Theories can, however, be *tested*. And one way to test Popper's claim is to try to see whether or not we can think of possible falsifying observations.

We can, with this in mind, now turn to the observational scenarios that Grünbaum presents to show that psychoanalysis is falsifiable.

V

Grünbaum claims that Freud's theory that paranoia is a defense against homosexual impulses can be falsified by epidemiological evidence showing paranoia in *avowed* homosexuals. This is interesting, but problematic. Freud's theory of paranoia is hardly a central plank of psychoanalytic theory,[43] and Freud himself held that paranoia is 'not usually amenable to analytic investigation.'[44] The example also raises a host of questions about the identity of mental states that would have to be resolved prior to any proper assessment of its merits. But before we consider such questions, it is necessary to raise a purely logical issue. For in order for paranoia in an *avowed* homosexual to count as a falsification of Freud's theory, the theory would, at least, have to claim that paranoia is *always* accompanied by repressed homosexual impulses.

Here, questions concerning the causal role of homosexuality in the psychogenesis of paranoia can be left aside. It will suffice if Freud claims that the two are constantly conjoined. But it is not clear that this is what he actually claims. In his discussion of the Schreber case, Freud says that homosexual impulses are 'frequently (perhaps invariably) to be found in paranoia.'[45] And in 'A Case of Paranoia Running Counter to the Psycho-Analytic Theory of the Disease,' he writes that 'we had not, it is true, asserted that paranoia is always without exception conditioned by homosexuality; but only because our observations were not sufficiently numerous.'[46] This suggests that Freud *wanted* to claim that paranoia is always accompanied by homosexuality, and perhaps even caused by it. But it does not quite add up to doing so. On the contrary, Freud is here explaining why he had *not* made that claim. But the discovery of paranoia in avowed homosexuals would not falsify Freud's theory unless it actually claims that paranoia is always and without exception accompanied by homosexuality.

But let us assume that the theory does say that paranoia is always accompanied by repressed homosexual impulses. Popper's reply might be that this claim is unfalsifiable since it is impossible to demonstrate that repressed impulses do not exist. Grünbaum, however, argues that the theory *is* falsifiable. For it would be impossible for avowed homosexuals to be paranoid, if paranoia is always accompanied by repressed homosexual impulses, because the homosexual impulses of an *avowed* homosexual would, by definition, not be repressed. But whether or not there exist avowed homosexuals suffering from paranoia is an empirical question that can be resolved through epidemiological research.

Grünbaum concludes that this part of Freudian theory is falsifiable, and that Popper's claim that Freudian theory is unfalsifiable is false.[47]

Grünbaum says that paranoia in an avowed homosexual would disprove Freud's theory. But what would Freud say? We believe today,[48] as Freud clearly suspected, that homosexuals vary widely in the intensity of their homosexual impulses—even when they consciously acknowledge them. Hence, Freud would undoubtedly want to look at the homosexual in question. But here, he would probably say that behavior alone reveals nothing about repression,[49] and he would insist upon using free association to seek for repressed homosexual impulses. But it would be difficult to prove the absence of *some* homosexual repressions by free association. And thus, it would be difficult to falsify this theory as Popper justly claims.

But wait a minute. Wouldn't free association be superfluous in this case? For isn't this case, after all, a case of *avowed* homosexuality?

But what exactly does Freud claim to be repressed in cases of paranoia? Homosexual *impulses*? Or the *belief* that one has them?

It may seem natural to understand Freud's theory as saying that paranoids repress the *belief* that they have homosexual impulses. But Freud talks about paranoids repressing the *impulses* themselves. The belief that one has homosexual impulses may be accompanied by a consciousness of them. But it also need not be. And *impulses*, in any event, are not beliefs—and nor are *beliefs* impulses.

Freud held that one can have impulses without believing that he has them. That, after all, is what his theory of neurosis is all about. He also held that it is possible for one's beliefs about his impulses to be mistaken. That is what his theory of repression is all about. But if this is true, then it should be child's play to construct a host of Gettier type examples[50] showing that one could both have homosexual impulses and believe that one has them—but believe it for the wrong reasons. And if this is possible, then it should also be possible that one could *profess* to have homosexual impulses and simultaneously *repress* the impulses themselves.

Consider, for example, Michael. Michael does in fact *have* homosexual impulses. He *believes* and *avows* that he has homosexual impulses. And he even engages in homosexual behavior. But Michael's belief that he has homosexual impulses is not due to his consciously feeling them—for Michael's homosexual impulses are in fact repressed. It is due instead to his acceptance of Freud's theory that *all* human beings have homosexual impulses. And Michael's homosexual behavior is not due to any conscious desire on his part to have homosexual relationships. It is due to his psychoanalyst's diagnosis that he has repressed homosexual impulses, and his prescription that he try to act them out. In this case, Michael would undoubtedly be an avowed homosexual—but, I would think, for all the wrong reasons.

If we now take the example one step further and imagine that Michael also suffers from paranoia, then we would have a case of an avowed homosexual paranoid who nonetheless also has repressed homosexual impulses.

But we really need not imagine all that much. For even if one is an avowed homosexual for all the right reasons, it does not follow that he is conscious of each and every one of his homosexual impulses. There is no reason why his awareness of some homosexual impulses should preclude his repression of others. And should such others exist, their repression might well be due to more threatening homosexual conflicts that have yet to be resolved. If heterosexual males generally repress their *heterosexual* impulses for their mothers, then it would seem possible that self-conscious homosexuals could repress their *homosexual* impulses toward specific persons as well. But if this *is* possible, then the existence of avowedly homosexual paranoids would prove nothing vis-à-vis Freudian theory.

Finally, while Grünbaum concedes the contextual dependence of Freudian theory and argues that contextual dependence is compatible with scientific status, he does not consider the effect that it might have upon this particular attempt at falsification. Freudians maintain that homosexual impulses are repressed and are an etiological pathogen in the psychogenesis of a psychosis because they are sexually/socially taboo. But few Freudians maintain that the taboo character of such impulses is necessary. Most Freudians regard taboos as culturally determined, and our repression of mental states that violate them as learned behavior. Indeed, many Freudians believe that a general recognition of our true polymorphic sexual identity would result in a brave new world in which no one would any longer feel the need to repress their homosexual impulses or their homosexual behavior.

But if it is possible to remove sexual/social taboos, then it is also possible to replace them. And if the taboo against homosexuality were replaced rather than removed, then its replacement might well emerge as a candidate for etiological status in the psychogenesis of paranoia. The existence of avowedly homosexual paranoids would, in such a world, at best be considered an anachronistic refutation of an outdated theory—one that held sway until, say, the early twenty-first century, and was recognized as falsifiable only after it had in fact been falsified, only after it had ceased to be the truth.

Popper acknowledged the possibility of avowedly homosexual paranoids as a potential falsifier of psychoanalytic theory.[51] But he apparently remained sceptical as to whether *Freud* would acknowledge it too. He pointed out both that the theory of paranoia was not part of the 'basic theory' that he was criticizing and that 'Freud could say of any apparently paranoid active homosexual that he is not *really* paranoid, or not *fully* active.'[52] This, of course, is fully consistent with the idea that what Popper was criticizing was Freud's way of rejecting criticism. And it leads us, finally, to Grünbaum's claim that Freud was open to the possibility of falsification and actively sought possible counterexamples to his theories.

VI

Grünbaum cites numerous passages regarding methodology from Freud's work to suggest both that Freud was an advocate of falsificationism and that Popper was seriously ignorant of his work when he criticized it in 1952, and when he reiterated his criticism in 1974.[53] He suggests, in fact, that Popper was either unaware that Freud had dealt with the problem of suggestibility[54] 'fourteen years before Popper was even born' or—as his chapter title 'Exegetical Myth-Making in Karl Popper's Indictment' insinuates—that he knowingly misrepresented the facts when he claimed that psychoanalysis is unfalsifiable.

It would be difficult to determine whether, to what extent, by what date, and with what understanding Popper read Freud. But the fact that he did not offer a detailed exegesis of Freud's works clearly does not mean that he was ignorant of them. And Grünbaum's claim that Popper was unaware of the fact that Freud had dealt with the suggestibility problem is at the least ironic, since the footnote by Popper that Grünbaum cites to support the idea *itself* refers to passages in which Freud discusses the problem.

Still, this charge of myth-making deserves some attention. Grünbaum correctly quotes Popper as saying:

> Years ago I introduced the term 'Oedipus effect' to describe the influence of a theory or expectation or prediction upon the event which it predicts or describes: it will be remembered that the causal chain leading to Oedipus' parricide was started by the oracle's prediction of this event. This is a characteristic and recurrent theme of such myths, but one which seems to have failed to attract the interest of the analysts, perhaps not accidentally.[55]

Now in my view, all Popper is saying here is that Freud and Freudian analysts have failed to take the problem seriously *enough*. For had they taken the problem seriously enough, then they would not have complete confidence in observations derived from free association alone. But Grünbaum, in his commentary on this passage, inexplicably attack's 'Popper's accusation that analysts are *oblivious* to the contamination problem.'[56] 'Thus,' he writes, Popper 'chides the Freudians for not having been aware, as he was, of the relevant moral of the Oedipus legend.'[57] And he then cites passages in which Freud discusses the problem of suggestibility in an effort to contradict what he calls Popper's 'incredibly uninformed and grossly unfair claim.'[58]

But who is being unfair to whom?

'Failed to attract the interest of' does not mean 'is oblivious to.' And it does not mean 'is unaware of' either. Moreover, in the very next sentence of Popper's footnote, *which Grünbaum also quotes*, Popper continues:

> (The problem of confirmatory dreams suggested by the analyst is discussed by Freud, for example in *Gesammelte Scriften*, III, 1925, where he says on p. 314: 'If anybody asserts that most of the dreams which can be utilized in an analysis ... owe their origin to [the analyst's] suggestion, then no objection can be made from the point of view of analytic theory. Yet there is nothing in this fact,' he surprisingly adds, 'which would detract from the reliability of our results.')[59]

Surely Popper knew that Freud was aware of the problem of suggestibility. And Grünbaum should know that he knew it too. But he nonetheless goes on to suggest that Popper actually doctored the text, saying that his 'citation from Freud borders on a sheer travesty':[60]

> Upon comparing Popper's excerpt to this original German wording or to S.E. 1923, 19: 117, it becomes evident that Popper simply truncated Freud's crucial sentence in a highly misleading way *without* any indication of this omission. Freud was responding to the criticism implied by the claim that most of the dreams that are interpreted in the course of an analysis are compliant dreams whose occurrence was induced by the analyst's expectation, and his response was as follows: 'Then I only need to refer to the discussion in my "Introductory Lectures [#28]," where the relation between transference and suggestion is dealt with, and it is shown how little the recognition of the effect of suggestion in our sense detracts from the reliability of our results.' Amid expressing surprise, Popper purports to be rendering this sentence in the following words: 'Yet there is nothing in this fact [of compliant dreams] which would detract from the reliability of our results.'[61]

Popper's citation is clearly truncated. But does it really border on a sheer travesty? Does it add or delete anything that would change or reverse the meaning of the text? I think not. For upon turning to Lecture #28, we find that Freud characterizes this criticism as 'groundless,' saying 'After all, his conflicts will only be successfully solved and his resistances overcome if the anticipatory ideas he is given tally with what is real in him.'[62] Grünbaum criticizes this argument in detail, while chiding Popper for failing to do so. He does not quite put it in these terms, but his criticism is that Freud's 'tally argument' is unfalsifiable.

But even if Grünbaum were right and Popper had never read Freud at all, and even if Popper had doctored all of the quotations he cited from Freud while not reading him, citing such passages from Freud does not, in itself, suffice to vindicate psychoanalysis from the claim that it is unfalsifiable. Psychoanalysis is a practical as well as a theoretical discipline, and there is a notorious and proverbial gap between theory and practice. So the fact that Freud makes certain comments about refutability does not, in and of itself, mean that Freud would actually be willing to *acknowledge* refutation. Jung, Adler, and Rank learned that lesson in a very hard way. Grünbaum, however, writes that:

> Even a casual perusal of the mere *titles* of Freud's papers and lectures in the *Standard Edition* yields two examples of falsifiability. The second is a case of acknowledged falsification, to boot. The first is the paper 'A Case of Paranoia Running Counter to the Psychoanalytic Theory of the Disease' (S.E. 1915, 14: 263–272); the second is the lecture 'Revision of the Theory of Dreams' (S.E. 1933, 22:7–30, especially pp. 28–30).[63]

But you cannot judge an article by its title, and we should not rely upon Grünbaum's 'casual perusal' either.

VII

In the first case that Grünbaum cites, Freud *thinks* about revising his theory and *entertains* the possibility of refutation, but never actually acknowledges refutation nor revises his theory at all. In fact, this case study shows Freud to be worried about the possibility of a paranoia not caused by repressed homosexual impulses for exactly *one* psychoanalytic session, only to 'discover' the expected homosexual repressions in the next. Of course, not every suspected refutation is a real one. But it is not so much the fact that Freud avoids refutation that is bothersome here as it is the *way* in which he avoids it. Through a breathless array of questionable associations and *ad hoc* assumptions—*including the assumption that his patient's account of the pertinent events are on several points and for various reasons false*—Freud 'deduces' his patient's expected repressed homosexual impulses in a way that would make Sherlock Holmes blush. Despite his disclaimer that 'the absence of a thorough analytic investigation makes it impossible in this case to go beyond a certain probability,'[64] Freud nonetheless writes:

> The patient mentioned in her first interview with me that she had immediately demanded an explanation of the noise, and had been told that it was probably the ticking of the little clock on the table. I take the liberty of assuming that this piece of information was a mistaken memory. It seems to me much more likely that at first she did not react to the noise at all, and that it became significant only after she met the two men on the staircase. Her friend, who had probably not even heard the noise, ventured the explanation, perhaps on some later occasion when she assailed him with her suspicions, 'I don't know what noise you can have heard. Perhaps it was the little clock; it sometimes ticks like that.' A subsequent use of impressions and displacement of recollections such as this occurs frequently in paranoia and is characteristic of it.
>
> I might go still further in the analysis of this apparently real 'accident.' I do not believe that the clock ever ticked or that any noise was to be heard at all. The woman's situation justified a sensation of throbbing in the clitoris. This was what she subsequently projected as a perception of an external object. Similar things occur in dreams. An hysterical patient of mine once related to me a short 'awakening' dream to which she could bring no spontaneous associations. She dreamt simply that someone knocked and then she awoke. Nobody had knocked, but during the previous nights she had been awakened by unpleasant sensations of pollutions: she had thus a motive for awakening as soon as she felt the first sign of genital excitation. There had been a 'knocking' of the clitoris. In the case of our paranoiac patient, I should substitute for the accidental noise a similar process of projection. I certainly cannot guarantee that during our short acquaintance the patient, who was reluctantly yielding to necessity, gave me a truthful account of all that had taken place during the two meetings. But an isolated clitoris-contraction would be in keeping with her statement that no contact

of the genitals had taken place. In her subsequent rejection of the man, lack of satisfaction undoubtedly played a part as well as 'conscience.'[65]

Grünbaum thinks that this paper shows that Freud was open to the possibility of refutation. But in my view, it was this very style of reasoning that led Popper to claim that psychoanalysis is unfalsifiable in the first place.

But perhaps Grünbaum's second example is more to the point—for this, according to Grünbaum, is supposed to be a case of *acknowledged* falsification. The case, moreover, pertains to Freud's theory of dreams, which, unlike his theory of paranoia, is undoubtedly a central plank of psychoanalytic theory. Popper discusses this case in section 18 of his *Realism and the Aim of Science*. He says that 'Freud was far less dogmatic than most of his followers'—before going on to criticize his 'way of rejecting criticism.'[66] But here it might be more instructive to learn from what Grünbaum has to say.

Early on in his critique of Popper Grünbaum says that 'Freud's 1933 "Revision of the Theory of Dreams" presents an acknowledged falsification by the recurrent dreams of war neurotics.'[67] But he defers further comment on this example until he himself is criticizing Freud one hundred eight pages, later. He then writes:

> True, in 1933, [Freud] acknowledged the existence of some exceptions to this universal claim [that wish fulfillment is the formative cause of any and all manifest dream contents] (S.E. 1933, 22:28–30), and he thus modified his wish fulfillment hypothesis. While retaining wish fulfillment as the impetus of dreaming, he acknowledged that it does miscarry with fair frequency. Hence, he then concluded that 'the dream may aptly be characterized as an *attempt* at the fulfillment of a wish' (S.E.1925, 20:46n; this footnote was added in 1935). In short, the motive for dreaming is still held to be a wish, but the dream that actually ensues is no longer claimed to qualify universally as its fulfillment. But let us defer comment on this rather minor modification and deal with Freud's unqualified generalization first.[68]

So what was first characterized as an 'acknowledged falsification' is here reduced to a 'rather minor modification.' But upon returning to the subject from yet a second deferral, Grünbaum concludes by quoting from Ernest Jones:

It may be pointed out, however, that none of these dreams were quite confined to an accurate presentation of the traumatic experience. One always found in them some other irrelevant feature which called for analysis, and which may well have signified a tendency to manipulate the traumatic memory in the direction of a wish-fulfillment, even if the patient waked in terror before this could be accomplished. Indeed it would seem possible to bring all the examples mentioned above under the broad tendency of abreaction.[69]

and, of course, from Freud:

We should not, I think, be afraid to admit that here the function of the dream has failed... But no doubt the exception does not overturn the rule. You can say nevertheless that a dream is an *attempt* at the fulfillment of a wish. In certain circumstances a dream is only able to put its intention into effect very incompletely, or must abandon it entirely. Unconscious fixation to a trauma seems to be foremost among these obstacles to the function of dreaming.[70]

I cannot imagine anything that would conflict more sharply with Popper's falsificationist attitude than Freud's notion that the exception does not overturn the rule. But Freud's 'rather minor modification' is minimized further by his retreat from wish fulfillments to *attempts* at wish fulfillment and, as Grünbaum justly characterizes it, by Jones' 'lame attempt to show that even the dreams of the war neurotics may well not require Freud's qualification after all.'[71]

But does Freud *really* acknowledge falsification as Grünbaum claims? Does he actually acknowledge that the dreams of war neurotics are not wish-fulfillments? And does he actually revise his claim that dreams are invariably the fulfillment of a wish? Grünbaum says that he does—even though the 'acknowledged falsification' turns out to be a 'rather minor modification' according to which dreams are not invariably wish-fulfillments, but *attempts* at wish-fulfillments. But upon checking Freud's 'Revision of the Theory of Dreams' I found reason to believe that he does not. This reason pertains partly to the passage deleted in Grünbaum's quotation of Freud, and partly to a second passage that he deleted without mention. Indeed, I do not even think that it would be accurate to characterize what Freud says there as an *attempt* at an acknowledged falsification. But to avoid further confusion, I will supply the material deleted by Grünbaum in context:

> With the traumatic neuroses things are different. In their case the dreams regularly end in the generation of anxiety. We should not, I think, be afraid to admit that here the function of the dream has failed. I will not invoke the saying that the exception proves the rule: its wisdom seems to me most questionable. But no doubt the exception does not overturn the rule. If, for the sake of studying it, we isolate one particular psychical function, such as dreaming, from the psychical machinery as a whole, we make it possible to discover the laws that are peculiar to it; but when we insert it once more into the general context we must be prepared to discover that these findings are obscured or impaired by collision with other forces. We say that a dream is the fulfillment of a wish; but if you want to take these latter objections into account, you can say nevertheless that a dream is an *attempt* at the fulfillment of a wish. No one who can properly appreciate the dynamics of the mind will suppose that you have said anything different by this. In certain circumstances a dream is only able to put its intention into effect very incompletely, or must abandon it entirely. Unconscious fixation to a trauma seems to be foremost among these obstacles to the function of dreaming.[72]

'We say that a dream is the fulfillment of a wish; but if you want to take these latter objections into account, you can say nevertheless that a dream is an attempt at the fulfillment of a wish. No one who can properly appreciate the dynamics of the mind will suppose that you have said anything different by this.'

Earlier I asked 'How high is the wall that separates bad science from nonscience?' There I suggested that the wall, at least according to Popper, is not very high at all. For an interesting metaphysical theory such as Freud's may provide a program for a scientific psychology. Grünbaum thinks that the above passage is an acknowledgement of a falsification. I think, on the contrary, that it is grist for Popper's mill.

But Freudians, in any event, should beware!

Falsifiability is always a mixed-blessing. False scientific theories are a dime a dozen, but a genuine pseudo-science is rather hard to find.

VIII

I am almost at the end of my story, but it does have a bit of a post-script, and I have not, in any event, yet told you what happened with *Metaphilosophy*. The long and the short of it is that when we submitted our review, the editor of the journal wrote to me saying that he was afraid that he could not publish it because it was the policy of his journal not to get involved in *political disputes.*

I confess that I was stunned when I read these words.

How is it that things in philosophy and science have gotten so bad that we can today regard such questions as whether or not psychoanalysis is a pseudo-science and whether or not someone has correctly quoted from someone else's text as political disputes?

Things might have ended there had I not written back saying that I did not understand what he could possibly mean by 'political disputes,' since I had nowhere in the article attacked Grünbaum's politics, and since I did not even know whether he was a Democrat or a Republican.

I am not quite sure whether he suddenly realized that he had misread our review, or whether he was just too embarrassed to ex-plain what he had meant by 'political disputes,' but he eventually wrote back saying that he would publish it after all. I admit that I almost immediately lost interest in the debate and that I have not kept up with the literature about it since publishing my review. For what is the point of such philosophical arguments if they are now regarded as political disputes, and if we are not prepared to ac-knowledge our mistakes and to learn from them?

I was, however, recently shown an article that Grünbaum pub-lished in the Vienna Circle Institute Yearbook[73] in which he men-tions me by name and quotes from the same passage that he mis-quoted fifteen years ago. I was happy to see that he has now changed his quotation, and I hope that it may even be as a result of my criticism. But I was sad to see that he continues to mislead his readers.

This time Grünbaum supplies one of the sentences that I had pointed out was missing, namely:

> We say that a dream is the fulfillment of a wish; but if you want to take these latter objections into account, you can say nevertheless that a dream is an *attempt* at the fulfillment of a wish.

But he apparently cannot bring himself to quote Freud's next sentence:

> *No one who can properly appreciate the dynamics of the mind will suppose that you have said anything different by this.*[74]

—which I had also pointed out was missing, and which shows quite clearly that Freud did *not* regard 'these latter objections' as falsifying his theory, or the idea that a dream is an *attempt* at the fulfillment of a wish as in any way a modification or revision of his theory. And he now deletes a sentence that he had originally quoted:

> But no doubt the exception does not overturn the rule.

—which I pointed out conflicts sharply with the falsificationist attitude.

So even now I sometimes wonder whether all of this was really worth the effort.

Nevertheless, I am also happy to find, *and to admit*, that I was mistaken to think that Grünbaum did not address my criticism that he had misrepresented both Popper and Freud. For I recently re-read his 1986 BBS reply to our review and found a passage in it that shows, absolutely and beyond the shadow of a doubt, both that he did respond to this charge and that he is ready and willing to acknowledge that he misrepresented them after all. I would like to call your attention to this passage, since it has, apparently, been missed by all of his other critics. So as to avoid further confusion, and also to set the record straight, I will here quote this passage, *à la Grünbaum*, in full. It reads as follows:

> What ... Notturno & McHugh say ... in ... criticizing ... my book ... is ... absolutely ... true.

Notes

1 This is a revised version of a paper that was presented at the Institute for Systems Analysis of the Russian Academy of Sciences in Moscow, Russia on 22 January 1992, and again at the Charles University Medical School in Prague, Czech Republic on 26 April 1995. An earlier version, co-authored with Paul McHugh, was published in *Metaphilosophy*, vol. 18, nos. 3 & 4, July/October 1987; a shorter version of which was published in *Behavioral and Brain Sciences*, vol. 9, no. 2, June 1986. The mottoes are from Sigmund Freud, *New Introductory Lectures on Psychoanalysis*, W.W. Norton Company, New York, 1933, p. 27; and from Karl R. Popper, *Realism and the Aim of Science*, 1983. Reprinted by Routledge, London, 1996, p. 168.

2 Adolf Grünbaum, *The Foundations of Psychoanalysis*, University of California Press, Berkeley, 1984, p. 278.

3 Grünbaum, *The Foundations of Psychoanalysis*, p. 278.

4 Grünbaum, *The Foundations of Psychoanalysis*, p. 278. The term 'psychoanalysis' is used in this paper, unless otherwise indicated, to mean the *theory* of psychoanalysis, and not the psychotherapeutic practice that is based upon it.

5 Grünbaum, *The Foundations of Psychoanalysis*, p. 278.

6 Grünbaum, *The Foundations of Psychoanalysis*, p. 278.

7 Grünbaum, *The Foundations of Psychoanalysis*, p. 103.

8 Grünbaum, *The Foundations of Psychoanalysis*, pp. 105–106.

9 Grünbaum, *The Foundations of Psychoanalysis*, pp. 113–116.

10 Grünbaum, *The Foundations of Psychoanalysis*, pp. 108–113.

11 Grünbaum, *The Foundations of Psychoanalysis*, pp. 118–125.

12 Grünbaum, *The Foundations of Psychoanalysis*, p. 105.

13 This is in sharp contradistinction to the views of Wittgenstein and the logical positivists, who maintained that metaphysical theories (including pseudo-sciences) are neither true nor false, but cognitively meaningless. Popper held that metaphysical theories may well be true or false, but that they are not *testable*.

14 I regard the ideas that scientific theories can be neither justified nor confirmed and that scientific knowledge need not be true as *the* most distinctive features of Popper's epistemology. Popper argued for it in *The Logic of Scientific Discovery* (1959. Reprinted by Routledge, London, 1995, pp. 93–94) in connection with Fries' Trilemma:

> The problem of the basis of experience has troubled few thinkers so deeply as Fries. He taught that, if the statements of science are not to be accepted *dogmatically*, we must be able to *justify* them. If we demand justification by reasoned argument, in the logical sense, then we are committed to the view that statements can be justified only by statements. The demand that *all* statements are to be logically justified (described by Fries as a 'predilection for proofs') is therefore bound to lead to an *infinite regress*. Now, if we wish to avoid the danger of dogmatism as well as an infinite regress, then it seems as if we could only have

recourse to *psychologism*, i.e. the doctrine that statements can be justified not only by statements but also by perceptual experience.

But Popper viewed psychologism, and the doctrine of immediate knowledge upon which it is based, as entailing an irrationalist epistemology. And he resolved the trilemma, contrary to Fries, not by embracing psychologism, but by abandoning justification as a criterion of knowledge. (For a more detailed discussion, see M.A. Notturno, *Objectivity, Rationality, and the Third Realm: Justification and the Grounds of Psychologism*, Martinus Nijhoff, Dordrecht, 1985.)

15 These two senses of 'falsifiability' are implicit throughout Popper's writings. But in *Realism and the Aim of Science* (p. xxii), he explicitly distinguishes them as such:

Hence, to repeat, we must distinguish two meanings of the expressions 'falsifiable' and 'falsifiability':

(1) 'Falsifiable' as a logical-technical term, in the sense of the demarcation criterion of falsifiability. This purely logical concept—falsifiable in principle, one might say—rests on a logical relation between the theory in question and the class of basic statements (or the potential falsifiers described by them).

(2) 'Falsifiable' in the sense that the theory in question can *definitively* or *conclusively* or *demonstrably* be falsified ('demonstrably falsifiable'). I have always stressed that even a theory which is obviously falsifiable in the first sense is never falsifiable in this second sense. (For this reason I have used the expression 'falsifiable' as a rule only in the first, technical sense. In the second sense I have as a rule spoken not of 'falsifiability' but rather of 'falsification' and of its problems).

16 See Karl R. Popper, 'Replies to My Critics' in *The Philosophy of Karl Popper*, edited by P.A. Schilpp, Open Court, La Salle, Illinois, 1974, p. 32.

17 Popper, 'Replies to my critics,' pp. 984–985.

18 Popper, *Realism and the Aim of Science*, p. 172.

19 Popper, *Realism and the Aim of Science*, p. 168.

20 Karl R. Popper, 'Science: Conjectures and Refutations' in Karl R. Popper, *Conjectures and Refutations*, 1963. Reprinted by Routledge, London, 1992, p. 37.

21 Popper, 'Replies to My Critics,' p. 984.

22 Grünbaum, *The Foundations of Psychoanalysis*, p. 103. In context, the passage from Popper ('Replies to My Critics,' p. 984) reads:

The difficulties connected with my criterion of demarcation (D) are important, but must not be exaggerated. It is vague, since it is a methodological rule, and since the demarcation between science and nonscience is vague. But it is more than sharp enough to make a distinction between many physical theories on the one hand, and metaphysical theories, such as psychoanalysis, or Marxism (in its present form), on the other. This is, of course, one of my main theses; and nobody who has not understood it can be said to have understood my theory.

23 Existential generalizations are statements of the form 'Such-and-such exists,' such as 'White swans exist.'

24 Universal generalizations are statements of the form 'All such-and-such are this-and-that,' such as 'All swans are white.'

25 Popper, *Realism and the Aim of Science*, p. 168.

26 Popper, *Realism and the Aim of Science*, p. 163.

27 Later we will have an opportunity to illustrate this via Freud's case study called 'A Case of Paranoia Running Counter to the Psycho-Analytical Theory of the Disease.'

28 Popper, *Realism and the Aim of Science*, p. 174.

29 See Popper, *Realism and the Aim of Science*, p. 32. See also Karl R. Popper, 'Conjectural Knowledge: My Solution to the Problem of Induction' in Karl R. Popper, *Objective Knowledge*, Oxford University Press, London, 1972; and Popper, *The Logic of Scientific Discovery*, pp. 93–111.

30 Popper, *The Logic of Scientific Discovery*, p. 34.

31 Popper, *Realism and the Aim of Science*, p. 159. See also Popper, 'Conjectural Knowledge: My Solution to the Problem of Induction.'

32 Grünbaum, *The Foundations of Psychoanalysis*, p. 103.

33 Grünbaum, *The Foundations of Psychoanalysis*, p. 106.

34 Grünbaum, *The Foundations of Psychoanalysis*, pp. 106–107.

35 Popper, 'Science: Conjectures and Refutations,' p. 38.

36 Popper, 'Science: Conjectures and Refutations,' p. 36.

37 Popper, 'Science: Conjectures and Refutations,' p. 36.

38 For further discussion, see Notturno, *Objectivity, Rationality, and the Third Realm*, pp. 134–136.

39 See Rudolf Carnap, 'Testability and Meaning' in *Philosophy of Science* 3, 1936, especially p. 427.

40 See Popper, *The Logic of Scientific Discovery*, pp. 251–252.

41 See Karl R. Popper, 'The Demarcation Between Science and Metaphysics' in *Conjectures and Refutations*, pp. 275–277.

42 Popper used to tell a funny anecdote to illustrate the difficulty that philosophers had in taking these ideas seriously. He attended a meeting of the Aristotelian Society when he first came to England in 1935 at which Bertrand Russell argued that we have to assume an a priori principle of induction, and that this set Kantian limits to empiricism. Popper was encouraged to speak in the discussion that followed and said in his broken English that he believed in learning from experience and in an empiricism *without* Russell's Kantian limitations, but not in induction. The audience apparently took this for a joke and laughed. He then went on to say that the whole problem was due to a false assumption, namely, that *scientific knowledge* was a species of knowledge in the sense of justified true belief, according to which if someone knows something then what he knows must be true. The audience also took this for a joke, or perhaps some sort of paradox, and laughed and clapped. (See Karl R. Popper,

Unended Quest, 1974. Reprinted by Routledge, London, 1992, p. 110. See also Popper, *Realism and the Aim of Science*, pp. 12–18.)

43 The central planks of psychoanalysis, according to Paul McHugh, are drive theory, the unconscious (with its assumption of psychic determinism), and the structural hypothesis (id, ego, super-ego). Dream theory is critical and basic because it was and remains a fundamental model of unconscious-conscious interaction and a unique source of data for the psychoanalyst.

44 Sigmund Freud, 'Certain Neurotic Mechanisms in Jealousy, Paranoia and Homosexuality,' 1922, in *Sigmund Freud: Collected Papers*, edited by Ernest Jones, Basic Books, New York, vol. 3, p. 234.

45 Sigmund Freud, 'Psycho-Analytic Notes upon an Autobiographical Account of a Case of Paranoia (Dementia Paranoides),' 1911, in *Sigmund Freud: Collected Papers*, vol. 3, p. 464.

46 Sigmund Freud, 'A Case of Paranoia Running Counter to the Psycho-Analytical Theory of the Disease,' 1915, in *Sigmund Freud: Collected Papers*, vol. 2, p. 153.

47 Grünbaum draws the following moral from this analysis: 'whenever empirical indicators can warrant the *absence* of a certain theoretical pathogen P as well as a differential diagnosis of the *presence* of a certain theoretical neurosis N, then an etiologic hypothesis of the strong form "P is causally necessary for N" is clearly empirically falsifiable.' (Grünbaum, *The Foundations of Psychoanalysis*, p. 109.)

48 See A.C. Kinsey, W.B. Pomeroy & C.E. Martin, *Sexual Behavior in the Human Male*, W.B. Saunders Company, 1948.

49 Sigmund Freud, *The Psychopathology of Everyday Life*, W.W. Norton & Company, New York, 1904.

50 Edmund Gettier has constructed counterexamples to the thesis that 'S knows that P' is true if-and-only-if (i) P is true; (ii) S believes that P; and (iii) S is justified in believing that P. These counterexamples are such that we would purportedly acknowledge that (i), (ii), and (iii) are satisfied while nonetheless denying that S knows that P. What these examples have in common is that S's true belief that P is true is 'justified' by reasons other than those which in fact render P true. Simply put: S has justified true belief that P—but for the wrong reasons. (See Edmund Gettier, 'Is Justified True Belief Knowledge?' in *Analysis* 23: 121–123, 1963.)

51 He wrote in *Realism and the Aim of Science* (p. 169. This paragraph was added in 1980) that:

The last sentence of the preceding paragraph [I cannot think of any conceivable instance of human behaviour which might not be interpreted in terms of either theory, and which might not be claimed, by either theory, as a 'verification.'] is, I now believe, too strong. As Bartley has pointed out to me, there are certain kinds of possible behaviour which are incompatible with Freudian theory—that is, which are excluded by Freudian theory. Thus Freud's explanation of paranoia in terms of repressed homosexuality would seem to exclude the possibility of active homosexuality in a paranoid individual.

52 Popper, *Realism and the Aim of Science*, p. 169.
53 Grünbaum, *The Foundations of Psychoanalysis*, pp. 107–113.
54 Grünbaum, *The Foundations of Psychoanalysis*, pp. 282–284.
55 Grünbaum, *The Foundations of Psychoanalysis*, p. 281.
56 Grünbaum, *The Foundations of Psychoanalysis*, p. 284. My italics.
57 Grünbaum, *The Foundations of Psychoanalysis*, p. 282.
58 Grünbaum, *The Foundations of Psychoanalysis*, p. 282.
59 Grünbaum, *The Foundations of Psychoanalysis*, p. 281.
60 Grünbaum, *The Foundations of Psychoanalysis*, p. 284.
61 Grünbaum, *The Foundations of Psychoanalysis*, p. 284.
62 Sigmund Freud, *Introductory Lectures on Psychoanalysis*, W.W. Norton & Company, New York, 1917, p. 452.
63 Grünbaum, *The Foundations of Psychoanalysis*, p. 108.
64 Freud, 'A Case of Paranoia Running Counter to the Psycho-Analytical Theory of the Disease,' p. 158.
65 Freud, 'A Case of Paranoia Running Counter to the Psycho-Analytical Theory of the Disease,' pp. 158–159.
66 Popper, *Realism and the Aim of Science*, p. 168.
67 Grünbaum, *The Foundations of Psychoanalysis*, p. 115.
68 Grünbaum, *The Foundations of Psychoanalysis*, p. 220.
69 Grünbaum, *The Foundations of Psychoanalysis*, p. 239.
70 Grünbaum, *The Foundations of Psychoanalysis*, p. 238.
71 Grünbaum, *The Foundations of Psychoanalysis*, p. 239.
72 Sigmund Freud, *New Introductory Lectures on Psychoanalysis*, W.W. Norton & Company, New York, 1933, pp. 26–27.
73 See *Scientific Philosophy: Origins and Developments*, edited by Friedrich Stadler, Kluwer, Dordrecht, 1993.
74 My italics.

10 The Choice between Popper and Kuhn: Truth, Criticism, and The Legacy of Logical Positivism[1]

> *Revolutions close with a total victory for one of the two opposing camps. Will that group ever say that the result of its victory has been something less than progress? That would be like admitting that they had been wrong and their opponents right. To them, at least, the outcome of revolution must be progress, and they are in an excellent position to make certain that future members of their community will see past history in the same way.*
>
> Thomas S. Kuhn

> *I may be wrong and you may be right, and by an effort, we may get nearer to the truth.*
>
> Karl R. Popper

I

Karl Popper died in 1994, and Thomas Kuhn died in 1996. With them, two of the greatest 20th century philosophers of science passed into history. In order to understand that history, it is necessary to understand their relationship to what came before them. Logical positivism is what came before Popper and Kuhn. And many people do not understand how their philosophies are related to it.

Michael Friedman's account is representative. Friedman writes that the 'official demise' of logical positivism 'took place sometime between the publication of W.V.O. Quine's "Two Dogmas of Empiricism" (1951), and that of Thomas Kuhn's *The Structure of Scientific Revolutions* (1962).'[2]

According to 'official' history, Popper was a minor logical positivist who introduced falsifiability as a criterion of meaning, but exaggerated his differences with Carnap and Neurath. According to 'official' history, the analytic/synthetic distinction was the lynchpin of logical positivism, it was cracked by Quine in the

1950's, and the philosophy of science then floundered about for approximately ten years until Kuhn provided an entirely new 'institutional' direction for the field.

This official history, like most official histories, is a convenient one. It has the effect, by emphasizing certain aspects and criticisms of logical positivism, and by ignoring certain others, of restricting the scope of its possible successors. And by fitting itself to Kuhn's model of theory change, it then corroborates the successor that it has itself already chosen.

Thus, we are told that the philosophy of science prior to the 1950s was dominated by one well-entrenched paradigm;[3] that this paradigm was confronted by severe anomalies from within;[4] that the field was then beset by a period of crisis;[5] and that this crisis was finally resolved through a revolutionary paradigm shift initiated by a quasi-outsider, quasi-initiate to the field.[6]

The story, as I have said, is convenient. But I would like to suggest an alternative.

The real demise of logical positivism began in the 1930's when Popper, in his *Logik der Forschung* (1934), argued that scientific laws can be neither verified nor confirmed, that the verifiability criterion is mistaken both as a criterion of demarcation and as a criterion of meaning, and that metaphysical theories are not only meaningful, but a necessary component of any science. The positivists acknowledged Popper's criticisms, but never quite recognized their fundamental significance.

Carnap continued to talk about the elimination of metaphysics. But he weakened his concept of justification, and then even his concept of truth.[7] This finally resulted in a transformation of his original bedrock foundationalism into what I like to call 'Floating Foundationalism'—a philosophy that retains the structure and function of bedrock foundationalism, but leaves the foundations themselves floating in midair. This, I suggest, was later transformed into the institutional approach, when Kuhn stressed the importance of scientific communities, arguing that truth and justification could no longer underwrite the authority of science, and that we would have to underwrite it with communal solidarity instead.

In my view, philosophers and scientists today are faced with a choice, but many of them are not very clear about what it is. There are many ways to describe this choice. It is the choice between whether we should, as philosophers and scientists, continue our rational, though ever fallible, search for truth, or resign ourselves to the dogmatic authoritarianism of The Scientific Institution. It is the choice between whether we should uphold the right of the individual philosopher or scientist to think and speak for himself, or demand that he subordinate his views to those 'officially' sanctioned by the community of scientists that form The Scientific Institution.

It is, in other words, the choice between Popper and Kuhn.

II

Perhaps I should put all of this into context. Logical positivism was one of the most influential philosophies of the twentieth century, and the verifiability criterion of meaning was its most distinctive doctrine. The verifiability criterion states that a sentence is both cognitively meaningful[8] and scientific if, and only if, it can be shown to be true on the basis of sensory experience or can be shown to be true on the basis of meaning alone. The positivists proposed this criterion both as a theory of meaning and as a demarcation between science and metaphysics. In this way, they proposed to distinguish science from metaphysics with a criterion of meaning that would equate meaningful discourse with science, and eliminate[9] metaphysics as meaningless.

Popper criticized the verificationist account of science in his *Logik der Forschung*. Science, according to Popper, is distinguished primarily by its *critical* approach, which, in epistemological terms, means the falsifiability of its theories. Popper argued that the verifiability criterion fails as a demarcation between science and metaphysics in at least two ways. It fails to account for the scientific character of scientific laws, and it fails to account for how old well-established scientific theories are replaced by new ones. More important, Popper argued that *any* attempt to verify or confirm or justify our knowledge, be it inductivist or deductivist, must ultimately lead to irrationalism, since it must ultimately appeal to cognitive authorities, and since the task of rationalism is to challenge such authorities.

Popper proposed criticism, instead of justification, as the method of rational discourse—and trial and error as the way to account for scientific change. 'Science,' according to Popper 'never pursues the illusory aim of making its answers final, or even probable. Its advance is, rather, towards an infinite yet attainable aim: that of ever discovering new, deeper, and more general problems, and of subjecting our ever tentative answers to ever renewed and ever more rigorous tests.'[10] Popper argued that scientific knowledge is both objective and rational, not because science and science alone is meaningful, but because its theories consist of statements that can be criticized by all, and because it uses deductive logic as its organon of criticism. The objectivity and rationality of science was, in this way, supposed to depend less upon the psychological traits of individual scientists than upon the institutions of science, whose purpose was to facilitate and protect critical discussion and the free exchange of ideas. Popper said that theories should be preferred for their ability to survive such critical examination. But he denied that a theory's survival of criticism ever means that it is justified, confirmed, or reliable.[11] All scientific knowledge is conjectural, tentative, and fallible. And no theory, regardless of how well it has survived criticism, should be regarded as final. On the contrary, Popper thought that the very suggestion that a theory is justified is pernicious to the growth of knowledge, since it encourages us to regard the theory as final and immune to testing, and since doing so may both impede new research and lead to scepticism and irrationalism when we find out that it is not.

Kuhn presented a somewhat different picture of science in *The Structure of Scientific Revolutions* (1962). It is not the critical approach that characterizes science, according to Kuhn, but the *uncritical* acceptance of what he called a 'paradigm.' Kuhn said that paradigms are 'universally recognized achievements that for a long time provide model problems and solutions to a community of practitioners.'[12] In so doing, he divided scientific inquiry into normal science and extraordinary, or revolutionary, science.

Most scientific inquiry, according to Kuhn, occurs within an accepted scientific paradigm. Hence, the term 'normal science.' Within normal science, fundamental presuppositions—including presuppositions regarding the scope and method of inquiry—are not in question, and the work of the normal scientist consists primarily in explaining unexplained phenomena in terms of his paradigm. Kuhn characterized normal science as exercises in puzzle solving—as attempts to fit the pieces of nature into the predefined patterns of the paradigm. These attempts may be regarded as tests, but they are, according to Kuhn, not so much tests of a paradigm as of a scientist's competence to provide an adequate fit. Not all puzzles, however, get solved. And as recalcitrant puzzles, or 'anomalies,' accumulate, the scientific community gradually enters into a period of crisis in which progress demands the revolutionary creation of a new paradigm that can explain what the old theory explained, and the anomalous phenomena as well. Kuhn regarded the creation and acceptance of new paradigms as irrational. Normal science is a rule-governed activity, but revolutionary science is not. More important, debates concerning paradigms are debates concerning the foundations of rational inquiry. They thus leave little common ground for non-question-begging comparisons of theories. 'Paradigm shifts,' for this reason, occur not through reasoned argument, but through a bandwagon process of ideological and political conversion that Kuhn likened to a religious experience. Hence, his celebrated thesis is that competing scientific paradigms are incommensurable.

There are many similarities between Popper and Kuhn—so many that one might think that the differences between them are unimportant. Popper and Kuhn were both concerned with the ways in which established scientific theories are replaced by new ones. They both saw the creation of new scientific theories as a response to problems that confront established theories when they are applied in new and unfamiliar contexts. They both rejected the inductivist idea that science grows through an accumulation and generalization of facts, and instead emphasized the logical and psychological priority of theory to observation. They both maintained that scientific change cannot be explained by logic alone, and that

we must, in order to understand it, be sensitive to the human values that govern the traditions in which scientific problems arise.
Finally, but perhaps most important, they both rejected the view
that science aims at or can achieve a final justified theory.

These agreements mark broad strokes in the history of philosophy, and I do not want to be misunderstood as denying or ignoring
the fact that they exist. Writ large upon the history of philosophy,
Popper and Kuhn fought many of the same battles against many of
the same enemies. There are, however, important differences. And
the attempt to get clear about these differences has proven difficult. Kuhn, for one, said that they resulted from a gestalt shift in
which he and Popper placed different emphases upon such things
as the possibility of falsification, the incommensurability of theories, and the existence of normal science.[13] But in my view, it is not
so much the emphasis that they place on falsification, incommensurability, and normal science that separate Popper and Kuhn, as it
is their attitudes regarding the role of truth, the value of criticism,
and the consequences of construing science as a social institution
whose members are defined in terms of their adherence to certain
beliefs.

The issue, at base, is whether science should be an open or a
closed society. And in what follows, I shall try to explain what I
mean.

III

Let me begin by dispelling a few misunderstandings. In *The Structure of Scientific Revolutions*, Kuhn claimed that Popper 'emphasizes
the importance of falsification, i.e., of the test that, because its outcome is negative, *necessitates* the rejection of an established theory.'[14] Kuhn said that the role that Popper attributes to falsification
is similar to the one that he [Kuhn] assigns to anomalies. But he
also said that 'anomalous experiences may not be identified with
falsifying ones,' and that he 'doubt[s] that the latter exist'[15]—since
no experience ever necessitates the rejection of a paradigm.[16] And
in his 'Logic of Discovery or Psychology of Research?' Kuhn

pointedly asked 'What is falsification if it is not conclusive dis-proof?'[17] There Kuhn claimed that both 'falsification' and 'refuta-tion' are antonyms of 'proof,' and, as such, imply the ability to compel rational assent from any member of the relevant profes-sional community.

Kuhn presented this as a fundamental criticism of Popper. But the issue is subtle, and it is important to see exactly what his criti-cism is. For his criticism it is *not* that Popper maintains the possi-bility of conclusive falsification. On the contrary, Kuhn quoted Popper that:

> In point of fact, no conclusive disproof of a theory can ever be produced; for it is always possible to say that the experimental results are not reliable or that the discrepancies which are asserted to exist between the experimen-tal results and the theory are only apparent and that they will disappear with the advance of our understanding.[18]

His criticism, on the contrary, is that 'having barred conclusive disproof' Popper 'has provided no substitute for it, and the relation he does employ remains that of logical falsification.'[19] Kuhn said that Popper's denial of the possibility of conclusive falsification is 'an essential qualification which threatens the integrity of his basic position.'[20] And he concluded that 'though he is not a naive falsifi-cationist, [Popper] may, I suggest, legitimately be treated as one.'[21]

Popper called this conclusion 'really astonishing.'[22] He said that 'It is exactly like saying: "Although Popper is not a murderer, he may, I suggest, legitimately be treated as one".'[23]

What is going on here? And why?

Kuhn apparently saw Popper's 'basic position' as an allegiance to logical analysis. But this is a distortion. And the fact that it is a distortion is something that Kuhn should have known. For in what immediately precedes the passage that Kuhn cites from *The Logic of Scientific Discovery*, Popper writes:

> I am quite ready to admit that there is a need for a purely logical analysis of theories, for an analysis which takes no account of how they change and de-velop. But this kind of analysis does not elucidate those aspects of the em-pirical sciences which I, for one, so highly prize. A system such as classical

mechanics may be 'scientific' to any degree you like, but those who uphold it dogmatically—believing, perhaps, that it is their business to defend such a successful system against criticism as long as it is not *conclusively disproved*— are adopting the very reverse of that critical attitude which in my view is the proper one for the scientist.[24]

And in what immediately follows the passage that Kuhn cites, Popper continues:

> If you insist on strict proof (or strict disproof) in the empirical sciences, you will never benefit from experience, and never learn from it how wrong you are.[25]

Contrary to Kuhn, Popper's 'basic position' is not an allegiance to logical analysis, but to fallibilism and the critical *attitude*.

But are logical falsification and conclusive disproof really identical, as Kuhn suggests?

Popper distinguished a scientific theory from a metaphysical theory by its falsifiability. But by this, he meant only that there must be at least one 'basic statement'[26] that contradicts it. Were such a basic statement true, then it would follow that the theory that it contradicts is false. But falsifi*ability* is different from falsifi*cation*. And it is an entirely different question whether an alleged falsification is ever conclusive or ever *necessitates* the rejection of an established theory.

We regard a theory as *falsifiable* if it contradicts some basic statement that is possibly true. We regard a theory as *falsified* if we think that a basic statement that contradicts it is true. Popper, insofar as this is concerned, emphasized that the acceptance of the basic statements that corroborate or falsify a theory is not logically or psychologically compelled. Such statements are not justified, but accepted or rejected as a result of free decisions that may be re-evaluated and revised at any time. It follows from this that *any* universal generalization can be regarded as falsifiable, *so long as its proponents are willing to admit that contrary empirical evidence is possible.*[27] And it follows from *this* that someone can always avoid falsification of his theory, simply by not accepting the truth of the basic statements that contradict it. Logic can tell us which statements follow from or contradict which, but it cannot force us to accept or reject a theory. Popper, insofar as this is concerned, consistently maintained that theories can never be *definitively* or *conclusively* or *demonstrably* falsified. The 'substitute' that he provided for conclusive disproof was simply the one that had always been there.[28]

IV

The second misunderstanding I want to discuss concerns Kuhn's claim that competing paradigms are incommensurable, which, according to Popper, is tantamount to the view that different theories are like mutually untranslatable languages.[29] Were paradigms like untranslatable languages, then they would not admit of the critical comparison that Popper regarded as necessary for rational discourse. Popper, insofar as this is concerned, likened paradigms to linguistic frameworks, and claimed that such frameworks *are* translatable and that Kuhn had exaggerated a difficulty into an impossibility. But while Kuhn accepted the analogy between paradigms and linguistic frameworks, he denied that he ever believed that competing paradigms were untranslatable.[30] Rather, he said that when paradigms compete:

> ... the parties to such debates inevitably see differently certain of the experimental or observational situations to which both have recourse. Since the vocabularies in which they discuss such situations consist, however, predominantly of the same terms, they must be attaching some of those terms to nature differently and their communication is inevitably only partial. As a result, the superiority of one theory to another is something that cannot be proved in debate. Instead ... each party must try, by persuasion, to convert the other.[31]

Kuhn did not deny the translatability of paradigms. But he did deny, and he seemed to think that Popper affirmed, the existence of a theory-neutral observation language that could provide a basis for a *non-question-begging* comparison of theories. Popper, however, was one of the first to criticize the idea of a theory-neutral observation language. According to Popper, all observation is and must be theory-laden—for an observer, at the very least, must know *what* to observe.[32]

Here it might seem as if we are in a position to defuse the debate concerning incommensurability. Kuhn did not claim that competing paradigms are untranslatable, but only that there is no theory-neutral observation language. His idea that Popper is committed to such a language may have been the result of hasty reading, but it is also a consequence of his view that Popper is, or at least ought to be, committed to conclusive falsification. And this, as we have already seen, is a mistake resulting from a distortion of Popper's 'basic position.'

Still, where Popper spoke of 'rational argument,' Kuhn talked about 'conversion' and 'persuasion.' And these terms, at least for philosophers and scientists, have traditionally marked opposite ends of the rhetorical spectrum. Thus, in *The Structure of Scientific Revolutions*, Kuhn said that scientists must 'commit' themselves to scientific paradigms; that they must do so on 'faith,' that they must try to 'convert' others, if at all, by 'persuasion';[33] and that paradigm shifts are made 'not by deliberation and interpretation, but by a relatively sudden and unstructured event like the gestalt shift.'[34] He said that 'there must be a basis … for faith in the particular candidate chosen,' but he also said that that basis 'need be neither rational nor ultimately correct.'[35]

So it is, perhaps, not too surprising that many philosophers have interpreted Kuhn as saying—and, indeed, have attributed the importance of his work *to* his saying—that 'paradigm shifts' are irrational.[36]

But Kuhn also said that his use of 'persuasion' is not as radical as it might first appear, and that the point he has been trying to make:

> … is a simple one, long familiar in philosophy of science. Debates over theory-choice cannot be cast in a form that fully resembles logical or mathematical proof. In the latter, premises and rules of inference are stipulated from the start. If there is a disagreement about conclusions, the parties to the ensuing debate can retrace their steps one by one, checking each against prior stipulation. At the end of that process one or the other must concede that he has made a mistake, violated a previously accepted rule. After that concession he has no recourse, and his opponent's proof is then compelling.

Only if the two discover instead that they differ about the meaning or application of stipulated rules, that their prior agreement provides no sufficient basis for proof, does the debate continue in the form it inevitably takes during scientific revolutions. That debate is about premises, and its recourse is to persuasion as a prelude to the possibility of proof.[37]

And he went on to say that:

Nothing about that relatively familiar thesis implies either that there are no good reasons for being persuaded or that those reasons are not ultimately decisive for the group. Nor does it even imply that the reasons for choice are different from those usually listed by philosophers of science: accuracy, simplicity, fruitfulness, and the like. What it should suggest, however, is that such reasons function as values and that they can thus be differently applied, individually and collectively, by men who concur in honoring them. If two men disagree, for example, about the relative fruitfulness of their theories, or if they agree about that but disagree about the relative importance of fruitfulness and, say, scope in reaching a choice, neither can be convicted of a mistake. Nor is either being unscientific. There is no neutral algorithm for theory-choice, no systematic decision procedure which, properly applied, must lead each individual in the group to the same decision.[38]

But then, what about all that talk about faith, conversion, and commitment?

Here again, part of the problem lies in Kuhn's characterization of logical proof. For according to Kuhn, the 'premises and rules of inference' in a logical proof 'are stipulated from the start.' Thus, the parties to a disagreement 'can retrace their steps one by one, checking each against prior stipulation.' And thus, one of those parties *must*, at the end of all that checking, 'concede that he has made a mistake, violated a previously accepted rule.' But if this is how Kuhn understood logical proof, then *of course* debates over theory-choice cannot be cast in a form that fully resembles it. For the premises of a logical proof are stipulated from the start *only* in the artificial examples and exercises that we find in logic books. In real life, premises are not so much *stipulated* as *assumed*. And in real life, the assumption of a premise is *always* tentative—no matter how obvious it might initially seem. For in real life, the use of a premise to derive a more obviously *false* conclusion might always be taken as its *reductio ad absurdum*—as a logical 'proof' that that premise is, in fact, false.[39]

Contrary to Kuhn, a logical 'proof' *always* requires judgment—either that its premises are true, or that its conclusion is false—and is *never* compelling as a 'neutral algorithm for theory-choice.' Logical 'proofs' are always double-edged swords that can, contingent upon that judgment, be used to 'show' either that their conclusions are true, or that their premises are false, or nothing whatsoever. And for this reason, they can, just like values, 'be differently applied, individually and collectively, by men who concur in honoring them.'

Popper and Kuhn no doubt attached their words to their ideas differently. And this too is part of the problem. Faith, according to Popper, is not belief in a theory that we cannot prove. It is belief in a theory that we are not willing to question. But if our only alternatives for theory-acceptance are faith and logical proof, then we will have no recourse but to faith. And this is the other part of the problem. For if Kuhn is right that only philosophers have seriously misconstrued the intent of his remarks about incommensurability, conversion, and faith,[40] it is because most philosophers regard faith and logical proof as mutually exclusive alternatives—*and because Kuhn, contrary to Popper, seems to have followed their lead in doing so.*[41] I think that we must, in light of his disclaimers about irrationality, conclude that Kuhn differed from these philosophers only by regarding faith as rational. This, perhaps, is what he meant when he said that 'there must be a basis ... for faith in the particular candidate chosen.' But even if this is what he meant, it does not quite explain what he meant when he said that this basis 'need be neither rational nor ultimately correct.' And even if we could explain *that*, it still would not explain what he meant by 'commitment' and why he believed that a scientist *must* commit himself to a paradigm instead of accepting it tentatively. It is this, more than anything else, that has led people to believe that Kuhn regarded the acceptance of paradigms as irrational.

V

This brings me to the role of normal science. Here I think that there is a real disagreement between Popper and Kuhn, though it is not the one cited by Kuhn. Kuhn claimed that Popper ignored the *existence* of normal science.[42] But this is simply not true.[43] Popper did concede that the distinction between normal and revolutionary science is something of which he has 'at best been only dimly aware.'[44] But he sharply rejected Kuhn's view that normal science is a distinctive or essential feature of science, and he characterized normal puzzle-solving research as 'a danger to science.'[45] And this, I think, is their real disagreement. As Popper put it:

> 'Normal' science, in Kuhn's sense, exists. It is the activity of the non-revolutionary, or more precisely, the not-too-critical professional: of the science student who accepts the ruling dogma of the day, who does not wish to challenge it, and who accepts a revolutionary theory only if almost everybody else is ready to accept it—if it becomes fashionable by a kind of bandwagon effect.[46]

And again, but more tellingly:

> ... the 'normal' scientist, as Kuhn describes him, is a person one ought to be sorry for... The 'normal' scientist, in my view, has been taught badly. I believe, and so do many others, that all teaching on the University level (and if possible below) should be training and encouragement in critical thinking. The 'normal' scientist, as described by Kuhn, has been badly taught. He has been taught in a dogmatic spirit: he is a victim of indoctrination. He has learned a technique which can be applied without asking for the reason why... As a consequence, he has become what may be called an *applied scientist*, in contradistinction to what I should call a *pure scientist*. He is, as Kuhn puts it, content to solve 'puzzles.'[47]

Some people say that this disagreement can be traced to the fact that Popper's epistemology is primarily prescriptive in nature, while Kuhn's is primarily descriptive. Kuhn, however, rejected this view. He wrote, in response to the question whether his remarks about scientific development should be read as descriptions or prescriptions, that:

> The answer, of course, is that they should be read in both ways at once. If I have a theory of how and why science works, it must necessarily have implications for the way in which scientists should behave if their enterprise is to flourish.[48]

Popper's epistemology, on the other hand, is neither descriptive nor prescriptive *in the methodological sense*. Whether or not the method of conjecture and refutation is an accurate description of the history of science is really quite irrelevant. And to say that the method of science should be that of conjecture and refutation is, in a way, to say that there should be no method peculiar to science at all.

Popper, in fact, was explicit that he was a *methodological* relativist.[49] The scientist can use whatever method he chooses, so long as he uses it critically and in an effort to discover truth.

In my view, the dispute about normal science is not about methodology, but about the value of criticism, and about the nature of the bond that unites scientists into a community.

Kuhn's idea that puzzle-solving research is the essence of science characterizes this bond in terms of shared *beliefs*. But since the scientific community cannot prove the truth of its beliefs, its members have no choice but to commit themselves to them uncritically. So in order to insure solidarity, the community itself discourages the critical attitude. Indeed, Kuhn was explicit that 'it is precisely the abandonment of critical discourse that marks the transition to a science.'[50] 'Scientists,' he wrote, 'sometimes correct bits of each other's work, but the man who makes a career of piecemeal criticism is ostracized by the profession.'[51]

Popper, on the other hand, characterized this bond in terms of the search for truth. He believed that it is only truth and the critical attitude that enables a scientific community to be an open society. For if it is really impossible to justify our beliefs, then it is only the critical search for truth that prevents the scientific community from deteriorating into a closed society that acknowledges inquiry only if it falls within the parameters of its own framework, and that ostracizes those whose criticism cuts too deep. This sort of community, in Popper's view, is both illusory and pernicious. For it is not the plurality of belief but its institutionalization that poses the worst threat to science. And here, it is truth and the critical attitude that emerge as our best hopes for keeping the growth of knowledge alive.

VI

This is the real difference between Popper and Kuhn. It is not about the possibility of falsification, or the incommensurability of theories, or the existence of normal science. It is about the nature of truth and, more particularly, about its place in science.

But it is *not* about our ability to infallibly discover the truth.

It is about the role that truth plays in scientific inquiry and in the-ory-choice.

Popper and Kuhn agreed that there is no such thing as an objective criterion of truth. But Kuhn took this to mean that truth plays no role at all in inquiry and theory-choice. Popper, on the other hand, maintained that truth plays the role of a regulative ideal.

Kuhn said very little about truth in *The Structure of Scientific Revolutions*, and the little that he did say seems, on the whole, to deny that truth plays any role in inquiry or theory-choice at all. Indeed, Kuhn seems to have been proud of this point. Toward the end of *The Structure of Scientific Revolutions* he points out that:

> … until the last very few pages the term 'truth' had entered this essay only in a quotation from Francis Bacon. And even in those pages it entered only as a source for the scientist's conviction that incompatible rules for doing science cannot coexist except during revolutions when the profession's main task is to eliminate all sets but one.[52]

Having pointed this out, he goes on to ask:

> Does it really help to imagine that there is some one full, objective, true account of nature and that the proper measure of scientific achievement is the extent to which it brings us closer to that ultimate goal?[53]

It is difficult, given the little that Kuhn said about truth, to know whether he objected to the idea that there *is* an account of nature that is *true*, or that there is *only one* such account, or that it is *full*, or *objective*.

There can, however, be little doubt that philosophers and scientists have traditionally regarded truth as a regulative ideal—or that they traditionally construed truth as one of the criteria of knowledge, and the denial of the possibility of determining truth as tantamount to scepticism. But the great scientific revolutions of the twentieth century, in particular the decline of Euclidean Geometry and Newtonian Mechanics, seem to have changed all that. If Kant's best candidates for certain true knowledge can be false, then what hope is there for determining the truth of any theory? Here, the view gradually emerged that one cannot speak of truth *per se*, but only of truth relativized to a particular theory. According to this view, theories themselves are neither true nor false; they are criteria by which we determine the truth or falsity of other statements. But since the most interesting and important questions concern the theories themselves, and since it was never too clear how a theory that is neither true nor false can determine the truth or falsity of other statements, philosophers soon came to regard talk about truth as superfluous.

But why can't we speak of truth *per se*? Why *must* we think of it as relativized to a particular theory?

I think it is undeniable—as will become apparent if you actually try to answer this question—that this sort of reasoning conflates the *concept* of truth with a *criterion* of truth by considering it nonsense to speak of truth in the absence of a decision procedure for determining whether or not a statement is true. And I think that it is also undeniable, though no doubt ironic, that this conflation was an essential ingredient of logical positivism. This, in fact, is what the verifiability criterion of meaning was all about. For if the meaning of a statement is really its method of verification, then to speak of statements *as* true, without any method to verify that they are true, is to speak with no meaning at all.

Kuhn said very little about truth, but his commitment to verificationism is clear from what he said about mistakes. For he described sharp disagreements in which people contradict each other—so that one might expect that *someone* was making a mistake—as being the result of 'gestalt shifts.' And when it came to paradigm shifts, Kuhn was 'not sure a mistake has been made' at all, or 'at least not a mistake to learn from.'[54] For Kuhn, making a mistake meant breaking an established rule, learning from mistakes meant learning to follow the established rules, and someone could learn from a mistake only because the group that established the rule could determine whether and when it has been broken.[55] Indeed, Kuhn found it 'difficult ... to understand' what someone could mean if he called the Ptolemaic system 'or any other out-of-date theory, a mistake.'[56] He said that 'At most one may wish to say that a theory which was not previously a mistake has become one or that a scientist has made the mistake of clinging to a theory for too long'[57]—and that anyone who says that a scientific paradigm, such as Ptolemaic astronomy, is mistaken must be implicitly referring to a misuse of *inductivist* rules.[58]

But why can't we just say that it is *false*?

Why do we need to think that the Ptolemaic system results from a failure to follow inductivist rules in order to believe that it is false? Isn't it the very nature of inductive inference that we can follow all the rules and still end up with a theory that is false? And if Ptolemaic theory *is* false, then isn't it a mistake to believe that it is not? And isn't it a mistake regardless of whether or not anyone ever discovers it? Not according to Kuhn. For talk about mistakes is meaningful for Kuhn only if we have a way to verify that they have been made. This means that mistakes are possible only relative to established rules. And this means that they can be made only in the rule-governed context of normal science—because extraordinary science begins where the rules leave off.

I am tempted to say that only an inductivist could believe that a false theory must be the result of a mistake in induction. But Kuhn denied that he was an inductivist. So let me just say that *I* find it difficult to understand what it means to say that 'believing that valid theories are the product of correct inductions from facts, the inductivist *must* also hold that a false theory is the result of a mistake in induction.' Does it mean that inductivists believe that a theory is valid *if* it is a correct induction from facts, or *only if* it is a correct induction from facts, or *if-and-only-if* it is a correct induction from facts? Does it mean that inductivists must hold that a theory is false *because* it is the result of a mistake in induction, or that it is the result of a mistake in induction *because* it is false, or that being the result of a mistake in induction and being false are one and the same thing? And this is just the tip of the iceberg. For what are *valid* theories supposed to be? Are they supposed to be *true* theories, as their contrast with false theories would suggest, or different from true theories, as Kuhn's idea that we need not talk about truth would suggest? And if valid theories are supposed to be different from true theories, then how are we to understand *false* theories? Are they supposed to be different from theories that are *not* true? Or are they still supposed to be understood in the ordinary sense of the word?

It would be a neat exercise in logic to articulate all of the possible interpretations that are hidden here and to state which of them yield inferences that are valid. But none of that, I fear, would help us to determine *why* Kuhn believed that a mistake is made only when someone breaks an established rule, or why he found it so difficult to *understand* what someone might *mean* when he calls the Ptolemaic system a mistake, or why he was so hung up on *rules*.

It is clear that those who accept verificationism should not regard the concept of truth as meaningful. But Popper did not accept verificationism, and he believed that we can use truth as a regulative ideal of science even though we can never determine that any particular statement is true.

A 'regulative ideal' is a standard or a goal or an aim that structures actions and decisions within a certain enterprise. Examples of regulative ideals are maximization of profit in capitalism, and winning in American football. To say that truth is a regulative ideal of science is simply to say that scientists try to discover truth, and decide to accept or reject a theory with reference to whether or not they think it is true. But it is not to say that this is the only thing that they do or that nothing else influences their decisions.

When put this simply, the idea that truth is a regulative ideal of science might appear to be trivial and uncontroversial. But this is not the case. Since Popper denied the existence of an objective *criterion* of truth, his appeal to truth as a regulative ideal is generally thought to be paradoxical. For if it is impossible to determine the truth or falsity of a theory, then how can we possibly use it as a standard for theory-choice? In my view, this paradox is *merely* apparent. And in what follows, I will attempt to explain why.

VII

The fact that it is possible to maintain a regulative ideal in the absence of a criterion for determining whether or not it has been achieved should really be obvious. For we do it all the time.

Consider the case of capitalism. To say that the regulative ideal of capitalism is the maximization of profit is simply to say that capitalists aim at maximizing profits. Confronted with competing strategies for maximizing profits, a decision will be made concerning which strategy will best achieve that goal. This, I suggest, is uncontroversial. But no one would ever suggest that such decisions are always successful. Despite the best laid plans of capitalists, businesses do fail.

What is, however, more interesting is that we can aim at maximizing profits, and we can base our practical decisions on that goal, without ever being able to determine whether or when our profits have been maximized.

Even were it possible to determine that one strategy for maximizing profits is better than another—which, in general, it is not since we are dealing with counterfactuals—*that* would still not suffice to determine whether it was the *best* strategy for maximizing profits, and, hence, whether profits had in fact been maximized. Capitalists, in the face of a possibly infinite number of such strategies, are committed to risk, and to bold guesses concerning which policy will prove most successful. But their commitment to the maximization of profits is meaningful and has real and important consequences. For, in practice, it might easily result in a decision to sacrifice quality in order to maximize profits—something that would be unthinkable were quality our regulative ideal.

This, I suggest, can help us to understand how truth can be a regulative ideal of science. We can adopt this ideal without ever being able to determine whether or when it has been achieved. And if we do adopt it, then our criticism and decisions concerning theory-choice will, in practice, be based upon what *appears* to be true, and not necessarily on what is. Appearances can be deceptive, and mistakes are always possible. This is our primary reason for saying that there is no objective criterion of truth. But the adoption of truth as a regulative ideal has clear implications for the conduct of scientific inquiry. For were we to adopt a different regulative ideal, then we might be willing to promote a theory that we think is false in order to achieve some other end.

VIII

I began this discussion by talking about the history of the philosophy of science, and by characterizing the choice between Popper and Kuhn as the choice between whether we should continue our rational search for truth, or resign ourselves to positivism and the authoritarianism of The Scientific Institution. I would like to end it by explaining what I mean.

Ever since Descartes, philosophers and scientists have regarded the justification of a theory as a criterion for its rational *acceptance*. But in the beginning of this century, the logical positivists introduced their verifiability criterion of meaning, and upped the ante by making justification a criterion for a theory's *intelligibility*. Kuhn's idea that paradigms can be meaningful despite the fact that they cannot be verified is clearly a step in the right direction. But it is not so clearly a step away from the verifiability criterion of meaning—let alone a step away from justificationism.

In my view, Kuhn's suggestion that paradigms are neither true nor false reveals a deep commitment to the verifiability criterion of meaning—as do his views regarding commitment, conversion, and incommensurability.

For when all is said and done, the reason why Kuhn can understand mistakes only in terms of established rules is the same reason why he can understand truth only in the context of a paradigm. It is because these rules provide the criteria for *determining* mistakes. It is because they provide the only way that we can *verify* that a mistake has been made.

But this is not Kuhn's only holdover from positivism. For the positivists also placed a strong emphasis upon community. They regarded communal collaboration as important for the production and justification of scientific knowledge, which they in turn regarded as important for the unity of science.

Neurath, for example, wrote that 'unified science is the outgrowth of comprehensive *collective labor*,'[59] and cast doubt upon the ability of 'isolated individuals' to achieve anything like it. And Carnap envisioned science as a community of co-workers in which 'each collaborator contributes only what he can endorse and justify before the whole body of his co-workers.'[60]

This emphasis upon community is what fuels Kuhn's conception of science as a *social institution*, and his attempt to define scientific knowledge, if not truth itself, in terms of the consensus of belief that is forged among its members. This is one of the features of Kuhn's philosophy that people find most attractive. But it is, in my view, a double-edged sword. For when we add to it Kuhn's ideas that scientists must commit themselves uncritically to a paradigm and that it is appropriate for 'the profession' to ostracize those who are too critical, or who disagree, then it becomes difficult to see how science, as Kuhn construes it, can uphold the freedom of thought. It becomes difficult, in fact, to see how the scientific community can help but degenerate into a closed society.[61]

IX

In my view, Kuhn's institutional picture of science is more of a continuation of logical positivism than a repudiation. Indeed, my own view is that Kuhn's institutional picture is, quite literally, logical positivism without the logic.

Their idioms are entirely different. But Kuhn's account of paradigms, his distinction between 'normal' and 'revolutionary' science, and his idea that competing paradigms are neither true nor false is a repetition of Carnap's account of linguistic frameworks, his distinction between their 'internal' and 'external' questions, and his view that the answers to external questions are neither true nor false.[62] Far from repudiating verificationism, Kuhn's own procedure, like Carnap's, was to reject, as meaningless, concepts—such as truth—whose meaning could not be reduced to the method of their verification.

More important, Kuhn's emphasis upon normal science and upon the communal aspects of scientific inquiry is both a repetition of Carnap's ideal of science as a community of co-workers, and part and parcel of Neurath's conception of unified science as a *collective labor*. It is easy to lose sight of this amidst all of the logical problems with logical positivism. But the institutional character of scientific inquiry was, in fact, one of the most important motivating conceptions of that quasi-political, quasi-philosophical unity of science movement. Of course, in Carnap's original version, the authority of the scientific institution was supposed to follow from the justification of its theories—and not the justification of its theories from the authority of its institution. But this gave way with Popper's critique of verificationism. And what eventually evolved was an account in which the internal (or normal) statements of science could be justified as true or false, but the external (or revolutionary) ones, which actually gave meaning to them, could be accepted only by consensus.

Far from spelling the demise of logical positivism, Kuhn's institutional philosophy of science is its living legacy—which is, perhaps, the reason why Carnap chose Kuhn as his 'official' successor when it finally became clear to all that the positivist emperor had no clothes.

X

Carnap said that Popper exaggerated his differences with the positivists. The 'official' historians of positivism who follow Carnap tend to repeat this view. I do not, however, think that their attempt to rewrite history can survive criticism. Popper shared the positivists' interest in the methodology of science. But he rejected their verifiability criterion of meaning, along with their idea that linguistic analysis can resolve the problems of philosophy. He also rejected their idea that scientific knowledge can and needs to be justified. Carnap spent much of his life trying to work out an inductive logic that would justify empirical theories. And Popper spent much of his trying to persuade Carnap that inductive logic is impossible. These are major differences in the philosophy of science, and Popper seems to have annoyed Carnap by talking about them. They no doubt agreed upon many things. But I think that it was Carnap, and not Popper, who was guilty of exaggeration.

The 'official' history of logical positivism is not simply a history written by and for the winners. It is also a history in which the losers *are* the winners—and in which the winners are also the losers. Indeed, the very idea that logical positivism should have an *official* demise and an *official* history means that its most debilitating features are still with us.

What was debilitating about logical positivism is the same thing that is debilitating about Kuhn's institutionalism.

It is the parochial policy, 'officially' endorsed by Kuhn, of making outsiders of those who criticize the insiders too sharply.

It is the obscurantism that rejects alternative theories as meaningless—as opposed to simply as false.

And it is the authoritarianism that insists that such theories—if not actually meaningless—*cannot* be rationally discussed.

All of this fits hand in glove with the policy of never admitting that you are wrong and that your opponents are right—as well as with the policy of using your power and position to ensure that the future members of your community will see its history in the same way that you do.

But what is most debilitating about both of these movements is that community, and politics, and power all become far more important than truth.

I would be the last to suggest that Kuhn *intended* these to be the consequences of his institutional approach to science. But that should not prevent us from recognizing that they *are* its consequences, and from fighting against them.

Most of us already know about the power of community and solidarity. We know that it poses a threat to our freedom of thought. And we know that it exists in most communities and, to the extent to which they are communities, in the institutions of philosophy and science as well. That is not in question. But what is in question is whether we ought to regard it as our model, or norm, or paradigm, of inquiry—whether we ought to promote it and to regulate our actions and decisions in accordance with it, whether we ought, in other words, to adopt it as our regulative ideal.

If philosophers and scientists ought to be committed to anything, then we ought to be committed to the defense of reason and the freedom of thought. We ought to be committed to the right of the individual to question the generally accepted beliefs of his community and to propose beliefs of his own that are different.

This means that our scientific institutions should exist for the sake of the individual—for the sake of our freedom of thought and our right to express it—and not the other way round.

There can be little doubt that science and philosophy involve contributions from many people. But my own sense is that pledging allegiance to community, and to solidarity of belief, and to The Scientific Institution is a big mistake.

Community and solidarity have many attractions. But they have always posed a threat to reason and to our freedom of thought. And reason and the freedom of thought is what I think science and philosophy are really all about. Our freedom of thought is something that we must always fight to preserve. And we can fight to preserve it only if we adopt truth as our regulative ideal. For when all is said and done, it is the power of truth and the critical attitude that will preserve science and philosophy as the open societies that we want them to be.

Notes

1 This is a revised version of a paper that has been presented, among other places, at the Center for Theoretical Studies in Prague, Czech Republic on 28 April 1995; at the Center for Analytic Philosophy in Tallinn, Estonia on 19 April 1997; at the Physics Faculty of Moscow State University in Moscow, Russia on 22 May 1997; and at a lecture organized at the University of Belgrade by the Philosophy Faculty and the Serbian Philosophical Society in Belgrade, Serbia on 18 March 1998. A Slovakian translation was published in *Acta Facultatis Philosophicae Universitatis Šafarikanae*, Filozofický zborník 3 (AFPh UŠ 70), 1996; and a Croatian translation in *Filozofska Istraživanja*, 62, God. 16, Sv. 3, 1996. The mottoes are from Thomas S. Kuhn, *The Structure of Scientific Revolutions*, 1962, second edition, University of Chicago Press, Chicago, 1970, p. 166; and Karl R. Popper, *The Open Society and Its Enemies*, 1945. Reprinted by Routledge, London, 1998, vol. 2, p. 225.

2 Michael Friedman, 'The Re-evaluation of Logical Positivism' in *The Journal of Philosophy*, vol. LXXXVIII, no. 10, October 1991, p. 505.

3 The verificationism of logical positivism.

4 Quine's critiques of reductionism and the analytic/synthetic distinction.

5 The decade of the 1950s, which was clearly a crisis in anybody's book.

6 Thomas Kuhn, and his emphasis upon the non-logical, sociological, psychological, historical—or, in a word, *institutional*—aspects of scientific inquiry.

7 See, for example, Rudolf Carnap, 'Testability and Meaning' in *Philosophy of Science*, vol. 3:4, 1936–37. Reprinted, with omissions, in *Readings in the Philosophy of Science*, edited by Herbert Feigl and May Brodbeck, Appleton-Century-Crofts, New York, 1953.

8 'Cognitively meaningful' means either true or false.

9 See Rudolf Carnap, 'The Elimination of Metaphysics Through Logical Analysis of Language' in *Erkenntnis*, vol. II, 1932, reprinted in *Logical Positivism*, edited by A.J. Ayer, The Free Press, New York, 1959. See also Carnap, 'Testability and Meaning.'

10 Karl R. Popper, *The Logic of Scientific Discovery*, 1959. Reprinted by Routledge, London, 1995, p. 281.

11 But the *Encyclopedia Britannica*'s article on Popper says:

> Popper argued ... that hypotheses are deductively validated by what he called the 'falsifiability criterion.' Under this method, a scientist seeks to discover an observed exception to his postulated rule. The absence of contradictory evidence thereby becomes proof of his theory.

> Someone ignorant of Popper's philosophy could only wonder, upon reading this passage, how Popper could hold such a silly theory of deduction. But this, I take it, is just one of the reasons why Popper opposed arguments from authority.

12 Kuhn, *The Structure of Scientific Revolutions*, p. viii.

13 Hence, Kuhn ('Logic of Discovery or Psychology of Research?' in *Criticism and the Growth of Knowledge*, edited by Imre Lakatos and Alan Musgrave, Cambridge University Press, Cambridge, 1970, p. 3) writes:

> Sir Karl and I do appeal to the same data, to an uncommon extent we are seeing the same lines on the same paper, asked about those lines and those data, we often give virtually identical responses ... Nevertheless (I am convinced) that our intentions are often quite different when we say the same things. Though the lines are the same, the figures which emerge from them are not.

14 Kuhn, *The Structure of Scientific Revolutions*, p. 146. My italics.

15 Kuhn, *The Structure of Scientific Revolutions*, p. 146.

16 But Kuhn appears to vacillate on this point. For no sooner than he says this, he writes (Kuhn, *The Structure of Scientific Revolutions*, p. 147):

> Popper's anomalous experience is important to science because it evokes competitors for an existing paradigm. But falsification, though it surely occurs, does not happen with, or simply because of, the emergence of an anomaly or falsifying instance. Instead, it is a subsequent and separate process that might equally well be called verification since it consists in the triumph of a new paradigm over the old one.

So while falsification surely occurs, falsifying experiences do not. But this is not as ironic as it first appears. For it is, in fact, important for Popper's anti-psychologism that observations and experiences play no role in a logical argument. For Popper, it is the statements that *report* observations, and not the observations themselves, that falsify theories.

17 Kuhn, 'Logic of Discovery or Psychology of Research?', p. 15.

18 Kuhn, 'Logic of Discovery or Psychology of Research?', p. 14.

19 Kuhn, 'Logic of Discovery or Psychology of Research?', p. 14.

20 Kuhn, 'Logic of Discovery or Psychology of Research?', p. 14.

21 Kuhn, 'Logic of Discovery or Psychology of Research?', p. 14.

22 Karl R. Popper, *Realism and the Aim of Science*, edited by W.W. Bartley III, 1983. Reprinted by Routledge, London, 1996, p. xxxiv.

23 Popper, *Realism and the Aim of Science*, p. xxxiv.

24 Popper, *The Logic of Scientific Discovery*, p. 50.

25 Popper, *The Logic of Scientific Discovery*, p. 50.

26 Popper places three requirements on basic statements—two formal and one material. The formal requirements are: (*a*) from a universal statement without initial conditions, no basic statement can be deduced; and (*b*) a universal statement and a basic statement can contradict each other. It follows from (*a*) and (*b*) that basic statements have the logical form of existential generalizations. The material requirement Popper places on basic statements is: (*c*) basic statements are testable, intersubjectively, by observation.

27 The point of falsifiability is to emphasize the importance of critical testing. In order for the test of a theory to be a test, it is necessary that some possibly true empirical statement, if actually true, would suffice to show that that theory is false. An example of a simple theory that *could* be falsifiable is 'All people with AIDS have HIV.' For so long as one does not maintain that HIV is an essential property for the diagnosis of AIDS, there would exist the possibility of finding someone with AIDS who does not have HIV. (It seems, however, that the presence of HIV *is* regarded as essential for the diagnosis of AIDS.) An example of a theory that is not falsifiable is 'All human actions are egotistic, motivated by self-interest.' This theory is not falsifiable because 'no example of an altruistic action can refute the view that there was an egotistic motive hidden behind it.' (Popper, *Realism and the Aim of Science*, p. xx.)

28 This is also contrary to Lakatos, who claims that Popper's thought evolved from the belief that scientific theories are conclusively falsifiable, to the belief that they are not. Lakatos calls the former position 'naive falsificationism,' and the latter position 'sophisticated falsificationism.' And he distinguishes between Popper$_1$, the naive falsificationist, and Popper$_2$, the sophisticated falsificationist. Ironically, Lakatos also distinguishes Popper$_1$ and Popper$_2$ from a third Popper, Popper$_0$, a dogmatic falsificationist who never existed, but was invented and criticized by the logical positivists. (See Imre Lakatos, 'Falsification and the Methodology of Scientific Research Programmes' in *Criticism and the Growth of Knowledge*.) I say this is ironic because Lakatos' Popper$_1$, judging from what we have quoted from *The Logic of Scientific Discovery*, is also an invention that never existed.

29 See Karl R. Popper, 'Normal Science and Its Dangers' in *Criticism and the Growth of Knowledge*, p. 56.

30 See Thomas S. Kuhn, 'Reflections on My Critics' in *Criticism and the Growth of Knowledge*, p. 267.

31 Thomas S. Kuhn, 'Postscript—1969' in *The Structure of Scientific Revolutions*, p. 198.

32 I say that Kuhn *seems* to think that Popper asserts the existence of a theory-neutral observation language, because Kuhn seems to vacillate on the point. On the one hand, he writes that Popper and he are 'correspondingly sceptical of efforts to produce any neutral observation language.' (Kuhn, 'Logic of Discovery or Psychology of Research?', p. 2.) On the other hand, he writes that many philosophers 'continue to assume that theories can be compared by recourse to a basic vocabulary consisting entirely of words which are attached to nature in ways that are unproblematic and, to the extent necessary, independent of theory. That is the vocabulary in which Sir Karl's basic statements are framed.' (Kuhn, 'Reflections on my critics,' p. 226.) Perhaps Kuhn wants to say that Popper, despite his denial of a theory-neutral observation language, is nonetheless committed to one.

It may, in any event, seem paradoxical for Kuhn to admit the translatability of paradigms but deny the existence of a theory-neutral basis for comparison. But the idea that communication and rational argument require the existence of a theory-neutral observation language is another residue of the traditional quest for certainty. It is a corollary to what I have elsewhere called 'The Clothesline Theory of Communication.' (See M. A. Notturno, *Objectivity, Rationality, and the Third Realm: Justification and the Grounds of Psychologism*, Martinus Nijhoff, Dordrecht, 1985, pp. 81f.) According to the Clothesline Theory, a necessary condition for communication is that the persons communicating grasp or apprehend the exact same meaning. But the material signs that are words are not themselves meanings. They are, rather, the clothing, or 'material garments,' of meanings. So in order to communicate, a person takes a meaning, dresses it in its material garments, hooks it to the clothesline, and sends it over to the person with whom he wishes to communicate. That person takes the clothed meaning off the line, undresses it, and apprehends the meaning. Since this theory holds that communication can occur only if communicators share the exact same meaning, it also holds that communication is always perfect or exact. And since a logical argument can be valid only to the extent to which the meanings of the signs which occur in it are fixed, it was only this exactness of communication that made justification via logical demonstration possible. But neither Popper nor Kuhn believes that knowledge is justified, let alone that it is certain. And both of them maintain that communication is rarely, if ever, exact.

33 Kuhn (*The Structure of Scientific Revolutions*, p. 158) wrote that:

> The man who embraces a new paradigm at an early stage must often do so in defiance of the evidence provided by problem-solving. He must, that is, have faith that the new paradigm will succeed with the many large problems that confront it, knowing only that the older paradigm has failed with a few. A decision of that kind can only be made on faith.

34 Kuhn, *The Structure of Scientific Revolutions*, p. 122.
35 Kuhn, *The Structure of Scientific Revolutions*, p. 158.
36 As Kuhn ('Postscript—1969,' p. 199), himself, puts it:

> A number of them ... have reported that I believe the following: the proponents of incommensurable theories cannot communicate with each other at all; as a result, in a debate over theory-choice there can be no recourse to *good* reasons; instead theory must be chosen for reasons that are ultimately personal and subjective; some sort of mystical apperception is responsible for the decision actually reached.

37 Kuhn, 'Postscript—1969,' p. 199.
38 Kuhn, 'Postscript—1969,' pp. 199–200.
39 Here, one need only recall Frege's failure to derive arithmetic from the 'laws of logic'—and, in particular, the fact that Russell's Paradox led Frege to reject his own Basic Law V—to realize that this tentativeness applies even in works that are supposed to be purely logical, and even to the assumed rules of logical inference: that these rules may also be rejected as false if their use leads to the derivation of a contradiction. (See Gottlob Frege, 'Appendix II: The Russell Paradox' in Gottlob Frege, *The Basic Laws of Arithmetic*, translated and edited by Montgomery Furth, University of California Press, Berkeley, 1967, pp. 127–143.)
40 Kuhn, 'Postscript—1969,' p. 198.
41 But, of course, it may also be because only philosophers have read the words that express this intent *critically*.

42 In 'Logic of Discovery or Psychology of Research?' (p. 6) for example, Kuhn writes that Popper:

> ... has characterized the entire scientific enterprise in terms that apply only to its occasional revolutionary parts. His emphasis is natural and common: the exploits of a Copernicus or Einstein make better reading than those of a Brahe or Lorentz; Sir Karl would not be the first if he mistook what I call normal science for an intrinsically uninteresting enterprise.

43 Normal science is clearly not the focus of Popper's inquiry. But *The Logic of Scientific Discovery* begins (p. 13) with the words:

> A scientist engaged in a piece of research, say in physics, can attack his problem straight away. He can go at once to the heart of the matter: that is, to the heart of an organized structure. For a structure of scientific doctrines is already in existence, and with it, a generally accepted problem-situation. This is why he may leave it to others to fit his contribution into the framework of scientific knowledge.

44 Popper, 'Normal Science and Its Dangers,' p. 52.
45 Popper, 'Normal Science and Its Dangers,' p. 52.
46 Popper, 'Normal Science and Its Dangers,' p. 52.
47 Popper, 'Normal Science and Its Dangers,' pp. 52–53.
48 Kuhn, 'Reflections on My Critics,' p. 237. This, I should note, is Kuhn's response to Feyerabend's claim that he is ambiguous as to whether he offers historical description or methodological prescription. (See Paul Feyerabend, 'Consolations for the specialist' in *Criticism and the Growth of Knowledge*, p. 199.)
49 See Popper, *The Logic of Scientific Discovery*, p. 15.
50 Kuhn, 'Logic of Discovery or Psychology of Research?,' p. 6.
51 Thomas S. Kuhn, 'The Relations between the History and the Philosophy of Science' in Thomas S. Kuhn, *The Essential Tension*, University of Chicago Press, Chicago, 1977, p. 10.
52 Kuhn, *The Structure of Scientific Revolutions*, p. 171.
53 Kuhn, *The Structure of Scientific Revolutions*, p. 171.
54 Kuhn, 'Logic of Discovery or Psychology of Research?', p. 11.
55 Thus Kuhn ('Logic of Discovery or Psychology of Research?', p. 11) writes that:

> It is a mistake to add three plus three and get five, or to conclude from 'All men are mortal' to 'All mortals are men.' For different reasons, it is a mistake to say, 'He is my sister,' or to report the presence of a strong electric field when test charges fail to indicate it. Presumably there are still other sorts of mistakes, but all the normal ones are likely to share the following characteristics. A mistake is made, or is committed, at a

specifiable time and place by a particular individual. That individual has failed to obey some established rule of logic, or of language, or of the relations between one of these and experience. Or he may instead have failed to recognize the consequences of a particular choice among the alternatives which the rules allow him. The individual can learn from his mistake only because the group whose practice embodies these rules can isolate the individual's failure in applying them.

56 Kuhn, 'Logic of Discovery or Psychology of Research?', p. 12.
57 Kuhn, 'Logic of Discovery or Psychology of Research?', p. 12.
58 Hence, Kuhn ('Logic of Discovery or Psychology of Research?', pp. 11–12) writes:

> If [the characterization of Ptolemaic astronomy as a mistake] does not immediately seem an odd usage, that is mainly because it appeals to the residual inductivist in us all. Believing that valid theories are the product of correct inductions from facts, the inductivist must also hold that a false theory is the result of a mistake in induction. In principle, at least, he is prepared to answer the questions: what mistake was made, what rule broken, when and by whom, in arriving at, say, the Ptolemaic system?

59 Otto Neurath, 'Sociology and Physicalism,' translated by Morton Magnus and Ralph Raico, in *Logical Positivism*, edited by A.J. Ayer, The Free Press, New York, 1959, p. 282.
60 Rudolf Carnap, *The Logical Structure of the World & Pseudoproblems in Philosophy*, translated by Rolf A. George, University of California Press, Los Angeles, 1969, p. vii.
61 Popper, in comparing the closed society to tribalism, said that the relatively infrequent changes that occur in tribal or closed societies are not based upon rational attempts to improve social conditions, but instead have the character of religious conversions. (See Popper, *The Open Society and Its Enemies*, vol. 1, p. 172.)
62 See, for example, Carnap, 'Testability and Meaning.' See also, Rudolf Carnap, 'Empiricism, Semantics, and Ontology,' in *Revue Internationale de Philosophie*, IV, 1920, reprinted in *The Linguistic Turn*, edited by Richard Rorty, The University of Chicago Press, Chicago, 1967.

Epilogue
What Is To Be Done?
or
Social(ist) Science and the Emergence
of Post-Communist Communism[1]

> *These methods lead, as we shall yet see, to this: the party organization is substituted for the party, the Central Committee is substituted for the party organization, and finally the 'dictator' is substituted for the Central Committee.*
>
> Leon Trotsky

> *One thing is clear: communism is not a paradise.*
>
> USSR Academy of Sciences

They used to tell the following joke in Moscow. A man goes to a clinic and says 'I need an ear, nose and eye doctor.' 'You must mean an ear, nose and *throat* doctor.' 'No,' the man insists, 'an ear, nose and *eye* doctor. I keep hearing things that I don't see, and something doesn't smell right.'

The title of my talk is 'What Is to Be Done? or Social(ist) Science and the Emergence of Post-Communist Communism.' It is a long title, and a presumptuous title, and it deserves an explanation. Karl Popper used to joke that social science began with the idea that we need a special science to get rid of our social problems—and now one of our greatest social problems is how to get rid of the social scientists. 'Now' was then in the sixties. But some things have not changed. And Popper, despite his famous optimism, was never too confident that we could actually get rid of the social scientists. Their interests and their power, he thought, had become far too entrenched to be easily removed.

Today science itself has become a social problem that is widely discussed by social scientists in the social sciences. Today the social scientists say that science is a social institution and that the sociological aspects of it are what count most in the social decision to accept or reject a theory. They tell us that truth and rationality are social constructs that do not really exist, and that the cognitive authority for our scientific theories—which is a social construct that *does* still manage to exist—depends upon nothing more than the solidarity of the scientific community that maintains it. They say that science begins where criticism leaves off, that 'normal' scientists must *commit* themselves to their beliefs, and that those who criticize them too persistently are and ought to be expelled from the scientific community.

It is with this in mind that I ask 'What is to be done?' and that I talk about social(ist) science and the emergence of post-communist communism. Social science is not necessarily socialist science. But it is undeniable that the idea of science, and particularly the idea of *social* science, played an important role in the development of scientific communism, and that most of the talk that we hear today about 'post-this' and 'post-that'—as well as the contempt that some people now feel toward anything that calls itself 'scientific'—is best understood in the context of its celebrated collapse.

It is easy today to forget that many people believed, less than a hundred years ago, that Czar Nicholas II ruled by divine right and, indeed, that he actually even communicated with the Divine—if not directly, then at least through the medium of Rasputin. It is also easy to forget that four-fifths of the Russian population, although officially emancipated, were *de facto* land serfs who had not yet learned to read or to write and who were encouraged not to think critically about social policy (or anything else for that matter), but to look toward their masters, as gods amongst men, for the truth, and to rely upon them for their survival.

The rise of communism in Russia did more to take advantage of this situation than it did to change it. Trotsky, I am told, was disturbed by the cult of leadership. He is said to have said that:

> These methods lead, as we shall yet see, to this: the party organization is substituted for the party, the Central Committee is substituted for the party organization, and finally the 'dictator' is substituted for the Central Committee.

And Lenin too is said to have found it disturbing, though there can be no doubt that he also found it convenient, and that he used it—called '*Starik*' at the tender age of thirty-three—for the success of his revolution.

It is difficult, in fact, to imagine how the October Revolution could possibly have supplanted the divine right of Czar Nicholas II, were it not for the serfs' submission to charismatic leaders, and were it not for the charismatic belief that these 'new men' had in the divine right of science.

The October Revolution meant that everything was subject to change, including social wealth, the forces and relations of production, the forms and methods of the class struggle, its impulses and motive forces. But 'the most important thing,' according to Lenin, 'is that the *laws* of these changes have been discovered, that the *objective* logic of these changes and of their historical development has in its chief and basic features been disclosed.'[2]

The most important thing, in other words, was that socialism had been set upon a *scientific* basis, and that its necessity and inevitability had been demonstrated, at least from the perspective of the materialist conception of history.

'Science,' for the Party, meant authority. It demanded that its philosophers and social scientists restrain themselves from freethinking, inquiry, and critique, because these things could only demoralize and confuse the workers, who intuitively understood the truth, which was, in any event, already articulated in the Party's scientific doctrines.

So what, exactly, has collapsed?

Today we hear many new stories about new people—about the 'New Russians' and the 'New Ukrainians,' and even the 'New Kazakhs' for that matter. So it is easy today to think that evil old scientific communism is dead and that everything now is new. But '*Stories about New People*' was also the sub-title of *What Is To Be Done?*—not the revolutionary pamphlet by Lenin, but the Chernyshevsky novel that so greatly influenced him. And people who meet the New Russians and the New Ukrainians and the New Kazakhs quickly realize that they are very much like the Old Russians and the Old Ukrainians and the Old Kazakhs: that they are often, in fact, the very same people, with the very same names, occupying if not the very same positions in their new post-communist societies, then the ones immediately above them.

Too many of the new post-communists seem to have replaced the old code-words of scientific communism with the new code-words of open society—and with the very same fervent belief, or the very same cynical one, with which they once adopted them: either with the firmly held belief that they would, by doing so, inevitably bring about a bright new glorious utopian, albeit post-communist, future; or with the belief that nothing really matters much at all.

It should thus come as no surprise, given the importance that scientific communism placed upon education, and upon theory and ideology, and upon establishing socialism as a science, that the newness of these new people is already reflected in new scientific textbooks that teach new scientific ideologies in their new scientific curricula. And it should come as no surprise that many of the new ideologies that have been proposed to fill the vacuum left by scientific communism continue to worship at the altar of social science.

The Party's demand that its members accept the authority of social science, and the reality gap that it caused, was clearly one of the most oppressive things about scientific communism. The Old Russians were fed a heavy diet of ideology by their social scientists. What they were told directly contradicted their own experience. And they were then forced to repeat it in order to survive.

One example, I hope, will suffice. As late as 1987, in a book entitled *Capitalism at the End of the Century*, the contributing team of Soviet social(ist) scientists wrote in its concluding section—the one reserved for the glories of scientific communism—that:

> The absolute movement of man's formation is the uninterrupted development of the individual, his creative enrichment and constant self-renewal. *The development of the individual is infinite, as infinite as the self-improvement of the communist system.* In the world communist community, the realm of freedom 'lies beyond the sphere of actual material production,' ceases to be dictated by external expediency and becomes an inexorable inner requirement. It is not merely the complete economic and political emancipation of

the individual, but the elimination of every type of alienation, including the confrontation between technical facilities and Nature.[3]

Imagine that! 'Not *merely* the complete economic and political emancipation of the individual!' Imagine that, when you know for a fact that you are deprived of the free flow of information, and of the freedom to travel, and of the freedom to associate with foreigners, or to move across the street, or simply to say what you think is true!

Imagine being made to repeat that freedom is an inexorable *inner* requirement in the world communist community!

But this, of course, was before the new educational reforms. Today the New Russians no longer teach courses in scientific communism. They teach 'politology' instead. Today we have 'culturology,' a new and fashionable social(ist) science that has replaced an old and newly out of fashion one. Today the New Russians can read in their new culturology textbooks that 'the personality of the man who initiates an enterprise becomes more and more liberated from traditions and presuppositions and gives itself to free self-expression in all forms.'[4] And they can, perhaps, take comfort in the fact that it all sounds so familiar, all too familiar, especially in the last chapter—where the one reserved for the glories of scientific communism used to be—which now paints the post-industrialist society or the post-technological society or the post-whatever society in the same comfortable, user-friendly, rosy, and fashionable shades of pink that were once used to describe the world communist community.

This, I hope, will explain, at least in part, what I mean by 'social(ist) science' and 'the emergence of post-communist communism.'

Is it really so surprising, given the significance that scientific communism placed upon social(ist) science, that the New Post-Communist Ukrainians are now debating the merits of *scientific* nationalism? Or that it is seriously proposed as a *new* ideological movement that is meant to unite them in their struggle to bring about the New Ukraine?

I think that it is hard to imagine how it could be otherwise. I think that only the most cynical, or those who harbor utopian dreams of their own, could expect that people who have relied for generations upon authority and have endured their hardships by dreaming about the future could change these habits of thinking and acting overnight.

And all of this makes it difficult for me to talk about the prospects for science and open society in the post-communist countries.

The Party's 'really existing socialism' was a messianic mix of authoritarian and utopian ideas that masqueraded as 'Truth' in a shiny red raincoat called 'Science.' Most post-communists have now experienced for themselves that Marxism is not true. Many of them have concluded from this that there is no truth. But many more are standing in line and looking to the West to tell them exactly what it is.

I know this first hand, because my wife and I have spent the past five years discussing the problems of science and the open society with philosophers and scientists of the post-communist countries. Kira and I have learned a great deal through these discussions. We have also had many gratifying experiences—all of which we owe, either directly or indirectly, to the vision, generosity, and good will of George Soros, who has provided the financial support for our discussions and for a wide variety of other projects aimed at making society in the countries of the former Soviet Union more open. We have met many talented and capable and good-hearted people at our workshops. Almost all of them want to live in a better world and in a freer and more open society. But we begin to feel uneasy when they seem too eager to adopt the philosophy of open society. And we feel even more uneasy when their talk about open society begins to sound more like the glorious communist future: when they say that all of their problems will be solved once they get the new 'scientific information'—and once they get to the open society.

We sometimes feel when this happens as if we are walking a tightrope between cynical opportunism on the one side and out and out indoctrination on the other.

The cynical opportunism is the easy part. Many of the post-communists we meet are quite literally desperate to get to the West. It is easy to understand why. I would not want to raise my child in the poverty and disease and hopelessness and hatred that surrounds them. Soros, for these people, is a way out—a ticket to

Budapest, and perhaps even further, maybe even to the kind of life that most people in the West take for granted. And they are often willing to say 'open society' for the fare. But their ideas about western social institutions are revealing. Some of them hear an all too familiar sound in the call for open society. It sounds, they say, like the call to welcome and embrace 'the highest socio-economic formation of society.' Many of them think that democracy means networking, that free trade means I scratch your back and you scratch mine, and that critical thinking is when you accuse and denounce your neighbors—though it is not always clear where they got these ideas and whether they regard them as good or bad.

Many others, however, are clearly ready to be indoctrinated. They talk as if open society were supposed to be paradise—and about 'the transition to open society' as if it were supposed to solve all of their problems once and for all. They talk about The Open Society and The Closed Society as if the West were completely open and the East completely closed, and not merely open and closed to different degrees. And they talk about Science as if it were synonymous with Truth. They talk, in other words, as if they are ready to welcome and embrace yet another messianic mix of authoritarian and utopian ideas. And it is, to be blunt, just a little bit frightening.

Open society is not democracy, free market, and rule of law. And no society is completely open or closed. The East is not trying to make the transition to open society. It has, on the contrary, already made it. Open society is not the promised land of milk and honey. It is the actual world of uncertainty and insecurity. It is not a new Utopia that we are trying to build, but a very old reality from which we have been trying to escape. We may, no doubt, regard it as an ideal. But it is an ideal that has plenty of problems, and the primary thing that recommends it is that our attempts to escape from it lead to something worse.

This is clearly what Popper thought.

Open society may aim at humanness and reasonableness and equality and freedom. But *The Open Society and Its Enemies*:

> ... attempts to show that this civilization has not yet fully recovered from the shock of its birth—the transition from the tribal or 'closed society,' with

its submission to magical forces, to the 'open society' which sets free the critical powers of man. It attempts to show that the shock of this transition is one of the factors that have made possible the rise of those reactionary movements which have tried, and still try, to overthrow civilization and to return to tribalism. And it suggests that what we call nowadays totalitarianism belongs to a tradition which is just as old or just as young as our civilization itself.[5]

It is the story of how we have repeatedly tried to escape from the 'strain of civilization.' It is the story of how our intellectual leaders have tried to help us to escape—either to protect 'the masses' who are not yet ready to deal with freedom and responsibility, or to protect their own power and authority—by replacing the values of rationality, critical thinking, and freedom of thought with the values of security, 'group-think,' certainty, community, and submission to the collective. And it is, in the end, the story of how and why these attempts ultimately fail and lead to something far worse than open society itself:

> We can never return to the alleged innocence and beauty of the closed society. Our dream of heaven cannot be realized on earth. Once we begin to rely upon our reason, and to use our powers of criticism, once we feel the call of personal responsibilities, and with it, the responsibility of helping to advance knowledge, we cannot return to a state of implicit submission to tribal magic. For those who have eaten of the tree of knowledge, paradise is lost. The more we try to return to the heroic age of tribalism, the more surely do we arrive at the Inquisition, at the Secret Police, and at a romanticized gangsterism. Beginning with the suppression of reason and truth, we must end with the most brutal and violent destruction of all that is human. *There is no return to a harmonious state of nature. If we turn back, then we must go the whole way—we must return to the beasts.*
>
> It is an issue which we must face squarely, hard though it may be for us to do so. If we dream of a return to our childhood, if we are tempted to rely on others and so be happy, if we shrink from the task of carrying our cross, the cross of humaneness, of reason, of responsibility, if we lose courage and flinch from the strain, then we must try to fortify ourselves with a clear understanding of the simple decision before us. We can return to the beasts. But if we wish to remain human, then there is only one way, the way into the open society. We must go on into the unknown, the uncertain and insecure, using what reason we may have to plan as well as we can for both security *and* freedom.[6]

Open society is a 'cross' and a 'strain.' It is something before which we may 'lose courage' and 'flinch.' It is the 'unknown,' the 'uncertain,' and the 'insecure.' We suffer from the shock of its birth. But there is no going back to the womb. We have tasted our freedom and reason, as well as our own fallibility. It may or may not be original sin. But it certainly is not a Utopia.[7]

So why do so many post-communists think that it is?

A large part of the answer is that they are post-communists. The world communist community made a habit of utopian thinking, and it is now a habit that is difficult to break. It can be seen in the widespread tendency to propose utopian solutions to our social problems, and in the equally widespread tendency to measure any proposed solution against the standards of Utopia. It is a habit that allows us to maintain any idea in the name of some glorious future yet to come and, simultaneously, to dismiss any new proposal out of hand—either as a piecemeal approach that does not quite solve *all* of our problems, or as an unrealistic utopian fantasy that is simply impossible to achieve. It is a voice that urges us to go along and not to rock the boat. For saying something beautiful, grand, and brilliant is far more important than saying something that is true. This is the reason why it never talks about its own fallibility, or about the problems that it cannot solve. And it is, in the end, the reason why 'open society,' in the mouth of a utopian thinker, is more likely to be a part of the problem than a part of the solution.

We can always pretend that open society is the new Utopia. We can pretend that our problems will all be solved once we get the new scientific information from the new scientific social scientists—and once we welcome and embrace free markets, democracy, and the rule of law. But we only set ourselves up for a new disappointment and for yet another new reactionary attempt to return to the closed society's promise of comfort and security if we do.

Popper wrote that 'the transition from the closed society to the open takes place when social institutions are first consciously recognized as man-made, and when their conscious alteration is discussed in terms of their suitability for the achievement of human aims or purposes.'[8]

Post-communists may dream of a transition to open society. But my own sense is that their dream is a part of the problem. They may not yet have what the West regards as market economies and real democracies. And they certainly do not have all the 'new scientific information.' But their grandfathers realized long ago that their social institutions were man-made. Indeed, the fact that they were unsuitable for the achievement of their purposes is the primary reason why they tore so many of them down.

Popper taught that all of life is problem-solving, and that life's problems will never all be solved. He also taught that the attempt to make heaven on earth invariably produces hell. This is the reason why he emphasized the importance of problems over theories and even over criticism in his later philosophy. Life continually presents us with new problems, and to think otherwise is to set ourselves up for disappointment, disillusionment, and all the defeatist, pessimistic, and post-modernist attitudes that come with it.

This is the reason why we feel so uneasy when we hear the new post-communists talk about the glories of the open society. And it is, ultimately, the reason why so many of the new post-communist countries are already experiencing reactionary movements, fueled once again by the social(ist) sciences, that would have them return to the heroic age of tribalism.

They thought that all they had to do to solve their social problems was to get rid of their local soviets, or the politburo, or the central planners, or the Old Russians, or scientific communism itself. And they are now suffering from the disillusionment of yet another reality gap. It is more difficult, they have found, to get rid of the social scientists. And more difficult still to get rid of themselves.

The new post-communists whom we meet sometimes ask me to define 'open society' or to say which society I think is most open. They would like me, of course, to say 'The United States of America.' But I do not have so neat and tidy an answer. Americans have what many regard as the world's strongest democracy and free market. But something is clearly wrong. When I left the States five years ago, the lead story in the Chicago press was about a nine year-old killer who continued to elude police for a second week.

Today, as I prepare to return, it is about two high school students who used automatic weapons, hand grenades, and explosives in a suicidal murder spree that took the lives of sixteen or more of their classmates and teachers, and left many more others wounded and, no doubt, traumatized for life. These are not isolated incidents. America now has one of the most violent societies in the world, and a growing number of Americans—and, what is most disturbing, a growing number of *very young* Americans—now prefer to express their thoughts and their hatred and their rage with guns instead of words. This is a problem that threatens the very heart of open society. Facing up to it, and to its causes, will not be easy. But it should, I think, make it clear that the once fashionable and simple-minded idea that the introduction of democracy and free markets would suffice to make post-communist societies more open is too simple-minded. Changes in our institutions are no doubt important. But open society begins at home, and even the best designed institutions can quickly become oppressive if the people who man them do not themselves have open minds—and open hearts.

If we want to improve our societies, and if we want to solve our problems, then we must first recognize that we have them. We must recognize that we ourselves are fallible and do not have all the answers. We must recognize that the solutions to our problems will not make heaven on earth. We must begin to propose solutions that can work in the world that we live in, and we must begin to evaluate them not by whether they make our world a Utopia, but by whether they make our life on earth any better than it was before and, if so, any better than their competitors would make it.

The new post-communists are the old pre-post-communists. They are people who have learned to rely upon experts, and who have been encouraged by social(ist) scientists—first from the East and now from the West—to believe that all we have to do is to rely upon the social(ist) scientists and that all of our social problems will be solved. They are, in other words, very much like ourselves.

And this, I hope, will also explain what I mean by 'social(ist) science' and 'the emergence of post-communist communism.'

What is an open society?

If you feel that your race and your ethnic heritage and your religion and your gender pose no obstacle to fulfilling your dreams—if you feel free to criticize your leaders openly and without fear of losing your life, or your freedom, or your home, or your job—if you feel that your leaders listen to what you say and take it seriously as an attempt to bring about a better world, instead of as a threat to their authority—and if what you feel is in fact true, then your society is more open than most.

But if you fear that you will be persecuted for your race or for your ethnic heritage or for your religion or for your gender—if you are afraid to speak your mind and fear that saying what you think will be taken as an offense, and that it may even cost you your life, or your freedom, or your home, or your job—if you fear that your leaders do not really care about you and your problems, but are instead interested only in preserving their own power—and if these fears are shared by your neighbors and seem to have some basis in reality, then the society in which you live, regardless of its political or economic structure, is closed.

In my view, social(ist) science and the belief in experts is still one of our greatest social problems—both in the East and in the West.

Its methods lead to this: the authority of science is substituted for rational argument, the solidarity of the scientific community is substituted for the authority of science, and finally political power is substituted for the solidarity of the scientific community.

In the end, it leads to post-communist communism, and to yet another form of closed society.

What is to be done?

There is no such thing as *the* open society or *the* closed society—and no such thing as a society that is completely open or closed. The battle for reason and the freedom of thought is a perennial one, and one that is apparently as old as mankind itself. But none of this gives us any reason not to try to make our societies more open, or not to try to put an end to our closed societies. The twentieth century, which has seen two world wars fought in defense of open society, is now drawing to a close. There has not been such a conflict in over fifty years, and there has been great progress toward making our societies more open. But as this book goes to press tribalism is once again on the rise. The intolerant are, more and more, terrorizing those who do not belong. We are once again confronted with growing numbers of people who prefer violence to reason. People are being driven from their homes by force. Those who refuse to leave are being killed. And the bombs are once again falling in Europe.

The future is open, and no one can know what is to come. But the future is, nonetheless, largely shaped by our actions, and our actions are largely shaped by the beliefs that we hold and by the philosophies we believe. The violence that we now witness in Europe is no doubt a failure of open society. But it is, at the same time, also a triumph. For it shows that we still have the will to fight for our freedom when it is threatened by tyrants, and that we still have the will to exercise our right not to tolerate the intolerant.

Tribalism may be beautiful when it is at peace and harmony with the world. But it is quite another thing when it begins to kill people who do not belong, or who do not want to belong. I refuse to call it by any of the more beautiful names that have been used to glorify it. And I fear that those intellectuals who have, in recent years, denigrated reason and the freedom of thought, and who have elevated the things that divide us into the many different groups to which we belong over those that unite us all as humans, may soon reap a heavy harvest.

What is to be done?

Put an end to our closed societies.

Notes

1 This is a revised version of a paper presented at the exhibition/conference organized by the Associazione Fondazione Karl Popper in Milan, Italy on 12 January 1997. The first motto is attributed to Leon Trotsky, and the second is from A.N. Yakolev, ed., *Capitalism at the End of the Century*, Progress Publishers, Moscow, 1987, p. 370.

2 V.I. Lenin, 'Materialism and Empirio-Criticism,' *Collected Works*, Vol. 14, 1977, p. 325.

3 A.N. Yakolev, ed., *Capitalism at the End of the Century*, Progress Publishers, Moscow, 1987, p. 369.

4 Y. Yerasov, *Social Culturology*, Aspect Press, Moscow, 1996, p. 541. (The passage quoted, as well as the title and author's name, is as translated by Kira Viktorova.)

5 Karl R. Popper, *The Open Society and Its Enemies*, 1945. Reprinted by Routledge, London, 1998, vol. 1, p. xiii.

6 Popper, *The Open Society and Its Enemies*, vol. 1, pp. 200-201.

7 Popper, *The Open Society and Its Enemies*, vol. 1, p. 201.

8 Popper, *The Open Society and Its Enemies*, vol. 1, p. 294.

Subject Index

Name Index